1,000,000 Books

are available to read at

www.ForgottenBooks.com

Read online
Download PDF
Purchase in print

ISBN 978-1-331-02495-8
PIBN 10134959

This book is a reproduction of an important historical work. Forgotten Books uses state-of-the-art technology to digitally reconstruct the work, preserving the original format whilst repairing imperfections present in the aged copy. In rare cases, an imperfection in the original, such as a blemish or missing page, may be replicated in our edition. We do, however, repair the vast majority of imperfections successfully; any imperfections that remain are intentionally left to preserve the state of such historical works.

Forgotten Books is a registered trademark of FB &c Ltd.
Copyright © 2018 FB &c Ltd.
FB &c Ltd, Dalton House, 60 Windsor Avenue, London, SW19 2RR.
Company number 08720141. Registered in England and Wales.

For support please visit www.forgottenbooks.com

1 MONTH OF FREE READING

at
www.ForgottenBooks.com

By purchasing this book you are eligible for one month membership to ForgottenBooks.com, giving you unlimited access to our entire collection of over 1,000,000 titles via our web site and mobile apps.

To claim your free month visit: www.forgottenbooks.com/free134959

* Offer is valid for 45 days from date of purchase. Terms and conditions apply.

English
Français
Deutsche
Italiano
Español
Português

www.forgottenbooks.com

Mythology Photography **Fiction**
Fishing Christianity **Art** Cooking
Essays **Buddhism** Freemasonry
Medicine **Biology** Music **Ancient Egypt** Evolution Carpentry Physics
Dance Geology **Mathematics** Fitness
Shakespeare **Folklore** Yoga Marketing
Confidence Immortality Biographies
Poetry **Psychology** Witchcraft
Electronics Chemistry History **Law**
Accounting **Philosophy** Anthropology
Alchemy Drama Quantum Mechanics
Atheism Sexual Health **Ancient History**
Entrepreneurship Languages Sport
Paleontology Needlework Islam
Metaphysics Investment Archaeology
Parenting Statistics Criminology
Motivational

THE EPIC OF THE INNER LIFE

BEING

THE BOOK OF JOB

*TRANSLATED ANEW, AND ACCOMPANIED WITH
NOTES AND AN INTRODUCTORY STUDY*

BY

JOHN F. GENUNG

BOSTON AND NEW YORK
HOUGHTON, MIFFLIN AND COMPANY
The Riverside Press, Cambridge
1891

Copyright, 1891,
By JOHN F. GENUNG.

All rights reserved.

The Riverside Press, Cambridge, Mass., U. S. A.
Electrotyped and Printed by H. O. Houghton & Co.

To

THE MEMORY OF

MY REVERED INSTRUCTORS IN HEBREW EXEGESIS

TAYLER LEWIS

AND

FRANZ DELITZSCH

PREFACE

THE kind reception accorded to an article on "The Interpretation of the Book of Job," published in the "Andover Review" for November, 1888, has encouraged the author to hope that a revision and completion of the study therein outlined may not be unacceptable to the reading public. In the carrying out of this work, thanks are due first of all to the editors and publishers of that Review, not only for their ready permission to make such use of that article as may seem necessary, but also for the hearty Godspeed that they have given to the undertaking. And now that the study has assumed the proportions of a book, some questions naturally arising about its form and the general treatment here adopted require, perhaps, the answer of a preface.

Those readers to whom the question-begging name Epic, displayed on the title-page, is a stumbling-block that must needs be removed before they can with complacency read further, are referred to pages 20–26 for a definition of the modified sense in which I have ventured to use the term.

The Book of Job, full as it is of religious edification, is also a poem, a work of literary art, to be read and judged as we would read and judge any poem, with the same favoring presuppositions, the same candor of criticism. It has long been my conviction that if we should make for it no demand but the literary demand, seeking in the broad diffused light of every day simply that unity of idea and treatment which we have a right to expect in every work of art, the book would prove itself not less sacred, rather more; while also it would gain greatly by stepping out of its age-constructed frame of abstruse erudition into common people's homes and hearts. Whether by the present Translation, Notes, and Introductory Study I have in any degree succeeded in verifying this conviction must be left to my readers to judge.

The question naturally arises, Why make a new translation? why not use the noble

Revised Version? Well, this is the answer that a prolonged study of the book has made increasingly evident: The Revised Version, being the work of a company of scholars, represents the average of their views; it is the somewhat colorless, or perhaps we may say low-relief, product of many minds, all of whom must sink to some extent their individual preferences in order to accommodate themselves to a common and composite result. The work as it lies before us is the verdict of a majority vote. But the original was presumably the work of one mind; such at least it must be presupposed until critical study compels another judgment. To get accurately at that one mind's idea, as a whole and in all its parts, it seemed to me necessary to pass the work anew through the crucible of a single mind, whose business it should be first to find what the book supremely stands for, and then, without having to trim and modify in obedience to divergent views, to estimate candidly and correctly every shading of expression, every degree of intensity, every transition, every connection, in the light of that dominant idea. Of course this necessitates retranslation. Translation is interpretation; it cannot be otherwise; it must take more or less the color of the mind that draws the idea out of the original. True as this is of all translation, it is especially the case in translation from the Hebrew, in which language the provisions for finer shadings of thought are so meagre, one particle, for instance, having often to do duty for a variety of relations. The Hebrew language presents its thought in great unsquared blocks, sublime and simple; and these the translator has to square and polish, so that they will joint together and make out of many one structure. The only way to do this effectually is to live with the author's mind, in self-effacing submission and obedience, until the power is obtained to follow all his sequences, anticipate his turnings and objections, gradually embody all his thoughts into a complex unity wherein every part shall be luminous with the spirit of the whole. This I have endeavored to do, not without a good deal of painstaking labor. And the present translation, whatever other merits or defects it may have, will, I think, be found at least homogeneous, the work of one mind interpreting one idea.

A new translation, from the "natural" point of view, is also justified, as seems to me, by the fact that there is a strong tendency in a company translation, made in the interests of Church and Christianity, to make every clause at all hazards a source of spiritual and homiletical edification. The custom of founding sermons on passages of Scripture, which latter for this purpose are torn from their connections, may be legitimate for religious instruction, but its operation is sadly unfavorable to the reading or translation of a book of Scripture as a homogeneous whole. My hope is, that the present attempt to translate the Book of Job, with the sermonizing instinct for the time being effaced, may prove not unfruitful in suggestion.

Having made the translation with care, I have then proceeded to treat it as if it were an English poem. That is to say, the notes are not devoted, in any great degree, to telling the reader just how this and that passage got itself done into English, or how many meanings Dillmann and Delitzsch and Ewald and Zöckler found admissible, or how much suggestiveness there is in a certain Hebrew root or idiom. Perhaps in so denying myself I have missed a good chance to display learning; but for this I do not care, being more concerned with the question what the ordinary reader wants explained. The notes are accordingly designed mainly to trace the sequences and interdependencies of the thought, and to solve briefly the difficulties inherent in the work of a remote age and land. In the numerous cross-references, too, from one part of the book to the other, the reader may see how predominant the endeavor has been to make the book interpret itself. The author of a book, after all, is his own best expositor.

As a further help to the reader, I have discarded the old division of the poem into chapters and verses, which often makes misleading interruptions to the connection, and have adopted a division into sections, according to the natural articulation of the thought, retaining, however, for facility in comparison, the old notation at the bottom of the page. To this division into sections with their subdivisions, a parallel, suggestive alike for its mechanical helpfulness and for its delicate fitness to the nature of the thought so articulated, may be seen in the notation of Tennyson's "Maud," which is a "monodrama" worked out by a connected series of lyrics; another, less closely indicated, in the "In Memoriam," which also portrays a progressive spiritual history by the lyrical method, its individual sections purporting to be "short swallow-flights of song." The value of these suggestions for the Book of Job is obvious. Its method, too, is strongly lyrical; and by choosing the same manner of division and subdivision as has given fitting physiognomy to the above-named poems, I set off the speakers' changing yet progressive moods in such wise that the eye as well as the mind of the reader can better discriminate them.

So much for what seems necessary to explain. If the other features of my book are not self-justifying, no preface can justify them.

AMHERST, MASSACHUSETTS.
February, 1891.

CONTENTS

I. THE INTRODUCTORY STUDY

	PAGE
PRELIMINARY — THE TREATMENT REQUIRED OF THE BOOK OF JOB	3
I. ITS CENTRAL AND RULING IDEA	8
II. ITS LITERARY CLASS — THE EPIC	20
III. CONNECTION AND CONTINUITY OF ITS PARTS	29
IV. CONSIDERATIONS REGARDING ITS ORIGIN	89

II. THE POEM

PERSONS	123
THE ARGUMENT	125
TRANSLATION AND NOTES	131

I

THE INTRODUCTORY STUDY

" The aim in expounding a great poem should be, not to discover an endless variety of meanings often contradictory, but whatever it has of great and perennial significance; for such it must have, or it would long ago have ceased to be living and operative, would long ago have taken refuge in the Chartreuse of great libraries, dumb thenceforth to all mankind. We do not mean to say that this minute exegesis is useless or unpraiseworthy, but only that it should be subsidiary to the larger way." — LOWELL, Essay on *Dante*.

STUDY OF THE BOOK OF JOB

"WHEN we see the natural style," says Pascal, "we are quite astonished and delighted; for we expected to see an author, and we find a man." Students who note merely the superficial traits of the Book of Job — its regular structure, its long colloquies, its argumentative tone — may easily discern therein only an author, employing an elaborate and somewhat artificial framework to group together for discussion certain hard problems concerning man's destiny and God's dealings with him on the earth. Is not this, as matter of fact, what we are directed to by the vast volume of interpretation which for ages has been lavished on the book? Whatever else we may find in it, we are taught to regard it first of all as a grand monument of reasoning, as a world-debate between Job and his friends, in which we are to look for a categorical decision telling men for all time why the righteous suffer. But surely its perpetual outflashings of the natural style, which will not

How the Book of Job may be superficially interpreted.

brook the restraints of mere dialectics, nor stay to build a coldly consistent structure of thought, should be accepted as an invitation to deeper search. These burning words are much more than a debate. If ever a book revealed a man, if ever through the indignant thrusts of controversy were heard the beatings of a warm human heart, it is in this story of the patriarch of Uz. So much, whatever problems have to be encountered later, is evident even to a hasty perusal. The task of interpretation is not easy; but let us at all events follow the line of least resistance. Studied as an argument cunningly put together by a skilled reasoner, the Book of Job is beset with difficulties well-nigh insurmountable. Studied as the utterance of a man like ourselves, who speaks out in the natural style what is in him, it is the clear and unambiguous voice of humanity, which finds echo in all the world.

How the "natural style," even at first test, makes against such interpretation.

To restore this book to its natural style, to read it without prepossessions in the broad light that falls on every man, seems to me the kind of treatment which it most needs to-day. For it has come down to us so thickly wrapped in a covering of associations erudite and dogmatic that it is in no little danger

The treatment proper to the book to-day,

as contrasted with the treatment we see it receiving.

of being lost to the one class for whom it was intended. "A noble book, all men's book," is what Carlyle says of it; yet to the plain reader it appears rather an arsenal of texts for the theologian, or a quarry of hard words for the commentator, or a dilapidated relic of antiquity to be carved and refashioned according to the notions of the critic. Right and necessary as such treatment is, perhaps, in its place, let it once get the upper hand, as indeed it seems very nearly to have done, and the book is degraded into one of those "things in books' clothing" which Charles Lamb accounted no books at all, being doomed thenceforth to stand by the side of other learned lumber filling up scholars' shelves, and preserving the credit of their libraries. Such a fate for the Book of Job were melancholy indeed. For the book was never written to satisfy an esoteric few. It came glowing from a large human heart, from the furnace of universal human affliction; and it is adapted to reach every soul that has thought and suffered. The more we penetrate beyond the mere skill of the author to communion in spirit with the man, the more will this universal character, this cry from the heart of humanity, far beyond the jargon of a class or the cunning performance of a pen, impress itself upon us.

Its universal human interest.

Time and space are annihilated, and the unreal vagaries of speculation seem outlived, as this echo of our own deep consciousness comes floating to us across the centuries. Such are the characteristics that inhere in Pascal's natural style. Such, too, are the marks of the true world-poem, of the poem which, though necessarily speaking in the dialect of a nation and an age, is the exponent of "those elementary feelings which subsist permanently in the race, and which are independent of time."

It is on these broad human lines, recognizing the man beneath the written word, that we will try now to study out the meaning of this Book of Job.

Object and result of the present study.

The study will indeed reveal great problems, whose filaments stretch out through the world of theological and philosophical inquiry; it will not fail to deepen our sense of the marvelous literary art which has presided alike over word and plan; but, what is of more intimate concern to us, it will disclose to our gaze in clearer outlines one of the great of the earth, a man of fears and doubts like ourselves, rising up against his doom, which is humanity's doom, and conquering his way to hope and peace. Invention or fact, the man Job is one of the guiding figures of the ages, a world's hero; whose words, the record of a great conflict and victory, we cannot afford to leave cloistered among the learned few.

Of the characteristics of the book which appear at first opening, none are more obvious than this, that its structural outline is twofold. On the one hand, its basis is simple narrative. It tells the story of a man eminently good, prosperous, and happy, who, at the instance of Satan, though himself perceiving therein only God's vengeful stroke, is suddenly deprived of everything — property, children, health, the world's esteem; who, nevertheless, though accused and deserted by relatives and friends, sturdily refuses to own that his affliction is due to sin, or that his punishment is just; and who, after many pains of doubt and conquests of faith, is commended by Jehovah and restored to twice his former prosperity. On the other hand, the main body of the work looks like pure discussion and argument: Job and his friends affirming and answering, reproving and recriminating, in three elaborate cycles of discourse; Elihu coming in, full of words, after the friends are silenced; and Jehovah pronouncing the final answer out of the whirlwind. So prominent is this second type of structure that it is no wonder the book

Two types apparent in its structure: narrative

and argument.

has been prevailingly judged by it; yet the question remains fairly open which of the two should be regarded as giving supreme law to the work; nor is the question less pressing, how the combination can also be a harmony — argument and action working together to set forth out of many one comprehensive, dominant idea.

Which type predominates?

How are the two interwoven?

Important questions these, with the satisfactory investigation of which are closely associated all the lines of inquiry that this study will open: the various considerations relating to the thought, the form, the connection of parts, and the origin, of the book before us.

Significance of these inquiries.

I.

First of all, it is important to inquire what in this book is most central, what the Book of Job supremely stands for; or, as the question is usually propounded, what is its *problem?*

I. Its central and ruling idea.

Any answer to this question, I suspect, which reduces the teaching of the book to an abstract proposition, or form of words, is bound to be unsatisfactory. The book is too much like life for that. In real life and experience things do not shape themselves to didactic ends. Good and

Difficulty of expressing this in a proposition.

evil, wisdom and error, are subtly interwoven with all events, but the pattern is not systematic; it is only in poetry that we are conducted unfailingly to poetic justice. To force on nature a didactic purpose is the mark of the inferior artist. The Book of Job evinces the consummate artistic genius that created it by reading like a transcript from life, with its struggles, its doubts, its eddying inconsistencies. The action reaches its end, not by the arrow-line of a homiletic plan, but through such gropings and stumblings, such gradual discoveries of the true way, as must content us all in this mystery-encompassed existence. We may not unfitly apply to it what has been said of Shakespeare's plays: " It teaches many lessons, but not any one prominent above another; and when we have drawn from it all the direct instruction which it contains, there remains still something unresolved, — something which the artist gives, and which the philosopher cannot give." Every one who has lived close to the beating heart of the poem must feel how it fades and shrinks by being turned into a mere moral tale. Like Mont Blanc, it radiates awe into many an enraptured beholder, as it rises glorious in the warm flooding sunshine that cheers the com-

J. A. Froude, Short Studies on Great Subjects, vol. i. p. 29.

mon world; but interpose the cloud of didacticism, and the next moment it stands a blanched, shivering, forbidding expanse of snows and chasms.

Nor are the grounds of this feeling wholly æsthetic. As a plain matter of interpretation, too, we find that any form of words, however felicitous, in which men attempt to imprison the poem's teaching and purpose fails to satisfy its whole idea; some of its choicest portions are sure to remain outside, ravelled and loose. It is chiefly for this unconfessed reason, I think, that modern critics have felt compelled *How such attempt reacts on criticism.* to manipulate the poem to suit their own ideas, — cutting out passages here, and making conjectural emendations there; assigning one section to the original author, who began well, and another to that *bête noir* of criticism, the later editor or transcriber, who bunglingly tried to steer the poem's thought into a new channel. Taking for granted that every part must at all events square with some supreme didactic idea, their suspicion naturally falls on whatever does not. They have confessedly no other ground to work upon that is decisive; apart from this the poem looks like a unity, nor is there sign of a record to prove later changes. And when the critics, having once given free rein to the refashioning spirit, have cut and carved to their hearts' content, there is nothing left but a torso.

To see how this works, let us examine the prevailing idea of the design, or problem, of the Book of Job, and follow it a little into its logical consequences. According to Professor Conant's view, the subject of the book is "The mystery of God's providential government of men;" or, to put it more specifically in Professor Delitzsch's words, which come essentially to the same thing: "Warum ergehen über den Gerechten Leiden auf Leiden? — das ist die Frage, deren Beantwortung sich das Buch Iob zur Aufgabe macht."[1] Now it is beyond doubt that this question, or some aspect of it, plays a large part in determining the course, or action, of the poem; Job's friends, for example, din it into his ears until he is fain to cry out, "I have heard many things like these." But does it play the leading part? that is, is this the most central and inclusive subject, to which all else is secondary, or is this itself a *motif* in the exposition of a deeper idea?

Illustrated from the prevailing view.

Conant's translation of Job, with introduction and notes, p. vii.

Delitzsch, Commentar über das Buch Iob, 2d ed., p. 3.

Let us see what results from making this didactic idea supreme.

[1] " Why does suffering on suffering befall the righteous? — that is the question to the answering of which the Book of ob devotes itself."

In the first place, this view subordinates the divine and presumably directive element of the book to the human; making the book centre in a question raised and discussed by human disputants, and regarding the Lord as appearing, in the theophany at the end, mainly in order to settle the point in dispute. At the same time, the question propounded by Satan at the beginning, "Doth Job fear God for nought?" and in fact the whole foundation laid in the Prologue, is ignored from the point where the discussion begins. Thus it cannot be said that the introduction really introduces. This fact operates to give a decided centrifugal tendency to the Prologue; nor, indeed, are there wanting those who would discard the Prologue as not belonging to the original design of the book. It does, in fact, seem to be a kind of intrusion, with its glimpse into heaven and the divine counsels, if, after all, the speculations of a company of bewildered mortals so completely overshadow it.

How this view subordinates the divine element to the human

and weakens the tenure of the Prologue.

A second and more fundamental result is, that this view commits the Book of Job almost wholly to the argumentative type of structure above mentioned; making it the record of a kind of debating club, wherein the question

How this view makes the book a debate; see above; p. 7

is discussed at great length, for and against, and is finally decided by the Lord from the whirlwind. Thus, with the narrative element practically ignored, the reader is left to work his way over arid fields of dialectics, in search of a Q. E. D.; and he may well wonder where a book that is so harnessed to the plodding tasks of prose could ever have got its acknowledged poetic power. Apart from this æsthetic objection, also, there are not wanting elements of the book, even in its purely controversial portions, which remonstrate against being pressed too rigorously into such a mould. For one thing, the Lord's assumed decision of the question, when we come to examine it, is no decision: it does not address itself to what the men are debating at all. In order to make it apply to the case, we have to resort to what may be *inferred* from this and that. This fact has not escaped the notice of interpreters; and Elihu, who is the wax nose of the critics, is brought in very opportunely, being as much of a refuge on one theory as he is a stumbling-block on others. And indeed his words sum up the discussion, it must be owned, more really than do the Lord's; for which reason he is regarded by some as fur-

and practically ignores the narrative element.

To such a debate the Lord's words are no decision;

and Elihu helps out only in defiance of the author's intent.

nishing "the first half of the positive solution of the problem." Thus it is given to him, as he plumed himself on doing, to set right both Job and his friends.

<small>Zöckler (Lange), p. 278.</small>

Yet here we encounter another difficulty; for Elihu is abruptly dismissed by the first word from the whirlwind as one who "darkeneth counsel by words without knowledge," and Job is singled out at the end, of all the disputants, as the only one who has "spoken of God the thing that is right." If the poem is a debate, its ending must be regarded as vague. Then further, when we come to examine into the manner in which the debaters answer one another we find little of that vigorous give and take which we associate with the close grasp and analysis of a question. The speakers wander wide of the mark that we have set for them; there is little real progress in the reasoning, and much that we have to explain, or excuse, on the convenient ground of Oriental discursiveness. Job, who is regarded as the uncompromising antagonist of all the others, not infrequently seems to give away his case; and once, indeed, he so closely reëchoes his opponents' thought that some interpreters have been inclined to give his speech to

<small>Section xxvi. 2, 3.</small>

<small>Section xxx. 5, 12.</small>

<small>Nor is the debate, as such, self-consistent.</small>

<small>See, for example, section xix. 12-45.</small>

Zophar. Then there is the twenty-eighth chapter, the magnificent praise of Wisdom, which certainly no one would consent to banish from the poem; yet into this scheme of a debate it fits so poorly, and seems with all its princely beauty so out of place, that it is conjectured by Professor Delitzsch to have been an insertion from the author's or some later editor's portfolio.

Section xix. 46–104.

We thus find that the debate theory, with its assumed main subject, "The mystery of God's providential government of men," does not result in an exposition so homogeneous as we could wish. Some parts of the poem are left in rather unstable equilibrium, while others have to be pressed quite arbitrarily into the scheme that we have made for them. The same fate would, I feel sure, befall any other abstraction, or general proposition, that might be taken as the supreme goal of the poem's teaching; the trouble lies with the didacticism itself rather than with any particular expression of it. Any object that contemplates being wrought out by discussion alone must of necessity leave the interpreter stranded far short of his ideal resting-point, which is only in that place where he sees all the parts of the book in their proper position,

General result of this view.

Unsatisfactoriness of any didactic object.

and doing what the deepest genius of the work requires.

It is no part of my present plan to enumerate the theories, sometimes grotesquely far-fetched, that have been imposed on this long-suffering Book of Job. Nor need I stay to describe at length the arithmetical style of interpretation, which works out the poem's problem, so to say, by the rule of three; laboriously computing the three sections of the book, the three parts of the poem proper, the three cycles of speeches, the three pairs in each cycle, the three discourses of Elihu,[1] the three strophes in many of the speeches, and the three temptations of Job. On this line of exposition the tendency, already mentioned, to assign one of Job's speeches to Zophar is augmented by the fact that thereby the third round of debate and the three-times-three speeches of Job and his friends are charmingly completed; and poor Elihu's tenure is made more precarious by the fact, forsooth, that he is a fourth speaker, who comes unintroduced by the Prologue. All this seems to me the sad result of trying to stretch a living poem on the Procrustean rack of a

A glance at certain mechanical interpretations.

How they affect the parts of the poem.

---

[1] So reckoned, I suppose, in order to preserve the general symmetry; though as matter of fact Elihu speaks four times.

dead, mechanical plan. I ought not, perhaps, to pass over Elihu with such slight notice here, seeing that just now in the critical realm he is everywhere spoken against; nor would I venture to leave him thus did I not hope to make clear by and by that the poem, as it now stands, has an artistic unity obvious enough to reconcile him fully to his place.

For an artistic unity the poem certainly has; let not the foregoing criticisms be taken as urged against that fact; a unity more comprehensive and poetic, and at the same time not less absolute, than could be obtained on the lines I have described. Only, that unity centres in a *person* rather than in a system of thought or reasoning; it is Job himself, the man Job, with his bewilderment of doubt, his utter honesty with himself and the world, his outreaching faith, his loyalty through all darkness and mystery to what is Godlike, who is the solution of the Job-problem, far more truly than Job's words, or the words of Elihu, or the august address from the whirlwind. How God deals with men, and how men may interpret his dealings; why God sees fit to afflict the righteous; these are indeed important questions, and not to be ignored; but more vital still is the question what Job *is,* becomes, achieves, in the fiery

Wherein centres the artistic unity of the poem.

trial of God's unexplained visitation. In the answer to that personal question lies the supreme answer to all the rest. It is not a mere author that we find here, but a man. And as we trace the progress of Job's soul, step by step, revealed to us through his own words and through the attacks of his friends, we shall be brought to a contemplation of greatness in life and character such as, for sublimity, it will be hard to parallel in literature, however highly we may value the divinest creations of an Æschylus or a Milton.

Thus, in the person and spiritual history of Job, we are brought back to the narrative basis which, so long as we consider only the discourses of the poem, we are in danger of ignoring. Under these discourses we are to trace not the building of a system, but the progress of a character, tried, developed, victorious; for they reveal how the patriarch works out, or perhaps we may better say embodies, the solution of a great problem.

How this does justice to the narrative element.

What, then, *is* the problem, if such is its solution? We need not look far for the answer to this question. The problem, propounded by Satan at the outset, and tested by permission of Jehovah, is, "Doth Job fear God for nought?" This is, of course, the sneer of utter selfishness against all that

Statement of the Job-problem.

is loyal and disinterested: it asks, in effect, Is there such a thing as whole-souled, self-forgetting service of God, just for His sake and for righteousness' sake? Nor is such a question, we must admit, very strange in a world where the fear of God is regarded as the sure road to worldly prosperity. Where such an idea prevails it is quite possible for piety to become, to all intents and purposes, merely a refined selfishness; how can we tell from the outside whether it is serving God for His sake or because such service is a paying investment? Yes: there is a place in history where the question just fits in; Satan has found the weak point in that Old Testament standard of piety and its reward. And Job's life, as it is traced in the glowing, indignant, faith-inspired words of his complaint, is the triumphant answer. Job *does* fear God for nought: that is, his integrity is no vulgar barter for wages, as Satan supposes, but deeply founded in the truth of things, — so deeply that he takes leave of friends, of family, of life, nay, of God himself, as he has hitherto regarded God, in order to be true. And if Job, a man like ourselves, has wrought out the answer, then the answer exists in humanity. There is such a thing as disinterested piety, and it contains

How it answers to the age in which it was propounded.

How Job solves it.

whole worlds of faith and insight. Or, to gather the history before us into a sentence:

The solution expressed in a proposition. THERE IS A SERVICE OF GOD WHICH IS NOT WORK FOR REWARD: IT IS A HEART-LOYALTY, A HUNGER AFTER GOD'S PRESENCE, WHICH SURVIVES LOSS AND CHASTISEMENT; WHICH IN SPITE OF CONTRADICTORY SEEMING CLEAVES TO WHAT IS GODLIKE AS THE NEEDLE SEEKS THE POLE; AND WHICH REACHES UP OUT OF THE DARKNESS AND HARDNESS OF THIS LIFE TO THE LIGHT AND LOVE BEYOND.

This, if we must chill it down from the glow of its personal and poetic utterance to a generalization, is what, as I conceive, the Book of Job stands for. But of this answer, as of the problem, the hero is as little aware as the rest. Wrought out in darkness and anguish, it is known only to those celestial spectators who rejoice, and to that scoffing spirit who is discomfited by it. For the answer is not put in words, nor made a didactic issue: it is *lived*.

II.

If, then, this poem centres in a hero, whose *II. Its literary class, the Epic.* spiritual achievements it makes known to us, we have thus indicated the literary class to which it is to be predominantly assigned. I regard this ancient book as the record of a sublime epic action, whose scene is not the tumultuous battle-field, nor the arena of rash adventure, but the solitary soul of a righteous man. It contains, though in somewhat unusual form, the governing elements of an epic poem.

This designation of the poem as an epic, however, is not to be made without some confession of how little, as well as how much, there is to justify it. *The word epic to be taken in a modified sense.* The whole genius of the Hebrew literature is so different from that of the Greeks that it is only by an accommodation of terms that we can apply to it the categories derived from the forms of the latter. This poem, for instance, looks at first sight more like a drama than an epic; it contains fairly individualized characters, and its thought is developed by means of dialogue or colloquy. It has been called a didactic poem; and such undoubtedly it is, if, as many think, it is preëminently a debate. Nor is there lacking in every part a lyric intensity which not infrequently seems almost to sweep the action away from its logical moorings into its own headlong utterance of a mood. Yet in spite of these untoward modifications, it is fruitful and significant to refer the poem to a prevailing type. "We may rely upon it," says *Matthew Arnold, Essays in Criticism, second series, p. 137.*

Matthew Arnold, "that we shall not improve upon the classification adopted by the Greeks for kinds of poetry; that their categories of epic, dramatic, lyric, and so forth, have a natural propriety, and should be adhered to. It may sometimes seem doubtful to which of two categories a poem belongs; whether this or that poem is to be called, for instance, narrative or lyric, lyric or elegiac. But there is to be found in every good poem a strain, a predominant note, which determines the poem as belonging to one of these kinds rather than the other; and here is the best proof of the value of the classification, and of the advantage of adhering to it."

To the view of the poem's class which I have ventured here to take, there presents itself at first thought a grave objection. The narrative, the action, seems lacking. The whole course of the poem is developed through what Job and Eliphaz and Bildad and the rest "answered and said." May there not, however, be an action disguised, an action wherein the speaker's words, like windows, reveal the great spiritual events that are taking place in the speaker's soul? I think I shall be able to show that there is, and a grand one. An unusual action it indeed is, for poetry; perhaps,

Seeming lack of epic action,

and how explained.

therefore, requiring just that union of structural types, the narrative and the argumentative, which I have already pointed out. Further, the Hebrew poetic style, with its basis the parallelism, which pauses at the end of every line and develops the thought by perpetual repetition and antithesis, is singularly unadapted to narration, — so unadapted, that when the Hebrew author has a simple story to tell, as, for instance, in the Prologue and Epilogue to our poem, he has spontaneous recourse to prose. On the other hand, for a sententious lesson, or *mashal*, for the brief and telling utterance of emotion, aspiration, precept, the Hebrew poetic style is a remarkably felicitous medium. Now in the Book of Job we have indeed a story, an action, but of very peculiar kind: the scene, so far as appears to the eye, only an ash-heap outside an Arab city, but to the inner view the soul of man, with all its warring passions, beliefs, convictions. It is the spiritual history of the man of Uz, his struggles and adventures, unknown to sense, but real to faith, as his fervid thoughts "go sounding on, a dim and perilous way." For portraying such an action, so as to lay the inmost thoughts and feelings of one soul upon another, this *mashal* style, with its trenchant

The Hebrew parallelism:

its disadvantages

and uses.

parallelisms, so far from being a disadvantage, is perhaps the unique and only adequate medium. Through it not the author speaks, but the man himself, laying bare the secrets of his own heart, and charging his words with his whole inner history. Curiously enough, a somewhat similar method of developing a narrative action has been largely employed by the poet of our own day who has done most to sound the depths of spiritual experience, Robert Browning, whose so-called "dramatic method" is merely his deliberately adopted way of bodying forth at once the inner and outer elements of a story, —

Browning, Sordello, beginning. "By making speak, myself kept out of view, The very man as he was wont to do, And leaving you to say the rest for him;"

and every student of Browning will testify to the wonderful vividness with which each one of his chosen characters is made to live a chapter of his life before our eyes.

But if so much is conceded to the dramatic element, why not frankly call the poem a drama? Well, I am not disposed to quarrel about the terms in which we are to designate its form; either term, epic or drama, has to be accommodated to a new application. Yet why call it a drama, and deny the term to the Platonic dialogues? for it is in these, I think, that our poem, as to structure, finds its nearest dramatic parallel. It is because the action, though to a degree dramatic in form, moves for the most part independently of the impact of mood on mood or of character on character, that I am unable to regard the poem as in the truest sense dramatic; and on the other hand, it is because of the vigorous onset of spiritual forces under the dialogue, self-moved even more than set in motion from other minds, valiantly meeting hostile doubts and trials, making memorable conquests in integrity and faith, that I discern in this testing and triumph of Job a predominating epic strain. Is it less truly epic than that conflict of temptation in the wilderness which Milton has sung, — a conflict whose weapons were piercing words and whose battle-ground was the soul of the Son of Man? I use the term epic, because, whatever its technical type, the poem is the embodiment of a veritable *epos*, of a history which, whether real or invented, lies at the very basis of pure religion, full of significance for its integrity and perpetuity. What I mean by this may be seen illustrated in the Prometheus Bound of Æschylus, which is truly the embodiment of a national epos, albeit in dramatic form. In that

Justification, nevertheless, of the term epic.

Milton's Paradise Regained.

Illustrated by Æschylus' Prometheus Bound.

poem as in this, quite apart from the dialogue or narrative manner of presentation, which is determined by the vogue of the age and the conditions under which the work is published, our paramount interest is centred in the legend or saga which lies at the foundation, in the heroic action which glorifies some revered name of universal tradition, and in the national or religious significance of the whole. These are marks of the epos ; and these are what give its basal literary character to the Book of Job.

That the poem before us was not the pure invention of its author, but founded on a Job legend or tradition, is the conclusion most in accord with what we know of the literary ways of the Hebrew writers. They wrote with practical objects in view, appealing from real life to real life, and not in order to please the world with the power or felicity of their literary achievements. Having a history marvelously rich in life-lessons, whose details and spirit had been faithfully instilled by fathers into generations of sons, they had a store of material which would ill brook to be supplanted by mere efforts of the fancy ; especially when, as in this case, the past was to influence the destiny of the future. It is into this treasure heap of tradition that Ezekiel dips, when, in threatening calamity on the rec-

The legendary basis of the poem.

reant land, he says, "Though these three men, Noah, Daniel, and Job, were in it, they should not deliver but their own souls by their righteousness, saith the Lord God." This we know because the Book of Daniel was not yet written: Daniel was a widely revered name; Noah was an historic name; and this mention of Job seems to derive its significance more from an age-filling tradition than from a book. *Ezekiel xiv. 14.*

"When we inquire, however," says Professor Davidson, "what elements of the book really belong to the tradition, a definite answer can hardly be given. A tradition could scarcely exist which did not contain the name of the hero, and the name 'Job' is no doubt historical. A mere name, however, could not be handed down without some circumstances connected with it; and we may assume that the outline of the tradition included Job's great prosperity, the unparalleled afflictions that befell him, and possibly also his restoration. Whether more was embraced may be uncertain." It was probably a tradition full enough so that to those who were familiar with it, as to the Apostle James's later age, could be said, "Ye have heard of the patience of Job, and have seen the end of the Lord." Further to un- *Davidson, Job (Cambridge Bible for Schools), p. xix.* *James v. 11.*

ravel the various threads, traditional and other, of which the book is woven together, could serve no practical end. Suffice it for us that out of these simple materials, because they represent a spiritual experience that taxes the whole gamut of expression to utter, some unknown author, grandly regardless of the technical restraints of drama or lyric or narrative, has given to the ages what we may regard as the Hebrew national Epic, expressed in a style and spirit peculiarly Hebrew.

As an Epic, Job an exponent of the national genius.
Every nation according to its genius. We often speak of that idea of symmetry and beauty whose evolution seems to have been the mission of the Greeks in the world, and of that idea of law and organism which we get from the Romans. Not only through their art and their institutions, but also through the spirit of their literature, these nations have impressed upon the world their distinctive character. We know also that no other nations have ever approached the Hebrews in their genius for apprehending spiritual truth. If the Hebrews were to give to the world an epic, would it be a story of battle and bloodshed, or of strange adventures beyond the seas? These by no means represent their national character. For the most genuine expression of their life you must look

under the surface, in the soul, where worship and aspiration and prophetic faith come face to face with God. And what epos could more truly gather into itself the most sacred ideal of such a nation than this story of Job, the man in whom was wrought the supreme test of what it is to be perfect and upright, who on his ashheap, a veritable Hebrew Prometheus, continued honest with himself, true to what he saw in the world, loyal to what his soul told him was divine, until the storm was past and his foe shrank baffled away? Is not such a theme worth singing?

The Epic of the Inner Life, — by this name we may designate the book before us. As such its significance is more than Hebrew; it extends far beyond national bounds to the universal heart of humanity; nay, it is with strange freshness and application to the spiritual maladies of this nineteenth century of Christ that the old Arab chief's struggles and victories come to us, as we turn the ancient pages anew.

The Epic of the Inner Life.

III.

That the narrative type of structure, which is the basis of the poem, also preponderates throughout, or at least is present in every part, so far as the peculiar poetic style will admit, is a not unreasonable conjecture. Let us see if this is so, by tracing what I have ventured to call its action, with special reference to its continuity and the interdependence of its parts.

III. Connection and continuity of its parts.

Job, a man perfect and upright, who has always feared God and shunned evil, and whose righteous life has always reaped its natural fruitage of honor and prosperity, is suddenly overwhelmed with the deepest afflictions; one stroke following hard upon another — loss of property, loss of children, and finally the most loathsome and painful bodily disease — until he can only long for death. At first he accepts his afflictions devoutly, attributing no injustice to God, and sharply rebuking any suggestion of disloyalty; but as months of wretchedness pass, and friends bring up in vain the commonplaces of explanation which he and they have hitherto held in common, his musing spirit finds itself girt round with a darkness and mystery wholly impenetrable. It is a problem which men's wisdom has not yet solved. Consider the difficulties into which he is plunged. Of the scene in heaven, where Satan has moved the Lord "to destroy him causelessly," Job has of course no knowledge. No Satanic agency is visible; all the data

Beginning and basis of the action.

Difficulties involved in Job's case.

point to God as the direct inflicter of the stroke. The four calamities occurring in one day cannot be an accident; the fire from heaven and the wind from beyond the desert cannot be casualties of this world, like the violence of men; and, most indubitable of all, his disease, elephantiasis, is universally regarded as the most dread sign of God's immediate visitation. It is taken for granted by all, Job, his wife, and his friends, that he is for some reason the object of God's wrath. Here, then, is Job's difficulty: God is punishing him, — and for what? He is conscious of no sin to deserve it; his "heart does not reproach one of his days." It is strange that he should perish without knowing his crime; strange, too, that the heavens should be shut to every call of his for explanation. To be so treated is to be shut off from the "friendship of God," which has always been the most cherished blessing of his life. But this is only the beginning of his distress. If he, a righteous man, is treated as if he were wicked, then the world is out of joint; the bounds of right and wrong, of justice and iniquity, are wholly confused; and where is the truth of things? Are the powers that work unseen arrayed after all on the side of evil, and against godliness? Is it falsehood that wins in this universe? Such is the labyrinth of "dreadful and hideous thoughts" through which Job must grope his way to the light.

The course that Job takes is set off very suggestively, by contrast, in the characters of the *dramatis personæ* with whom he is associated.

Of these, the most deeply contrasted to Job is Satan, the Accuser, at whose instigation the trial of his integrity is made. In studying this character, we need to dismiss from our minds, for the time being, the Satanic traits that come to light in other parts of Scripture, and confine ourselves to the record before us. The being who appears here so familiarly among the sons of God is no Miltonic Satan, no monster of black malignity and unconquerable hatred. The most striking trait of his character seems to be simply restlessness, unquiet. In his "roaming to and fro in the earth and walking up and down in it," and in his eagerness to try experiments with Job, we are reminded of that New Testament evil spirit, who being cast out of a man "walketh through dry places, seeking rest." A homeless, unquiet spirit: may we not say, then, that in Satan our author portrays a spirit unanchored to any allegiance, a spirit who has lost his moorings? Being attached to no

Contrast between Job and Satan.

Satan's character.

See Luke xi. 24.

Father of spirits, to steady him and give him principle, all his regards centre in self-gratification; having no goal beyond the present, he lives simply to appease the restlessness of the moment. So we find him, naturally enough, a mocking, detracting, reckless, impudent being, observing and criticising all things, yet sympathizing with none, caring for no sufferings, responding to no deep movements of heart, — what Goethe calls a "schalk."[1] For a being like this, such a thing as disinterested goodness is simply non-existent; he has no faculty to comprehend it. When he asks the sarcastic question, "Doth Job fear God for nought?" and when he lays the wager with God to sever the patriarch from his allegiance, he is merely speaking out of his own shallow selfishness, and interpreting men as good or evil, just as it happens, for a price. In polar contrast to this stands Job. His soul is so deeply anchored to what is good and true that the idea of barter, of work and wages, finds no room in the calculation, — nay, so deeply that he is forced to

Job's contrasted traits.

---

[1] Goethe's imitation of this opening scene of the Book of Job, in his Prologue to *Faust*, brings out the traits of Satan's character in several suggestive ways, which will be traced more particularly in the notes to this section of the translation.

cut loose from what his friends say of God, to take his life in his hand and remonstrate with God himself, as he looks out on a confused world; and thus, putting uttermost faith in goodness, he " voyages through strange seas of thought alone," finding radiant landing-places of faith one after another, until a new world is discovered in which he comes to see that being anchored to the good and true is being anchored to God after all.

The other contrast is afforded by the friends who come to visit him. They represent, with its outcome in character, the kind of philosophy that the whole devout world, Job with the rest, has hitherto held, a philosophy which ages of wisdom and reflection have evolved. A philosophy, moreover, that through a long period of national prosperity has crystallized into a very comfortable and convenient creed, well adapted to fair weather and to the routines of life. That God deals with men by an unchanging and in the main calculable law, — good receiving its sure reward in prosperity, wickedness receiving its unfailing desert in woe, — this we may depend upon as the principle on which to build our life. It is a good belief by which to key men up to law and duty, a very effectual

Contrast between Job and his friends.

The friends advocates of the Wisdom philosophy: compare below, pp. 92, sqq.

police regulation for the world. But the fierce light of Job's affliction, so strange and undeserved, opens his eyes to see in this philosophy imperfections hitherto unsuspected. *Job takes issue with the Wisdom doctrine.* First of all he sees that it rests on an incomplete induction of facts: for there are afflicted righteous, — he is one, — and there are unpunished wicked, filling the land with their evil deeds. Then, secondly, — and here is where his self-forgetting integrity evinces its insight, — he sees that this belief may be so held, nay, is actually so held by these very friends, as to become merely a refined sort of work-and-wages theory. Serve God, and you will prosper; if woes come, betokening God's displeasure, turn to God anew, and prosper again. If this were all, — and it very nearly sums up the friends' creed, — we might with only too much reason ask, Does such a believer fear God for nought? But to Job's quickened spiritual sense this is not all. The old imperfect wisdom must be lifted to a higher than worldly plane. In the black shadows that surround him come flashes of unspeakable things, new resting-places for faith, truths that the unchastened soul cannot appreciate. Here, then, is the contrast: the friends, who have never been quickened by suffering, are conventional, speculative believers, their God a traditional God, remote, undelighted-in, their creed a hide-bound system, essentially worldly and selfish, for the sake of which they deny both the righteousness of Job and the mystery of evil that is in the world; Job, whose affliction has startled him with the sense that God's face is darkened, turns loyally to God as flowers turn to the sun, is in agony of doubt until he can identify God with goodness and love, and seeking supremely after light, reality, personal communion, advances with increasing insight until at the end he can say, "I had heard of Thee by the hearing of the ear, but now mine eye seeth Thee."

The action foreshadowed in these contrasts. The voyage of Job's soul to God, his anchorage and his light, which is the action foreshadowed in the foregoing contrasts, we are now ready to trace somewhat in detail.

How Job first relieves his heart in words. The first feeling of a soul thus plunged into undeserved misery we can readily divine, — the sense of utter bewilderment. This is the feeling that finds expression in Job's first speech, wherein he opens his mouth and curses his day.

Section ii. Weariness of life, passionate desire for death with its rest and its oblivion, which are the emotions that shape his utterance, are after all but the surface-waves of his agitation;

its deep cause lies in his feeling that his life has lost its guidance and direction. He is like one whose way, hitherto free and clear, is suddenly shut in by cloud and darkness.

> "Wherefore giveth He light to the wretched,
> And life to the bitter in soul? ...
> To a man whose way is hid,
> And whom God hath hedged in?"

*Section ii.
41, 42, 47, 48.*

It is worthy of remark that Job's question is not, why he is punished, but why a life so bitter and dark should have been given at all. Punishment implies desert, or if not desert, then injustice. To have given his affliction the name of punishment would have set him at once in the attitude of seeking for its cause, either in himself or in God. That the cause should be in himself, either as wicked, or even as unconsciously corrupt through the innate sinfulness of men, has never entered his mind; on the contrary, one great element of his bewilderment is his consciousness of the watchful solicitude with which he has hitherto led a life of faithful integrity before God: —

> "For I feared a fear, and it hath overtaken me;
> And what I dreaded is come upon me.
> I was not heedless, nor was I at ease,
> Nor was I at rest, — yet trouble came."

*Section ii.
51-54.*

No more is he ready to fasten the cause, even by remote implication, upon God. His friends have not been at him yet with their theodicies; and Job is unwilling to theorize or to accuse where there is no ray of light. The only outlet for his overburdened heart, in this opening speech, is just to sigh over a life that contains no reason for living.

Effect of Job's speech on the friends. Thus, with the mournful comfort that sympathizing friends are still about him to share his woe, Job pours out the bitter fullness of his soul. As he pauses, however, he is surprised to find, not murmurs of sympathy, but silence and averted faces. The three friends have scented evil. Here is a man who when the stroke comes is *not* all submission, does not own that it is clear and deserved. He must be set right, let friendship stand or fall. Accordingly, with very conciliatory words, as of one who would do an unpleasant duty in the gentlest way, Eliphaz, the eldest and wisest of the three, takes him in hand, and reminds him of his inconsistency: —

Section iii. 2-9.
"If one essay a word with thee, wilt thou be offended?
Yet who can forbear speaking?
Behold, thou hast admonished many,
And thou hast strengthened feeble hands;
Thy words have confirmed the faltering,
And bowing knees hast thou made strong;
But now it is come upon thee, — and thou faintest;
It toucheth thee, and thou art confounded."

Then he goes on to read Job a lecture, in which he presents — in general terms, *Eliphaz's discourse.* and leaving Job to make his own applications — the prevailing doctrine, hitherto unquestioned, of sin and retribution. It is the most elaborate discourse of the friends, and anticipates substantially their whole argument, Elihu's included. It is the argument that everything in the world comes by justice and desert; that punishment has its sufficient cause in sin, open or secret; and that thus in God's wrath we may read and measure man's wickedness. This is what Job has always accepted as the fundamental principle of the Hebrew philosophy; nor is it to be called untrue, so much as inadequate and aside from the present case. Of course it can have but one implication. To talk of sin and punishment now, though in ever so general terms, is merely to accuse Job of sin. It is meaningless otherwise. So little is this implication disguised that forthwith Job is solemnly admonished to make his peace with God — as if he had ever been at war with God! But there is the tell-tale leprosy; the friends cannot get over that. If it does not mean that some one has sinned, it seems to mean something about God which it were impiety to think of.

The three friends all ply Job in turn with essentially the same interpretation of the case, their one object being at all hazards to justify God. They vary mainly in the manner of enforcing their views. Eliphaz, who assumes the calmest and most judicial tone, draws his arguments from the universal "natural law in the spiritual world:" —

Essential identity of the three friends' arguments.

Eliphaz.

"Bethink thee now: who that was guiltless hath perished?
And where have the upright been cut off?
As I have seen, — they that plough iniquity,
And that sow wickedness, reap the same."

Section iii. 12–15.

He has also a deep spiritual view, revealed to him as he says by a vision, of the corruption that lurks unseen in the heart, rendering even angels unclean, and making desert of punishment an inevitable accompaniment of the creature. Such Calvinism before Calvin as this, which reappears more than once in the friends' arguments, is the hardest blow directed at Job's sturdy consciousness of innocence; it "poisons the wells." Bildad, whose anger is roused by Job's assumption of righteousness and complaint to God, emphasizes the perfect justice that orders all things: —

Section iii. 22–43.

Bildad.

"Will God pervert the right?
Or will the Almighty pervert justice?   *Section v.*
If thy children have sinned against Him,   *4-7.*
So hath He given them over into the hand of their transgression," —

and corroborates his words by quoting from the wisdom of the ancients. Zophar, who is still more incensed by Job's passionate remonstrances with God and call for explanation, urges the folly of seeking the mystery of God's ways: — *Zophar.*

"But oh that God might indeed speak,
And open His lips against thee,   *Section vii.*
And show thee the hidden things of wisdom, —   *8-18.*
For there is fold on fold to truth; —
Then know thou, that God abateth to thee of thine iniquity.
   Canst thou find out the secret of God?
Canst thou find out the Almighty to perfection?
Heights of heaven; — what canst thou do?
Deeper than Sheol; — what canst thou know?
Longer than the earth is its measure,
And broader than the sea."

So by their triply bulwarked argument the friends seem to take away all of Job's standing-ground. If he falls back on what his heart assures him of his innocence, he is confronted by the unescapable corruption of the creature; if he besieges the heavens for some explanation of his undeserved misery, he is driven back by the mystery which forbids profane approach. All that is permitted to him is to bless the brazen hardness by which he is **en-compassed**, and to call it justice.

To these arguments of the friends Job does not reply at length until all have spoken. He is musing onward in a way of his own. Yet he marks what they say, and it has its effect in kindling his own thoughts, which in this part of the poem rise to their highest intensity. Nor does it occur to him to deny their assertions: to what they say he answers, "Of a truth I know it is so,— who knoweth not things like these?" And yet from the beginning their well-rehearsed words are strangely insipid; familiar to him always, they have suddenly shriveled into the commonest commonplace, with no vitality, no power to reach the source of his trouble:—

Before answering, Job gives free course to his own thoughts.

"Doth the wild ass bray over the fresh grass?
Or loweth the ox over his fodder?
Can it be eaten — what is tasteless, unsalted?
Or is there savor in the white of an egg?
My soul refuseth to touch!
They are as loathsome food to me."

Section iv. 9-14.

It breaks his heart, too, to see his friends turning away from him, just at this time when a friend's open heart would be a haven of refuge. Job has evidently built a great deal on the love of friends; and as this

His plea for friendship.

fails him we shall see, in the sequel, how he builds more, but on foundations that are out of sight. Plaintively he beseeches them to return and show him wherein he has erred, to look with brotherly eyes into his case. *See section iv. 48-61.* But there is no comfort in them. They are judging him by the visitation that has overtaken him, and think that they are justifying God by withholding sympathy where God has apparently withdrawn favor. It is a case wherein they deem that they must choose between God and friendship; but strange it is to Job that their attitude toward him should be determined by an intellectual theory rather than by that natural brotherly affection which is "likest God within the soul."

Meanwhile, one thing is left to Job: to be honest with himself, to respect his own convictions of right, to cherish the integrity that has always been his life. *His one resource: honesty with himself.* The desire to leave this intact and beyond the reach of temptation sharpens even his longing for death:—

> "Oh that my request might come!
> And that God would grant my longing *Section iv.*
> That it would please God to crush me; *15-21.*
> That He would loose His hand and cut me off.
> For then it would still be my comfort,—
> Yea, I should exult in pain, though He spare not,—
> That I have not denied the words of the Holy One."

Here, then, at the outset Job has struck the key-note; has reached the intrenchment where the battle is to be fought out to the end: loyalty to his own ideal of godlike and holy. It is with trembling consciousness of his own weakness that he sees the long conflict before him; but to live necessitates it.

See section iv. 22-27.

As the friends go on with their pitiless exposition of God's dealings with men, Job is becoming aware of the full significance of his case. It is a season of testing, when his own state, physical and spiritual, the doctrines in which he has always believed, and the interpretations that the friends are pressing upon him, all come up in a disordered review before his mind and gradually crystallize into a definite conclusion. Eliphaz has already recounted what was revealed to him by vision, and intimated that Job, by his anger, is losing the ability to see as the immortals see. But Job will not let himself be cut off from the judgment of his own case. He avers that in calling himself righteous he is speaking out of a spiritual perception of good and evil that is still sane and true. Strong in such confidence, he addresses himself to the enigma before him. He cannot understand why that unknown sin of his, if in-

Job thinking order out of chaos.

Section iii. 44-47.

Section iv. 59-61.

Section iv. 100-106.

deed he is guilty, a sin which at the worst is so venial that forgiveness may be sought almost as a right, should be pursued relentlessly, like a heinous crime, down to death. Then, too, why will such a God give no account, no explanation, no standard for man to live by? Bildad says that nevertheless God is just; but in such a mystery as this where is justice to be found? If this is justice, why, then justice means God's arbitrary will, God's infinite caprice; and the only way one can recognize justice is by noting which way God's favor happens to set. No man can maintain his ways before such a tribunal. Let him have never so righteous a cause, it is but the turn of a hand for God to prove him perverse. Nay, and into what hideous confusion does such a government throw the whole world! No resource left for what has been called righteousness; the bounds of good and evil, of right and duty, are wholly obliterated. With such a state of things Job will not have alliance. Thus, in recording his protest against a world so governed, he reaches his everlasting No.[1]

The spirit of section vi.

Job's everlasting No.

---

[1] The expression is adopted from Carlyle, whose chapter on The Everlasting No, in *Sartor Resartus* (Book ii., chapter vii.), reproduces with remarkable vigor the spirit of Job's protest. In both Carlyle and Job we trace the same fearlessness

Nothing can exceed the tremendous energy of Job's arraignment of God, as it is given in the ninth chapter. The whole chapter ought to be cited to illustrate it; here are a few lines:—

To which section vi. 1-69 corresponds.

"Is the question of strength,— behold, the Mighty One He!
  Of judgment,—'Who will set Me a day?'
  Were I righteous, mine own mouth would condemn me;
Perfect were I, yet would He prove me perverse.
Perfect I *am*,— I value not my soul — I despise my life —
It is all one — therefore I say,
Perfect and wicked He consumeth alike.
If the scourge destroyeth suddenly,
He mocketh at the dismay of the innocent.
The earth is given over into the hands of the wicked;
The face of its judges He veileth;—
If it is not He, who then is it?"

Section vi. 36-47.

Nor does he stop with mere censure in the third person. Turning directly to God, with

of death, the same honesty of spirit, the same remonstrance against a supposed unrighteous order of things, though Job's is the sweeter and more temperate spirit. "Thus," says Carlyle, "had the EVERLASTING NO pealed authoritatively through all the recesses of my Being, of my ME; and then was it that my whole ME stood up, in native God-created majesty, and with emphasis recorded its Protest. Such a Protest, the most important transaction in Life, may that same Indignation and Defiance, in a psychological point of view, be fitly called. The Everlasting No had said: 'Behold, thou art fatherless, outcast, and the Universe is mine (the Devil's);' to which my whole Me now made answer: '*I* am not thine, but Free, and forever hate thee!'"

THE INTRODUCTORY STUDY 47

amazing boldness he brings the Creator himself to that bar of judgment which his standard of justice, his sense of the godlike, has erected : —

"Is it beseeming to Thee that Thou shouldst oppress;
That Thou shouldst despise the labor of Thy
　　hands,
Whilst Thou shinest on the counsel of the
　　wicked?"

*Section vi.
75-77.*

A sorely bewildered heart it is, bewildered by its very integrity, that speaks through these burning words!

This is the passage, in especial, that commentators have referred to, when, taking exception to God's own dictum, they have maintained that Job did not always "speak of God the thing that is right," but sometimes what is wrong, even blasphemous. But consider: Job is not arraigning that God who is recognized as truth and holiness; rather, he is speaking *in the interests* of truth and holiness, against that conventional God whom his friends have created before his eyes out of their arid theologies, the God who by His own confession has been "moved against Job to destroy him causelessly," and of whose mysterious visitation, whatever its purpose, no man has yet found a meaning in which the consciously up-

Are Job's words blasphemous.

See section i. 103.

right soul can rest. It is the *godlike* in Job rising up in remonstrance against an apparently misgoverned world. *Is* it, then, so far out of the way?

Prometheus, a god, chained on Mount Caucasus, could defy the rage of a god whose enmity and supremacy he was destined to outlive; Job, a mortal ready to die on his ash-heap, does not defy, does not hate, does not forswear allegiance, but sends into the darkness the immortal protest of the creature against what is ungodlike and unjust. I confess the hero of the old Hebrew epos seems to me the sublimer of the two.

Job compared with Prometheus.

Thus, by the time two of the friends have spoken, their words, combined with Job's anguish and bitter sense of wrong, have pressed from him his remonstrance against what he must recognize as the unjust order of things. As yet he has not called in question the truth of what they say. But when the third friend, Zophar, follows in the same hard strain, with his angry rebuke of Job for daring to call himself pure, and for presuming to pry into the secret of God, Job's eyes are suddenly opened. He begins to see that they do not know everything after all; that, in fact, their spiritual insight is no more to be trusted than his own:—

Job's eyes opened to his friends' error.

> "Of a truth, ye are the people,
> And wisdom will die with you!
> I also have understanding, as well as you;
> I am not inferior to you;
> And who knoweth not things like these?"

Section viii. 2-6.

What is true in their argument is not new; the "things like these" are the long-established commonplaces of doctrine. That the whole world is God's handiwork; that when He doeth there is no undoing; that He deals with righteous and sinful, with wise and foolish, with individual and nation, just as He will, — these things none will question. Accordingly, his first answer to them, after hearing what all have to say, is to recapitulate and indorse their general position, summing up with these words: — *Section viii. 15-56.*

> "Behold, all this hath mine eye seen;
> Mine ear hath heard and understood it well.
> What ye know, that know I also;
> I am not inferior to you."

Section viii. 53-56.

But all this has failed to touch his real issue with them. In spite of the abstract correctness of their doctrine, they are wholly wrong. *What the friends' error is.*

> "But ye too, — forgers of lies are ye;
> Patchers-up of nothings are ye all."

Section viii. 59, 60.

For as he sees them maintaining God's justice through thick and thin, and denying Job's righteousness in order to do it, the thought flashes upon him that their term righteousness is merely a conventional name for *the winning side;* they are calling his transparent integrity sin, not because what is righteous in their nature compels them to see it so, but because, forsooth, he is a leper. They have found out by this affliction which way God's favor seems to point, and they are hastening to ally themselves with it and be safe. Such a selfish use of God rouses Job's soul to stinging rebuke: —

<small>Section viii. 63-76.</small>
"Hear ye now my rebuke,
And listen to the charges of my lips:
Will ye speak *what is wrong*, for God?
And will ye, for Him, utter deceit?
Will ye respect His person,
Or will ye be special pleaders for God?
Would it be well, if He should search you out?
Or will ye mock Him, as man mocketh man?
He will surely convict you utterly,
If in secret ye are respecters of persons.
Shall not His majesty make you afraid,
And the dread of Him fall upon you?[1]
Your wise maxims are proverbs of ashes;
Your bulwarks turn to bulwarks of clay."

Thus, piercing by the insight of truth to the heart of his friends' life, Job finds that they are *not* serving God for nought; they are shrewdly calculating where

<small>Job's break with his friends.</small>

---

[1] "There is nothing good that is not entirely honest. Better for a man that all the world should grin at him for ever, than that, failing in honesty, God should laugh him to scorn but only once." (Selkirk, *Ethics and Æsthetics of Modern*

the chances of reward and prosperity lie, and shaping their views of right and wrong accordingly. This is enough; no more alliance with them. From this point onward Job's attitude towards his friends is changed. He no longer regards them as wise, nor does he let any more words of theirs go unquestioned. Henceforth he regards them as spiritually blind, —

"For their heart hast Thou hid from understanding," — *Section x. 57.*

and treats them with the scorn due to those whose pretensions have far outrun their wisdom: —

"But you — all of you — return ye! and come now!
For I shall not find a wise man among you." *Section x. 69, 70.*

He can no more look for help from friends; the question lies henceforth between his soul and God.

Nor has this encounter with the selfishness of his friends left Job the man he was. It has carried him over from the everlasting No to the everlasting Yea. *Job's everlasting Yea.* Farewell, now, fear and complaining; farewell trust in the outworn maxims of men: face to face with death and the worst that his unseen enemy can do, Job turns solemnly from his fellows, and commits himself anew to the righteousness that has hitherto been his life, in supreme faith that its issue, though at present he sees it not, must be salvation:—

Section viii. 77-84.
"Be silent; let me alone; and speak will I,
Let come upon me what will.
Wherefore do I take my flesh in my teeth,
And put my life in my hand?
Behold — He may slay me; I may not hope;
But my ways will I maintain to His face.[1]
Nay, that shall be to me also for salvation,
For no false one shall come into His presence."

It is an appeal from the God who works in the impenetrable darkness without to the God who has put holy impulses within, and a trust in the guidance of that honest human heart which "condemns him not."

Compare I John iii. 21.

Section viii. 85-88.
"Hear, oh hear my speech,
And let my declaration sound in your ears.
Behold, now have I set in order my cause;
I know that I shall be justified."

[1] To maintain his ways, to be true in the face of God and the iron universe to that perfect and upright ideal which has hitherto shaped his life, is in Job's soul the supreme imperative, compared with which the desire for restored health and property or any earthly happiness never once comes to mention. "There is in man a Higher than Love of Happiness: he can do without Happiness, and instead thereof find Blessedness! Was it not to preach forth this same Higher that sages and martyrs, the Poet and the Priest, in all times, have spoken and suffered; bearing testimony, through life and through death, of the Godlike that is in Man, and how in the Godlike only has he Strength and Freedom? . . . Love not Pleasure; love God. This is the Everlasting Yea, wherein all contradiction is solved: wherein whoso walks and works it is well with him." (Carlyle, *Sartor Resartus*, B. ii., chap. ix.)

This declaration we may regard as the bedrock, so to say, of the Book of Job. To appreciate what it means for Job to make it, reflect that the wisdom of man, the testimony of the past, the utterance of trusted friends, have all raised their voice in unison with a mysterious visitation of God to declare the contrary. Job is launching out into the darkness alone, staking life and destiny on the belief that the powers that work unseen, in spite of inexorable appearances, are for righteousness.

Doth Job fear God for nought? The sneer of Satan is more than answered.

But having traced the progress of Job's soul to this point, let us be clearly aware what is done, what remains. And, in fact, we find that he still has, as Browning expresses it, "all to traverse 'twixt hope and despair." The achievement that we have noted thus far has been mainly negative. By remonstrance against an arbitrary God, and by reaction against the self-seeking theology of his friends, he has reached a landing-place where he can say, "I know that I shall be justified." That is much to say; but how or when? His suffering remains a fact, all too palpable; he is at the gates of death, with no outlook; and all his importunate demand for explanation of the mystery is

Estimate of Job's progress thus far.

Mainly negative.

but "shouting question after question into the Sybil-cave of destiny, and receiving no answer but an echo." Where shall he find some *pou sto* whereon to lift the weary weight of the problem that presses upon him?

To see how, even along with his negative remonstrances, he has been taking steps toward evolving a positive solution, let us turn back a little and trace some elements of the poem hitherto unmentioned.

The problem all comes from his absorbing quest for that divine presence and communion from which this affliction has seemed to shut him out. "But I, — to the Almighty would I speak, — I long to make plea unto God," is the constant burden of his desire. Two questions there are, to which his mind turns and returns with pertinacious inquiry, and whose answer he must in some way find, on his soul's way to God and light. In his musings on these questions we may trace what may be called Job's positive achievements in faith, his impetuous efforts to enter the darkness that closes him round and *create* what he sees ought to be. This part of the action constitutes its most remarkable and significant feature; it admits us, as it were, behind the veil of God's world-plan, where we get a glimpse of revelation in the making.

Basis of a positive solution of his problem.

And we see therein the part that man plays, as co-worker with God; for what the book before us reveals of unseen things comes not through the whirlwind; it reaches us by way of that darkened yet loyal and yearning heart of Job.

The first question — implicit, of course — is, How to bridge the chasm that has opened between his soul and God? *The question how to approach God.* From the beginning of his affliction this question has presented itself in various forms until it has become agonizing. God has fenced up his way, that he cannot pass. To his frantic inquiries why he is afflicted, God vouchsafes no answer. Then the friends, failing him as comforters, go on portraying a God who is a grotesque projection of their own hard selves, a Being throned above all judgment, all defense of the creature; until Job is constrained to raise against such a conception his everlasting No. It is in the midst of this protest that constructive faith begins to image a solution, — negative at first, fond dwelling of fancy on a state of things that he must confess is not, but how good if it were. It is the idea of a Daysman between him and God, who could represent the cause of both.

" For He is not a man, like me, that I should answer **Him**,
 That we should come together in judgment;

Nor is there any Daysman between us,
Who might lay his hand on both of us;
Who might remove His rod from upon me,
That the dread of Him should not unman me.
Then would I speak, and would not fear Him;
For as I am now, I am not myself."

Section vi. 62-69.

How necessary he considers to be the office that a Daysman should fulfill is seen in the request that he urges, as soon as his solemn committal to his righteousness brings him to a point where, having "set in order his cause," he can address himself definitively to God:—

"Only these two things do not Thou unto me,—
Then will I not hide myself from Thy face;—
Remove Thou Thy hand from upon me,
And let not Thy terror unman me;
Then call Thou, and I will answer Thee,
Or I will speak, and return Thou answer to me."

Section viii. 91-96.

Here is the need, the feeling of which has evidently sunk deep into Job's heart. If only there were in God something like man to appeal to!

The second question, or questioning, centres about the enigma of death. Like many a perplexed soul after him, Job has to beat his wings against the barriers of the grave. Even if he were a transgressor, the mystery is that God will not "look away from him," will not forgive his sins and leave him alone. Why pursue him so cruelly, if he is

The question of death.

destined so soon to drop into "the jaws of vacant darkness and to cease?" In this very fact that God watches and judges such a "driven leaf" as man, and pursues him out of the world, there is a strange inconsistency. The care seems so out of proportion to the object; it is like bending all the forces of the universe to pick up a straw. Who shall solve such a discrepancy? Yet stay; here is what *would be* a solution, if it were only true, which, alas, he cannot say: suppose man should live again after death, as the tree that is cut down sprouts anew!

> "Oh that Thou wouldst hide me in the grave,
> Wouldst keep me secret till Thy wrath is past,
> Wouldst set me a time, and remember me!
> If a man die — might he live again?
> All the days of my service would I wait,
> Until my renewal came;
> Thou wouldst call, and I would answer;
> Thou wouldst yearn after the work of Thy hands!"

Section viii.
137-144.

This solution, like the other, is suggested only negatively, only as a radiant fancy, at first; but both are germinating seeds, and when we meet them again they will have grown, by a kind of unconscious cerebration on Job's part, into greater things.

So much has Job achieved, in protesting and creating, by the time the three friends have spoken once. They are of course moved to answer; but it makes little difference now what they say. It is not so certain to Job as it once was that they have the secret of wisdom. Until they all have spoken again, he does not address himself to their arguments at all, being engaged in exploring the new region that his questioning and his faith have opened. Let us first follow him.

Summary of argument as it stands at the end of section viii.

Eliphaz having spoken a second time, Job, stopping for only a word in scorn of his unavailing speech, turns to the ever-present subject of his affliction. So severe, so pitiless, so inveterate is his anguish, that he can only count its inflicter as his enemy; and that enemy he can do no other than identify with God. He seems to tax the power of language to its utmost to portray the deadly conflict that God is waging with him. Yet, by a strange antinomy, he draws steadily nearer to God for refuge. The very whirlwind and tempest of his remonstrance seems only to lay bare more and more the inner deeps of his essential godliness. Nay, he seems almost to divide God against Himself, to set God the Advocate over against God the Chastiser, in his eager confidence that his hu-

Examination of Job's words continued.

Job's faith imaging an Advocate on high.

man ideals and affections *must* be represented on high, and that he must have a Friend who is the friend of righteousness.

> "Earth, cover not thou my blood,
> And let my cry have no resting-place!
> Even now, behold, in heaven is my Witness,
> And mine Advocate is on high.
> My friends are my scorners,
> But unto God mine eye poureth tears,
> That HE would plead for man with God,
> As the son of man for his neighbor."

Section x. 41-48.

Is not this the Daysman, whom Job was so despairingly dreaming of a little while ago, now no longer in fancy but in full assurance? Job has advanced from despair to confidence; he has a representative on high. *See section vi. 64.*

But that equally obtrusive fact of death recurs: here he stands, with an Advocate in heaven, but with his life's plans broken off and the eternal darkness at hand. *The recurring thought of death.*

> "If I have any hope, the grave is my house;
> I have spread out my bed in the darkness;
> To corruption I have said, 'My father thou!'
> 'My mother, and my sister!'— to the worm.
> And where is now my hope?
> Yea, my hope — who shall discover it?
> Will the bars of Sheol fall down,
> When together there is rest in the dust?"

Section x. 76-83.

Here he pauses while Bildad makes his second

speech ; and then, with the recurring thought of God's enmity, comes upon him the crushing consciousness that his soul is alone, alone in the ruins of a life; friends, brethren, wife, kinsfolk, servants, all have forsaken him. One despairing cry he sends forth, —

Section xii. 12-41.

> "Have pity on me, have pity on me, O ye my friends,
> For the hand of God hath touched me!"

Section xii. 42, 43.

and then all at once he breaks out into that avowal which for all the ages since has remained the supreme utterance of the Book of Job, which gathers into one mighty assurance the solution of all his problems, the final reach of his aspiring faith, revealing in one view the Advocate on high, the vindication beyond death, God his restored friend, — and binding all together with the exultant word, *I know.*

The Redeemer passage.

> "Oh that now my words were written!
> Oh that they were inscribed in a book!
> That, with iron pen, and with lead,
> They were graven in the rock, for ever!
> I know that my Redeemer liveth;
> That He shall stand, survivor, over the dust;
> And after my skin is gone, they will rend this body,
> And I, from my flesh, shall see God.
> Whom I shall see, I, for myself;
> Whom mine eyes shall behold, a stranger no more.
> For this my reins consume within me!"

Section xii. 46-56.

As helping on toward this supreme landing-place of Job's faith, consider what a part the idea of friendship has played. It is one of the leading, though less obtrusive, *motifs* of the poem. Just in proportion as the friends failed him, — as they became deceitful like a dried-up brook, as they would not turn back and acknowledge his integrity as it was, as they turned from companions to scorners, as they persecuted him like gods, — just in that proportion, along with his faith in the triumph of righteousness, Job's faith images also a triumph of love, a finding of divine friendship, until one strong element of this last declaration is his assertion that some time God will be "a stranger no more." It exemplifies Tennyson's description, in "The Two Voices," of man struggling through darkness to find the meaning of his mysterious endowments: —

The idea of friendship in the Book of Job.

> "He seems to hear a Heavenly Friend,
> And thro' thick veils to apprehend
> A labor working to an end."

Tennyson, The Two Voices.

The struggle is over. From this point onward Job no more inquires into God's mysterious enmity and remoteness, nor into the unsolved enigma of death. He has laid up these questions in

How much is settled by Job's knowledge of a Redeemer.

that future where life's problems are all answered.[1]

Return to the friends' arguments. But there remains the present world, the world that all our experiences move in, with its perplexing facts; and the friends in the meanwhile are saying about it things that demand reply. Let us return to them.

See, for example, section xi. 4, 5. They are naturally enough angered at being treated as spiritually blind, and at having their wise maxims contemned. On their side, too, they regard Job's words, so daring in remonstrance, so importunate in inquiry, as exceedingly dangerous, irreverent, blasphemous. "Nay," says Eliphaz,—

Section ix. 6-11.
"Nay, and thou bringest piety to nought,
And lessenest devotion before God;
For thine iniquity teacheth thy mouth,
And thou choosest the tongue of the crafty.
Thine own mouth condemneth thee, and not I;
And thy lips testify against thee."

Their anger against Job, together with their

---

[1] Surprise has often been expressed that Job, having reached such prophetic certitude of blessedness beyond this life, does not make more of the idea in his succeeding argument. I think it is to be explained partly on the ground that this is an idea not argued out but believed in, and partly because Job goes on to other things not requiring such a solution. And so much may be said for the potency of the Redeemer idea, that from this point the doubts that have hitherto oppressed him absolutely disappear.

reactionary impulse to put their arguments in the directest contrast to him, leads them, in this second round of speeches, into intemperate, unconsidered language. *Namely, in sections ix., xi., and xiii.* However his piety may seem to be tottering to its fall, *they* will declare against wickedness so that none can misunderstand or misinterpret their position with reference to it. In the lurid pictures that all in turn give of the awful fate of the wicked, it seems to me the writer's obvious intention to make the friends overreach themselves by assertions which, though not without a nucleus of truth, are so exaggerated as to be grotesquely false to observed facts. Their position amounts to willful denial of what, if they will but open their eyes, they cannot but see.

As in his first answer to them, Job waits till all have spoken, and he has drawn their fire, so to speak; then he turns upon them. Not in anger, — the problem is too awful for that, — but *Job's answer, given when all have spoken, section xiv.* in shuddering amazement, Job portrays to his friends what indeed is palpable to every one who will be honest with himself and the world: the wicked prospering, becoming old, and dying in peace, apparently just as secure and just as favored as the righteous.

"They fill out their days in weal;

Section xiv. 24-29.
And in a moment they sink down to the grave.
And yet they said unto God, 'Depart from us;
The knowledge of Thy ways we desire not.
What is the Almighty, that we should serve Him?
And what gain we, if we pray to Him?'"

Nor does he own this because he inclines to their ways:—

Section xiv. 30, 31.
"Behold not in *their* hand is their weal;
The counsel of the wicked — be it far from me!"

it is mere honesty to facts that compels the confession. The friends have let their imagination riot in terrific descriptions of the death of the wicked, and of the perpetual fear that paralyzes their lives, in contrast to the tranquil security of the righteous; but to Job it is the absolute *equality* of righteous and wicked before God, so far as this life reveals, that is so inexplicable:—

"Shall any teach knowledge unto God,—

Section xiv. 43-52.
Him — who judgeth them that are high?
One dieth in the fullness of his strength,
All at ease and quiet,—
His vessels full of milk,
And the marrow of his bones well moistened;
And another dieth with a bitter soul,
And hath never tasted of good.
Together they lie down, in the dust,
And the worm spreadeth a covering over them."

This is his answer to them, in which he shows them how entirely a figment of the mind is their theory. So strongly has this view seized upon his soul that, stopping for only a partial reply to Eliphaz's third speech, he goes on to give, in calmer mood, a detailed picture of what he has already outlined, the world apparently void of divine judgment, and filled with a perfect impunity of lawless wickedness, — a picture whose truthfulness he seals with a challenge, — *Namely, in section xvi. 34-91.*

> "If it be not so, who then will prove me false,
> And make my words come to nought?" *Section xvi. 92, 93.*

Eliphaz's third speech, which is a kind of Parthian shot, betrays the natural irritation due to the consciousness that he is employing the last weak runnings of his argument. He accuses Job directly of various sins such as are natural to his eminent position in life, sins which Eliphaz has not discovered as a fact, but *deduced* from Job's condition; then he censures Job's avowal of the evils in the world, as indicating a secret hankering after wicked ways, — as if in order to keep one's self from evil one must deny its existence. In these considerations the friends' argument reaches its *reductio ad absurdum*. Eliphaz then concludes with a beautiful exhortation to Job to remove iniquity *Eliphaz's third speech, section xv.* *Lines 8-27.* *Lines 28-39.* *Lines 40-59.*

from his tents and reconcile himself to God. This exhortation we may regard as the final

The friends' final appeal. appeal of the friends, as they see Job drifted so far from them. Nor does it go unanswered. To the charge of sin Job

Job's response. replies later; but this exhortation elicits an immediate answer, in which he gives utterance once for all to his unchangeable attitude before God: —

Section xvi. 4-13.
"Oh that I knew where I might find Him! —
Might come even unto His dwelling-place!
I would set in order my cause before Him;
And I would fill my mouth with arguments.
I would know the words He would answer me;
And I would mark what He would say unto me.
Would He plead against me in the greatness of His might?
Nay; but surely He would give heed unto me.
There it would be an upright man pleading with Him,
And I should be delivered for ever from my Judge."

The calm height to which his faith by this time has led him is suggestively indi-
How Job has advanced. cated in the way in which he confronts again that old problem, once so disturbing, of God's hidden face and refusal to be found. Now it hardly moves him, while he can say, —

Section xvi. 18, 19.
"For He knoweth the way that is mine;
He is trying me; I shall come forth as gold."

The lesson of the disciplinary value of God's

chastisements is generally regarded as Elihu's contribution to the question: does Elihu reach a point higher than this?

I called Eliphaz's exhortation the friends' final appeal. Bildad indeed speaks once more; but what he says is a virtual confession of defeat. His few words are a feeble echo of Eliphaz's favorite doctrine of man's innate depravity, the doctrine that dies hardest, so to say; but so manifestly aside from the present case that Job ridicules them in unmeasured terms:— *Bildad's third speech, section xvii.*

> "How hast thou given help to the powerless!
> How succored the nerveless arm!
> How hast thou counseled the unwise,
> And made known truth in abundance!
> To whom directest thou words?
> And whose breath goeth forth from thee?"—

Job's answer, section xviii. 2-7.

and then in turn carries on the same strain at some length, as if to show how easy it is to compose sublime — yet inapplicable — descriptions of God's power. To take this view of the passage need not belittle the utterances of either Job or Bildad, which as matter of fact are true and full of eloquent beauty; it merely reveals by a striking illustration how entirely the friends have mistaken the issue. *In section xviii. 8-28.*

Zophar fails to appear the third time. Is

he needed? Have we not reached the friends' natural stopping-place?

Zophar does not speak a third time.

So Job is left alone and victorious. What now remains? He has committed life and destiny to the issue of righteousness; he has gazed unflinchingly into this present evil world, and blinked none of its evils; he has by a creative faith made triumphant discoveries in the world above and beyond. What has he yet to do? Evidently to fit himself, so to speak, into the sum of things, to find by that same creative faith the road through this life, where so often wickedness gets the pay, and goodness the affliction. It is to this task, this sober survey of a perplexing world, that Job now addresses himself.

Job continues his discourse,

in a survey of the present world.

He begins with a solemn asseveration of his mental and spiritual soundness whereby he is able to see things as they are; and anew he commits himself unalterably to righteousness: —

"As God liveth, who hath taken away my right,
And the Almighty, who hath embittered my soul, —
For yet whole is my breath within me,
And the spirit of God in my nostril, —
So surely my lips speak not perverseness,
Nor doth my tongue murmur deceit.
Far be it from me that I should justify you;

Section xix. 2-11.

> Till my breath is gone will I not let depart my integrity from me.
> My righteousness I hold fast, and will not let it go;
> My heart shall not reproach one of my days."

In such a survey of the world, the first thing that calls for solution is the problem of the wicked, who are so secure in this life, and who at the end, in a ripened old age, are gathered in like all others. *The problem of the wicked considered, section xix. 12-45.* It would be strange, after all the assertions and denials, if he should leave them without a final word, to clear up what has caused him such trembling dismay. Nor does he. Here, then, is the truth about them. The wicked, after all, *have not the future;* their life, not being founded on the truth of things, cannot count on hope or permanence. They are not anchored to God; all is precarious, unsafe, unstable. Besides, whatever else they gain, the blessing paramount, that which alone, whether now or hereafter, gives value to life, namely, delight in God and sweet dependence on His will, they miss entirely; it is to them a thing nonexistent. No greater woe than this is conceivable to Job. And this judgment of his, while it raises spiritual estimates to a plane immeasurably above that of the friends, also throws light on his own standard of living;

"Be mine enemy as the wicked man,
And he that riseth against me as the unrighteous.
For what is the hope of the godless, when He cutteth off,—
When God draweth forth his soul?
Will God hear his cry,
When distress cometh upon him?
Doth he delight himself in the Almighty?
Doth he call upon God at every time?"

Section xix. 12-19.

The picture that Job then draws of the wicked, which some have tried to give to Zophar, merely follows this view into detail. It is a statement, in vivid poetic form, of what we call the logic of events, of the truth which we see inlaid in the history of all human affairs, that whatever does not make for righteousness does not make for permanence. Its drift is not unlike that of Bildad's first speech, of which Job has already said, "Of a truth, I know it is so." The friends had a nucleus of truth; only they erred by overstatement and by purblind application; Job has found the key of things, and he follows it out by the standard of the unseen and eternal.

In section xix. 24-45.

If, then, the security of the wicked is only a seeming, what is the reality? If their course is folly, what is the true wisdom of life, by which we may

The true wisdom of life, section xix. 46-104.

walk calmly through the mystery that surrounds us, and solve it for ourselves, however baffling the enigma of the world? Here comes in the twenty-eighth chapter. Is such a topic out of place, or must we call it an interpolation from the author's portfolio? *See above, p. 15.* Rather, it answers the question that most naturally arises here, and gives the practical lesson in which the Book of Job both begins and culminates. The hidden wisdom, the way that no creature has found, —

> "GOD understandeth the way thereto,
> And He knoweth its place.
> For He looketh to the ends of the earth; *Section xix. 92-104.*
> Under the whole heaven He seeth.
> When He gave the wind its weight,
> And meted out the waters in a measure, —
> When He gave a law to the rain,
> And a way to the flash of the thunder,
> Then did He see, and declare it;
> He established it, yea, He searched it out.
>   And unto man He said,
> Behold, the fear of the Lord, that is wisdom,
> And to shun evil is understanding."

Thus Job, the man perfect and upright, who feared God and shunned evil, has held fast to the integrity with which *Summary.* he began, until he has not only answered Satan's question, but solved for every man the problem of life. His solution is not new, nor does it contradict the wise precepts of the friends. And yet it *is* new; for it comes now with a whole world of fact and experience behind it, reporting that in the most searching trial this rule of life has stood the test. To fear God and shun evil is wisdom, in spite of the affliction that righteousness suffers, in spite of the prospered wickedness that is rampant in the world. And in the deepest sense, too, the solution *does* contradict, if not the friends' words, yet the friends' whole false attitude toward God; for with Job, to fear God and shun evil is not to fear and shun appearances, or to trim the sails according to the way in which the breeze of God's favor seems for the time to set; it is to be true to the soul's ideal of the godlike, in scorn of consequence.

They say Job was impatient. If patience means holding one consistent mind through a hard experience, and if patience has her perfect work in believing and enduring, *was* he impatient?

Was Job impatient?

Having reached this firm landing-place, with clear view of the way through this world's confusion, and with confident outlook toward the vindication beyond death, Job, as is natural, takes a retrospect of his former happy and honored life, now so inexplicably plunged into misery. Let us bear in mind that he still regards himself as

Job's retrospect, section xx.

standing on the brink of the grave, with no hope more in this life. What he bears in his hands now he brings to submit to the award of that Divine Friend, whom he is to see hereafter. This fact gives a new significance to these three beautiful chapters in which he brings his words to a close. In them he gathers up the threads of his life, one after another, for God and man to judge, and at the end, full of that overmastering desire for God's presence which all along has supremely inspired him, he stands ready for the word that shall vindicate him and make him blessed: — *Job's readiness to meet God at the end.*

" Behold my sign! let the Almighty answer me!— And the charge that mine Adversary hath written! *Section xx. 187-192.*
Surely I will lift it upon my shoulder;
I will bind it unto me like a crown;
I will declare to Him the number of my steps,
I will draw near unto Him like a prince."

Except half a dozen lines, which not improbably have become dislocated in transcription, these words are the last of Job's stout-hearted defense before God and the world. The testimony is all in; and now, as the veil of flesh is ready to drop away, Job is fully prepared for the unseen meeting beyond.

With Job's words ended, and with the friends put to silence, evidently at this point the action is ready for its *dénouement*. What shall this be? If the poem is really a finished work of art, as all its features thus far have indicated, we naturally expect the ending to be directly related to the main issue, and significant enough to bring its deepest elements to solution. We have seen how signally this test fails, if we regard the main issue as the decision of a debate on the question why the righteous suffer: the address from the whirlwind, with all its sublimity, does not really touch the question; nor can Elihu be made to furnish an answer without a great deal of accommodation and inference. But I think we have become aware also of an issue far deeper than this, an issue, not of words and reasoning, but of life. The controversy of the friends with Job has revealed an antagonism too deep and radical to be settled by debate or by any verbal decision. The nature of this antagonism Satan indicated at the outset, when he charged Job with serving God from selfish motives. It is the question of serving God for reward, or serving God disinterestedly, that is at stake; a question for whose answer we must look below words and forms, into the deepest currents of life. In his own person Job has indeed given a thorough refutation to the charge;

but in the battle that he has had to wage with his friends, he has dragged to light one after another their hidden motives, *See above, p. 50.* until he has made it evident that *they* illustrate just what Satan sneered at. The friends are not fearing God for nought. Their whole theory of religion is based on the idea of barter. So deeply is this idea ingrained in their life that, as we have seen, they have hastened without scruple to desert Job and break all the ties of friendship, in order to get on the favorable side of God and keep their prospects good; so deeply that they have interpreted the mystery of wickedness, not by the fact, but by what they think God would like them to say. This deep antagonism between the friends and Job has manifested its effects in their general attitude before God. Job's attitude has been emphasized at every step, — supreme longing for the restoration of God's presence. "Oh that I knew where I might find Him!" has been the constant burden *See section xvi. 4.* of his cry; and beginning with his despairing wish for a Daysman, his creative faith has kept on until he knew that somewhere beyond this life he would see God as his friend. The whole determination of his life is toward God. The attitude of the friends is no less evidently the opposite. They are orthodox and dogmatic;

they are zealous for the forms and decorums of religion; but they manifest no hunger for direct communion of spirit with God. Their God is a tradition, their religion a conventionalism. They are perfectly content with Teufelsdröckh's "absentee God, sitting at the outside of the universe and seeing it go," so long as they secure an honorable and prosperous way through life. Now what kind of a *dénouement* shall bring such an antagonism as this to solution? Do we not naturally look for some scene wherein the two contrasted classes shall stand, as it were, naked before God, the thoughts of their hearts revealed, not judged in words, but judging themselves by their spontaneous, uncalculated conduct?

The kind of dénouement required.

If such is the reasonable expectation, what could more fully answer to it than the theophany which actually follows? It comes as a surprise to all of them, Job and the friends alike. Job is looking for a meeting somewhere out of human view, where his integrity shall be recognized as it is. The friends are looking for nothing at all, unless it be some flash of divine wrath against him whom they regard as so bringing piety to nought. A surprise, it makes of course also that profound and heart-

How the theophany, sections xxvi. and xxviii., fulfills this requirement.

shaking impression which cannot but result when the mortal comes face to face with the supernatural. "We may disbelieve," says an eminent student of the human mind, "in any manifestations of the supernatural; but we cannot but believe that were their occurrence possible, they would profoundly affect the mind. Humboldt says, that the effect of the first earthquake shock is most bewildering, upsetting one of the strongest articles of material faith, namely, the fixedness of the earth. Any supernatural appearance must have this effect of shaking the foundations of the mind in an infinitely greater degree." Some illustration of this we have already seen indicated in Eliphaz's vision, where, when the spirit glided before his face, he was overwhelmed with fear and trembling, and built the creed and conduct of a lifetime on the communication he then received. Of much profounder significance than any vision of spirits, and of correspondingly greater effect, must be the sublime theophany of the whirlwind. It is like setting up a divine judgment throne on the earth; it brings the glory of a holiness and truth wherein each man may see himself, and wherein the thoughts and ideals of each heart must necessarily be revealed. The way in which men

Bucknill, The Mad Folk of Shakespeare, p. 8.

See section iii. 22-43.

meet such a dread ordeal will show, through a shrinking abjectness and terror on the one side, who at heart is selfish and would be left alone ; and on the other side, through a reverent awe and joy, who, having the real determination of heart toward God, rejoices to be warmed and lighted by the sunshine of His presence.

For such a scene as this Job is fully ready, his righteous life disclosed in epitome, his record on his shoulder. But the friends? They have retreated, one by one, before the searching fire of the patriarch's words, until they have nothing more to say. In order that we may see the power of the Divine Presence manifested at once on both classes, the friends, or at least the spirit and principle that they represent, must needs pass likewise in review and summary before the reader. If this did not come to pass, the action would be lacking in a very important and necessary connecting link.

Job ready for the theophany; the friends not yet ready.

Here, then, and as I judge with precisely this significance, intervene the discourses of Elihu.[1] In the character of Elihu the author

---

[1] If the discourses of Elihu form no part of the original poem, but were added, as the critics assert nowadays, by a subsequent editor, then all I have to say is, I prefer to study the poem in its latest edition. From the point of view here taken, the writer who added such a finishing touch as this was a master in his art, one who could be fully trusted to

presents the friends' side of the question, freed from the heats and disturbances of controversy, and brought to its best expression. Neither in word nor in general attitude is he at issue with them. The only reason why his wrath is kindled against them is because their arguments have not been strong enough to convict Job; he represents confessedly what they would have said, but failed to say. He stands on the same presuppositions; he reasons concerning the same inaccessible, unapproachable God; he finds the same wicked tendencies in Job; he points Job to the same goal of restoration, discipline, renewed prosperity. He is merely directing Job in a little more minute terms than they

The discourses of Elihu, sections xxi.–xxv., and how they identify him with the cause of the friends.

compose the whole poem, as indeed I am willing to believe he did. In other words, I do not think the critics who would expel Elihu have made out their case. From their conception of the poem's scope and purpose he is in the way; they cannot help desiring his absence. Deduct the influence of this fact, and the other arguments urged against him, arguments drawn from his alleged Aramaisms, his peculiarities of speech, and the like, are confessedly inconclusive. He *is* undeniably a little tedious; he has words and idioms of his own; his character is individualized in a way quite different from that of the friends; but all this, whether so intended or not, but serves to adapt him more exquisitely to the part he has to play. What the critics would take away on the score of its lack of harmony with the rest is more than made up by dramatic fitness and skill.

have used to take proper measures for reinstatement in a life of earthly ease and comfort. So far as we can see he has no more idea of serving God for nought than have the friends. Even his exhortation to Job to accept affliction for the sake of discipline, true and sound as it is, is quite consistent with the idea of getting as distinguished from that of giving.

The conception of the character of Elihu is to be interpreted with a twofold reference: to the friends, whose cause and life he represents; and to the coming theophany, which is to bring, as it were, his spiritual testing.

Twofold significance of Elihu's part.

As the champion of the friends' cause, he possesses the advantages that inhere in youth and fresh, enthusiastic energy. To him the world of ideas has just opened, full of intense interest; he is not hide-bound by the timid conservatism of age or by the oracles of the past; he has a vigorous, constructive mind, fired by zeal and insight. Many of his words are truly noble. His discourse is rich in helpful things; he directs Job especially to the secondary revelations of God's will, — by dream, by vision, by the chastisement of suffering, — and seeks thus to lead the patriarch to repentance and devout submission. All this we may freely concede;

Elihu as the champion of the friends' cause.

for we will remember that the issue of the poem is not the issue of goodness with wickedness. Both sides alike represent righteousness and devout service of God; it is only the motive of such service, selfish or disinterested, that Satan has called into question. And what Elihu says, noble though it is, but serves to identify him, as to standard and goal, with the friends; it is what consists with a merely conventional faith and a traditional God.

As related to the subsequent theophany, the conception of Elihu's character is not without a certain grim humor, apparent especially in the sharply accentuated contrast between his extravagant pretensions at the beginning and his ludicrous abasement at the end. He opens his discourse with a long account of the wonderful thoughts he has and the wonderful things he is going to do. Then, identifying his thoughts with God's thoughts, he sets up definitively for Job's Daysman the one whom Job had so longed for to stand between him and God : —

Elihu as preparing for the theophany.

Section xxii. 2-38.

> "If thou art able, answer me;
> Set words in array before me, take thy stand.
> Behold I, according to thy word, stand for God;
> Out of clay am I moulded, also I;

Section xxii 47-52.

Behold, *my* terror shall not unman thee,
Nor will my burden on thee be heavy."

Compare this with Job's words in section vi. 62-69, and it is obvious what he has in mind. Elihu's idea of a Daysman is a wise interpreter of life, a מֵלִיץ מַלְאָךְ, "a messenger, an interpreter," not necessarily supernatural, but "one of a thousand," exceptionally gifted, and authorized by his gifts to speak, — such a one, in short, as he himself feels inspired to be. As he proceeds, he feels increasingly that he is the champion of God, the channel of God's word to Job, through which the whole controversy is to be settled.

Section xxii. 84, 85.

"I will fetch my knowledge from afar,
And to my Maker will I ascribe justice;
For of a surety my words are no lie; —
It is the Perfect in knowledge that is with thee."

Section xxv. 4-7.

So he continues his discourse, eloquently defending the Perfect in knowledge; until across the desert is seen a storm rising. With great beauty he begins to descant on this, and so long as it is an ordinary storm he employs it, with no little assumption of wisdom, to Job's edification. But as it nears, its phenomena become so exceptional that his experience can no longer account for it: it seems to betoken that God is indeed coming, as Job has fervently desired, and as the friends have rather savagely wished for

Section xxv. 55 sqq.

him. Whereat Elihu's words become confused; he begins to retract his pretensions, stammers an attempt at propitiation, and breaks off abruptly, paralyzed by terror : —

"Give ear unto this, O Job;
  Stand, and ponder the marvelous things of God.   *Section xxv. 97-121.*
Knowest thou how God layeth command upon them,
And maketh shine forth the light of His cloud?
Knowest thou the poisings of the thick cloud,
The wonders of the Perfect in knowledge? —
Thou whose garments are hot,
Because from the south the earth lieth sultry still, —
Canst thou spread out with Him the skies,
Firm, as a molten mirror?
. . . O teach us what we may say to Him!
We cannot order it — it groweth so dark . . .
Hath one told Him that I am speaking . . .
Or hath a man said . . . for he shall be swallowed up!

. . . .

  And now they no longer see the light, —
That splendor in the skies,
For a wind hath passed, and scattered them.
. . . From the north a golden glory cometh . . .
Oh, with God is terrible majesty!
The Almighty — we have not found Him out;
Vast in power, and in judgment,
And in abundance of righteousness; —
He will not afflict;
Therefore do men fear Him;
He regardeth not any wise in their own conceit."

Thus the self-appointed Daysman shrinks away before the test, and we hear no more from him. A humiliating retreat for one who set out so valiantly and self-confidently to defend God.[1]

The opening words from the whirlwind dismiss Elihu abruptly, —

The Lord's address from the whirlwind, sections xxvi. and xxviii. Section xxvi. 2-5.

"Who is this, darkening counsel
With words, — but without knowledge?"

Then the Lord addresses Job: —

"Gird up thy loins now, like a strong man,
And I will ask thee; and inform me thou."

The dread Presence is here; and Job stands at last before Him who seemed so far off, yet to whom in all darkness Job's spirit turned, as the needle to the pole. What now shall the divine revelation be?

Not what Job expected; not perhaps what

---

[1] At the end of Browning's *Caliban upon Setebos*, which is his portrayal of a brutish being's speculations on God, there is a striking though grotesque parallel to this closing scene of Elihu: —

"What, what? A curtain o'er the world at once!
Crickets stop hissing; not a bird — or, yes,
There scuds His raven that has told Him all!
It was fool's play, this prattling! Ha! The wind
Shoulders the pillared dust, death's house o' the move,
And fast invading fires begin! White blaze —
A tree's head snaps — and there, there, there, there, there,
His thunder follows! Fool to gibe at Him!
Lo! 'Lieth flat and loveth Setebos!
'Maketh his teeth meet through his upper lip,
Will let those quails fly, will not eat this month
One little mess of whelks, so he may 'scape!"

our curiosity seeks. We look for the veil to uproll and disclose mysteries beyond human research; Job expects a hearing and a justification. And what is it? Just the unending miracle that passes before our eyes every day. In the heavens above, in the earth beneath, in the great events of creation and phenomena of nature, in the myriad life that fills land and air and ocean, we are made to see that there is Wisdom and Power sufficient for everything, to make every creature fulfill its part in one infinite purpose and will. No esoteric disclosure for some exceptionally favored disciple, but what every one may lift up his eyes and see. No apologies for mysterious dealings, nor little systems of men corrected, but the perpetual self-justifying course of a harmonious universe. Is it not sublimer so? Would we desire the God of the ages to measure reasoning with mortals, and argue out a case? Nay, it was more than genius, it was inspiration, that kept the author from such a fatuity. *Character of the divine revelation.*

Job hears, and makes his own application. He had stood ready, like a prince, bearing the record of his righteous life on his shoulder. But what seemed his worth, when he had only his friends to compare with, seems in the infinite *How Job meets the Lord's words.*

light very small. When the LORD pauses for his answer, he has no word to say. No claim more of merit and a triumphant cause; no clamor for explanation; all has melted away in reverence and humility, being absorbed in the one blessed consciousness that God is no more a hearsay but a seen reality.

"I had heard of Thee by the hearing of the ear,
But now mine eye seeth Thee;
Wherefore I loathe me and repent
In dust and ashes."

Section xxix. 9-12.

Thus Job meets the test with that worship which is at once rapture and pain; takes his place, so to say, with submission and self-abnegation, in the sum of God's creatures, content to fulfill his part with the rest.[1] This is his vindication: to go on, with enlightened eyes and chastened spirit. It is altogether in keeping that in this vision, so profound in its influence, self is lost, and reverent, trustful, penitent love abides.

[1] In the long train of creative works by which the Lord teaches Job of Himself and His ways, we are reminded of Milton's reflections in the Sonnet on his Blindness: —

"His state
Is kingly; thousands at his bidding speed,
And post o'er land and ocean without rest."

Nor is the lesson that Milton draws for his own conduct dissimilar to the submissive attitude here taken by Job: —

"Who best
Bear His mild yoke, they serve Him best."

What, now, has become of that problem which most interpreters have taken as the central theme of the Book of Job, — "the mystery of God's providential government of men?" In denying to it the supreme significance, it would be temerity, not to say blindness, so to insult the critical mind of the ages as to banish it altogether. Nor does Job himself ignore it. Has he not asked virtually the same question? —

How the Job-problem, as generally propounded, is answered. See above, p. 11.

> "Why are not judgment times determined by the Almighty?
> And they that know Him — why see they not His days?"

Section xvi. 34, 35.

And all this time, though he knew it not, he has been living the answer. The grand conclusion, the sum total, is expressed not in words but in life: "Now mine eye seeth Thee." Need one whose eyes are opened by such a hard schooling ask why it was given? The answer is self-evident. Less than such stern discipline would not have produced such beauty and strength of human character. Less than such severe chastening would not have quickened Job's vision to see how subtly selfish motives may work to impair the friendships and the wisdom of earth, and how sufficing is the refuge provided in the eternal Love beyond this life. And the answer thus embodied in the patriarch's experience is a world-answer, pointing to that mystery of travail and suffering which everywhere underlies the deepest insight, the highest achievements. Shall we ask why God invades our ease and scourges us onward and upward to the table-lands of vision? The new horizon and the purer air and the stronger muscles are the sufficient reason. "The spirit of man is an instrument which cannot give out its deepest, finest tones, except under the immediate hand of the Divine Harmonist."

The Epilogue, section xxx. Then comes the Epilogue. Job is commended; prays for his friends, who are forgiven at his intercession; is restored to health and double prosperity. The friends were righteous for the sake of worldly good; Job was righteous for the sake of God. At the end of his long quest he found God and worldly good too; the greater brought with it the less. Some think his restoration is an artistic blemish; that it would have been a nobler ending if he had been left suffering. It would be a blemish if this paltry reward were the end which Job sought, and for which the poem existed. But the quest has already reached its supreme end in the vision and restored favor of God; this is merely its incidental addition. And at least the old poet has put God and prosperity in the right relative places, in remarkable anticipation of the precept, "Seek ye first the kingdom of God and His righteousness; and all these things shall be added unto you."

IV.

One more inquiry remains, the inquiry as to its origin. What must have been the age, and what the nation, out of which such a book could grow? What general vogue of thinking could have environed such colossal thought? Genius may indeed be a mighty tree, growing from an unseen germ to be the one commanding object of the plain; but it is rooted in the same soil that nourishes the shrubs at its feet. A great work of literature both feeds its age and is fed by it. What the book returns, in transmuted and vitalized form, to its generation is what it has already gathered out of the hopes and needs and problems that surround it. Not that the highest literature is merely the echo of the people's surging thought, and no more; we cannot say this of Tennyson and Browning and Whittier and Emerson to-day: it is rather the utterance of those who, making the universal cause their

IV. Considerations regarding its origin.

A poem's relation to its age.

own, stand nearest the light, and bring the people's inarticulate longings to expression. The poets of an age, when they let their open and genuine hearts speak, are its truest seers. In them we hear, not one man alone, but the vast body of the time, pervaded by a spirit of hope or doubt or inquiry; a spirit voiceless, until the Æolian strings of the poet's heart feel and answer to its breathings; a spirit unguided, until the seer's own disciplined and originative personality conducts it to its dimly sought rest. This is the truth to-day, and has been ever since we could first trace the connection of literature with history; may we not say that something like it was equally a truth twenty-six centuries ago? And when this Book of Job comes home to the general spir-itual need as freshly as if it had been written to meet the maladies of this nineteenth Christian century, may we not say that its involution is equal to its evolution, and that there was a great heart of the people in that old time, out of which the book grew and to which it thrilled responsive, as it does to ours?

Such relation to be sought for Job.

Yet when by external tests we endeavor to fix its age, we find the book very baffling. Generations of scholars have ransacked the ten centuries from Moses to

Difficulty of determining its age.

the Babylonian Exile to find a place where it would fit in. It seems to move in a region unconnected with any period of history or custom that we are acquainted with. It was because the book has no traceable contact with Mosaic legislation and ritual that it was conjectured by old interpreters to be the work of Moses' middle age, when he was a shepherd in Midian. It is because the book speaks in the Wisdom dialect, as did Solomon and his compeers, that some students trace in it a shadowy contact with Solomon's age. It is because for the lesson of the book, intensely individual though it seems, a national occasion and significance must at all hazards be postulated, that its composition is by many assigned to a time near or within the Exile period. But none of these indications can be regarded as conclusive. Nor is it easier to account for what the book contains than for what it omits. It evinces knowledge, not slight nor casual, of Arabian deserts, Judæan mountain ravines, mines of the Sinai peninsula, beasts and plants of the Nile region; it contemplates modes of life both pastoral and urban; it purports to represent a distant patriarchal time, yet breathes the air of a later civilization. For the historic setting of such a product as this we must look, I think, be-

Where to look for its historic setting.

neath the vicissitudes of wars and dynasties, beneath the surface of political movements, legislation, ecclesiastical affairs, to that stratum of national life where there is least to record, yet where most truly history is made, that subsoil of thought and custom where the great body of the people live and work and think. In such tranquil surroundings, if we can penetrate thither, we shall find the influences that lie at the roots of the Book of Job.

But are there obtainable data enough, after all these centuries, to help us conjecture, by the creative imagination, something of that faraway "spirit of the age" to which the Book of Job supposably answers? Let us gather up what there is, and see.

One fact we may take with confidence as the starting-point of our inquiry, — the fact that the Book of Job belongs distinctively to the so-called Wisdom literature of the Hebrews; being indeed, of all the products of that literature, the grandest in the reach and ripeness of its thought, and the completest in its literary form.

Job a work of the Hebrew Wisdom.

What the Hebrews called Wisdom corresponds to what other nations call philosophy. The books classified under that name contain the thoughts of earnest and observant minds on life, on con-

The Hebrew Wisdom or philosophy.

duct, on worldly prudence, on divine things, on the mystery that encompasses the world. And they introduce us to a class of men, of whom otherwise little is known, the "wise men," who in an unofficial way, and with objects less purely religious, taught and had influence along with priests and prophets in shaping the spiritual life of the Hebrew people. "The law shall not perish from the priest," said the men who rejected Jeremiah's prediction of evil, "nor counsel from the wise, nor the word from the prophet." Each of these three classes had its work to do in the Hebrew state, and each has left its record in the Hebrew literature. The Law and the Prophets, mighty as are their influence and doctrine, leave an important part unsupplied; they are supplemented, as they need to be, by the utterances of Wisdom. *Jeremiah, xviii. 18.*

And a fitting supplement these are; for just as through law and prophecy comes to us the voice of the divine, through the Wisdom literature we hear the voice of the human. It is man thinking for himself, interpreting what he sees about him and above him by the free exercise of reason, spiritual insight, faith. The note of law is authority; the note of prophecy is, "Thus saith the Lord." In both of these that which is *The human character of Wisdom.*

above takes the initiative, it lays behest on man without coöperation of his, adapting itself to human limitations, but not reflecting them. In Wisdom the initiative is taken by man; its note is inquiry and discovery. It is the result of man's efforts, crude and short-sighted, it may be, but his own, to think God's thoughts after Him, and shape the world anew by the ideal of man's constructive heart. Whatever it generalizes from the world of experience is the fruit of its honest and open-eyed observation. Whatever conclusions it reaches regarding man's duty and destiny rest on visible and verifiable facts. And whenever it pushes its inquiries out into the mystery beyond this world, it keeps within the bounds of a rational faith and insight, as it interprets the things it beholds, or boldly pronounces on that which ought to be. This it is which gives such universal human interest to the literature of Wisdom. It is a literature that embodies, not the oracles of priests and prophets, who, having the nearer vision, speak as exempt from doubt and mistake, but the halting yet progressive thoughts of men like ourselves, who, surrounded by a world of perplexing experience, must interrogate for its meaning the native insight with which every man is endowed. When such men give counsel, the universal feeling of comradeship provides ears to hear. And whatever revelation of the unseen is achieved by their yearning faith is revelation indeed.

Essentially a people's literature, then, is this Hebrew Wisdom; this, too, in the more natural and ordinary sense. Not an official utterance, it rises out of the people's every-day work and practical affairs, giving voice to the thoughts with which their lives are most conversant. To kings and laborers alike it gives direction and guidance: gathering wisdom for men when they go to the temple for prayer, and when they go to the city-gate for counsel; walking with them in the field where they toil, and in the market-place where they bargain. Its note is eminently individual;[1] herein lies one of its distinctive characteristics. Law and ritual are prescribed for the congregation; prophecy addresses itself to the nation at large, reading the nation's history in the divine light. The counsel of the

Wisdom, a people's literature.

[1] Wellhausen, in his article on "Israel" in the *Encyclopædia Britannica*, makes this strong individualism of the Book of Job an argument for its post-exilic origin, because he regards the pre-exilic literature as suffused only with the national consciousness. But I think he does not take sufficient account of the fundamental difference between the Wisdom literature on the one hand and the Law and the Prophets on the other. Wisdom was always individual even from its beginning, as truly so before the Exile as after; and the argument for the age of the Book of Job must be made up on other grounds.

wise concerns man as man; and in no other department of the literature are we brought so near the great heart of the nation, so near to men's common and secular pursuits, as in this, where untitled and unmitred men take upon themselves to speak out freely and in the natural style what is in them. For this very reason, also, no other literature is so hard to connect, in our reading of it, with national events. To find its era and origin we must find how it answers to the general pervasive spirit of an age.

Beginning of the culture of Wisdom in Solomon's time.

The beginnings of the Wisdom culture we trace to the age of Solomon, a period when, as never before and perhaps as never after, the Hebrew nation broke through the shell of its narrow exclusiveness and became awake to broader and more cosmopolitan interests. Solomon himself, with his keen devotion to knowledge, his judicial mind, and his "largeness of heart," was the impulse-giving centre. Through his enterprises in commerce, in art, in internal improvement, in foreign intercourse, a new and larger spirit pervaded the air and began spontaneously to blossom into literary expression. Inquiring what such a rich and varied world meant, and what were the laws of its successes and failures, men began to formulate their observations into generalized maxims, such as we see in the Book of Proverbs. This book, which contains the earliest Wisdom utterances that have come down to us, is the natural literary evolution from those "dark questions" which Solomon put to the Queen of Sheba, or exchanged with Hiram, King of Tyre; and in the aphoristic *mashal* style therein exemplified is set the type for all the succeeding Wisdom literature. How much of the thought of that nascent time remains to us in written product it is impossible to say; but its spiritual attitude and tendency was of a type so distinctive, and so expressive of the character of the age and its king, that down to the days of its latest development, only a century before Christ, the works of the Wisdom literature still legitimated themselves by the name of the wise son of David. The Book of Proverbs, the Book of Job, the Book of Ecclesiastes, and the two apocryphal books of Sirach and the Wisdom of Solomon, which make up the extant body of the Hebrew Wisdom, possess, with all their differences in style and doctrine, a unity of character answering to the free spirit of judgment and inquiry impressed upon that literature at its birth.

But a beginning is only a beginning; we cannot expect a literature, however vigorous the impulse of its inception, to leap into existence full grown. The proverbs and riddles and dark questions with which Solomon and his court amused themselves, though they embody many an earnest interrogation of life and the world, are still ages away from that ripened and seasoned product apparent in the Book of Job. Before we reach that supreme achievement we must allow time enough for the Poor Richard maxims about diligence and prudence and industry and temperance which form the staple of the early *mashal* to have passed from truths into truisms; time enough for the Wisdom utterance to have developed from detached observations into a body of philosophy, and then to have hardened into an orthodoxy, with its intolerance of new things, and its disposition to make life or perdition depend on what a man thinks; time enough for the culture of Wisdom to have long departed from courts and palaces, and to have become the occupation of a recognized guild, with its blue blood, its sacred traditions, its learned nomenclature; time enough for the philosophy to have become so international that it is taken as no strange thing for an author to represent Edomites and Hauranites and Aramæans as speaking in a common religious dialect which in no way interferes with the dis-

How great a development must be allowed for in Job.

Marks of later culture in Job.

tinctive cult of any nation. When we bear in mind how tenaciously theological views once established hold their ground, contesting to the death every inch of advance, we shall be slow to reckon the period as brief which covers the progress of ideas from Solomon to Job. For not only does the book bear all the marks of development just described, it sig- nalizes also a new period of doubt succeeding to the first age of discovery and generalization. *How Job represents a new period of doubt.* In its pages the Wisdom hitherto accepted is becoming old and stale. Its sages are repeating their lessons by rote: lessons faultless in rhetoric, but no longer thrilling hearts to vital response, and too inflexible to adapt themselves to new experiences. The Book of Job exists largely in order to call into question that very foundation truth, which is to Wisdom what Newton's law is to astronomy, that both righteous and wicked receive in this life the fruit of their deeds, prosperity or destruction. A new induction of life must be made, for in that principle there are two fatally weak points. A weak point first in its assumption of fact; for so far as this life reveals there is no difference between the fate of the righteous and the fate of the wicked. Open your eyes and see every- *Weak points in the earlier Wisdom. See above, p. 35, also p. 19.*

where the wicked dying in a prosperous and honored old age; and is not Job himself, the man perfect and upright, suffering a misery which if this standard is true is injustice? A second weak point it betrays in its fruit of character. For under such a law of life men, reckoning surely on prosperity as the reward of their righteousness, will put up their righteousness in the market to be sold for a price; so that the mocking spirit roaming to and fro in the earth may with only too much reason ask, "Doth that well-rewarded man serve God for nought?" Satan may be narrow and selfish, but he has sharp eyes. He sees, what also we see, that when we make God over from a personal Sovereign to a law of nature, forthwith from servants we become masters, and begin to mould that law to our own selfish purposes. That was no small discovery to make, in those early days; requiring, not only acumen on the part of the individual, but a reënforcing readiness and sympathy in the spirit of his age; and the fact that the author of the Book of Job has made it indicates that the meditative years had passed through a long maturing process, until some of their best-established ideas, over ripe, were ready to fall.

But to give definite date to such a development as this, to locate it at its precise point in the ages, is extremely hard, not to say wholly uncertain. The tides of the spirit, which we are endeavoring to trace, are not easily estimated by years. Besides, all this belongs to the class of events of which little note is taken in the more pretentious records that we call historical. We see its fruits in literature, and to some extent in the coloring of political progress; but to find its habitat we must, as I have intimated, turn aside from courts and capitals, with their alternations of good and wicked administrations and their fitful vogues of piety and idolatry, to those quieter regions where men think more and live a less changeful life. We have not reached the real heart of Israel, that Isaiah's "remnant" which was the idolatrous nation's sole redemption, when we have merely traced what was going on at Samaria and Jerusalem. While in these capitals of Israel and Judah long lines of kings were creating some surface agitation by playing their little games of war and diplomacy; while priests were working out their elaborate rituals for the public religious service; while prophets were strenuously seeking to guide political affairs according to principles of faith and righteousness; in those smaller towns and country places which could on occasion fur-

Difficulty of assigning a date to such purely intellectual product.

nish a herdsman of Tekoa to prophesy or a Barzillai the Gileadite to serve with his substance the cause of a fugitive king, there was all the time, we must believe, a deep undercurrent of constructive, progressive thought, flowing and broadening from its remote source in the ages, channeling its way through the reality that alone can vitalize any forms; on which current many earnest minds, unheeding the world's fluctuations, were borne steadily forward toward their spiritual rest. Among these minds, and with such tranquil surroundings, dwelt the wise men who wrought at the problems of life.

On what kind of a world, then, looked out the wise man who wrote for us the Book of Job? In the first place, as the whole atmosphere of the book makes evident, it was a world of tranquil, settled conditions of life; these seem to fill the whole background of the writer's consciousness. When Job looks back upon his life of helpful activity among his neighbors and dependents and of wise counsel in the city-gates, and when Eliphaz says, —

Background of the Book of Job; the social state recognized.

Section xx. 1-50.

Section ix. 33-37.

"that which I have seen will I declare;
Which wise men tell, and have not hidden, —
Things heard from their fathers,

Unto whom alone the land was given,
And no stranger hath passed among them," —

we seem to hear, not the voice of these characters alone, but the voice of an author whose dwelling-place has for ages been remote from invasions and national upheavals. Such places there must have been, many of them, in the land of Judæa, where one dynasty occupied the throne continuously from David to the Babylonian Captivity, and where the whole history is notably lacking in the interest due to stormy and revolutionary annals. In such regions Peace under her olive could without interruptions maintain her traditions and dwell among high thoughts.[1] But, secondly, the very region and era which would furnish such congenial field for the culture of Wisdom would also be pervaded by an atmosphere in which such Wisdom, if unvitalized by doubts and new discoveries, must inevitably grow old and crumble. For that same settled permanence gave abundant opportunity for the rich to extend their

[1] Nothing is clearer to my mind than that the Book of Job contemplates a period not of adversity, but, if anything, of too uniform and uninterrupted prosperity. Those who, assuming that it is a "national dramatic poem," project it into a time of hardship when, like the Captivity for instance, the lesson is needed that a righteous and favored *nation* may nevertheless be afflicted, seem to me to be doing violence to the whole presupposition on which Job, as a wise reformer of his age, is establishing a broader and deeper truth.

possessions and grow more selfish and heartless, while the hungry poor were obliged to tread the rich man's wine-press or roam the wastes for bread. Society would crystallize into classes, with their tyrannies of the powerful over the weak, and of the aristocratic over the humble. To oppress the needy, or, what comes to the same, to let them stand shivering and hungry at the rich man's door would become, even with the nominally righteous, more and more a matter of course; while with the unscrupulous and wicked the harshness of the unfeeling creditor and the secret sins of the luxurious idle would find their natural nesting-place. All this, which but follows the universal tendencies of human nature, reads almost like a transcript from the book we are studying. Consider what kind of social state that must have been wherein Eliphaz could so naturally predicate just these sins of Job merely because the latter was rich; wherein professed sages who had their lesson only by rote were blind to any iniquity that existed apart from its doom of misery, while at the same time the pure soul of Job, touched with the feeling of human wretchedness, was quivering with dismay to see landmarks removed, cloth-

Compare section xvi. 36-59.

Compare section xvi. 60-73.

Section xv. 8-27.

Sections ix., xi., xiii.

Section xiv.

ing stripped from the needy debtor, famished and thirsty toilers in the very fields and wine-vats of the wealthy, and yet apparently no flash of divine judgment against such enormities. The age on which our author looked was not especially idolatrous or apostate, nor were the forms and decorums of religion lacking; it was an age whose easy prosperity, too long unwatched and undisturbed, was becoming heartless, callous to social ills, heedlessly worldly.

Section xvi. 36–59; xix. 25 (where see note).

And for such a social state what spiritual guidance and admonition existed? The wise men sat in the city-gates and went in and out among the people; what did they teach? As far as we can judge, merely a wisdom that followed the age instead of leading it, that cherished dead tradition instead of striking out new truths for new and living needs. The venerable Proverbs of Solomon constituted its basis; and these, with their thrifty laws of success, might easily have become popular as a rich man's book, making it so natural, as they do, for men to draw the comfortable conclusion that (because righteousness is the means of prospering in the earth therefore prosperity is the evidence of righteousness.) But in addition to these there must have been accumu-

State of Wisdom instruction in Job's time.

The Proverbs of Solomon.

lated a considerable body of Wisdom, several specimens of which have been preserved in the book before us. Bildad and Eliphaz quote explicitly from it, to prove the transitoriness and the present misery of the wicked; Job quotes a passage of similar import, in order to refute it; and it is not unlikely that Job's description of God's ways in history and Bildad's description of His mysterious dealings above, to which latter may be added Job's continuation in the same strain, are transcripts from a philosophy familiar to all the sages of the time. To the same spirit, though probably now first published, may be reckoned the oracle of Eliphaz's vision, and perhaps Job's praise of Wisdom. Elihu, rich in words but obeying unconsciously the dominant traditions, tries to bring Wisdom up to date in order to fit Job's case; he, and indeed all the friends, may be regarded as finger-posts of the spiritual teaching of Job's time. And what do we discern in it, beyond the lines already laid down in the Solomonic Wisdom? The *maskal* is more finished and rhetorical; from a detached apothegm of two lines it has become a continuous and highly wrought picture; but it is still ringing changes on the same old theme of righteousness and reward, wickedness and woe; and in reconciling the obvious discrepancies of the world it has advanced only far enough to invent a doctrine of innate corruption, which makes every man wicked enough to deserve whatever punishment he gets. It is a wisdom that occupies the social heights, looking down upon miseries with which it does not sympathize; and it has so lost vitality that it leaves the world heedless and undisturbed. Corresponding with this is the spiritual state of its teachers. *The wise men and their spiritual state.* Their God has become a hearsay, their teaching a conventionalism. Zealous to justify God in all His ways, no calamity could be greater to them than to meet God face to face. Thus along with their age they have become unspiritual and worldly; and deep beneath their philosophy there lurks the dry-rot of a selfishness which eats away their sensibility to the highest and truest things.

Such a state of things as this brings its inevitable reaction. Sooner or later Satan's question of motive must come to the front. Sooner or later also such a spirit, permeating the remote corners of society, must begin to leaven the nation's affairs, and to attract the attention of the *How this state of things meets its reaction.*

prophets. The first of these, the question of motive, has been raised and nobly answered by the author of the Book of Job; who, in all the splendor of the later *mashal*, has conceived and written what is at once a masterly arraignment of Wisdom's weak points and a creative solution of the world's problem, so woven together in portraying the character of a historic hero as to make a world-epic, a sublime monument of universal literature. But, meanwhile, has all this social background of our poem been otherwise lost to history? Let us see. During the prosperous days that culminated in the reign of Hezekiah, in the kingdom of Judah, a country prophet, Micah, looking upon the same secluded scenes that we have imagined for our author, spoke such burning words as these: "Woe to them that devise iniquity, and work evil upon their beds! when the morning is light, they practice it, because it is in the power of their hand. And they covet fields, and seize them; and houses, and take them away: and they oppress a man and his house, even a man and his heritage." Such sin as this was apparently the crying evil of that time; for we hear also Micah's greater contemporary, Isaiah, from his point of observation at the capital,

In the Book of Job.

In the prophets.

Micah ii. 1, 2.

Isaiah v. 8.

saying, "Woe unto them that join house to house, that lay field to field, till there be no room, and ye be made to dwell alone in the midst of the land!" Exactly this unchecked covetousness of the landed proprietors, with its attendant cruelty to the poor, we have seen before: it is the first great evil specified by Job, in his detailed survey of his surroundings; nor can the friends ignore it, blind as they are to many things, when they see men dwelling in desolated cities, and seizing on houses that they would not build. The general religious condition, too, recognized by these prophets, is not at variance with what we have already traced as connected with our poem. It is not idolatry and apostasy that they denounce, so much as that formalism which freely dedicates worldly goods and neglects moral obligations, which is scrupulous to observe new-moons and sabbaths, but is all foulness and extortion within. "Seek judgment, relieve the oppressed, judge the fatherless, plead for the widow," is Isaiah's summary of man's duty; and Micah's conclusion of the matter might be taken as the motto of the Book of Job: " He hath showed thee, O man, what is good; and what doth the LORD require of thee, but

Section xvi. 36-59.

Sections ix. 54; xiii. 37.

See Micah, vi. 6-8; Isaiah i. 11-17; v. 7.

Isaiah i. 17.

Micah vi. 8.

to do justly, and to love mercy, and to walk humbly with thy God?" Nor can we fail to be struck by the remarkable parallelism between the blind subserviency to a traditional Wisdom on the part of Job's friends and the kind of teaching that Isaiah observed in his age: "Forasmuch as this people draw nigh unto me, and with their mouth and with their lips do honor me, but have removed their heart far from me, and their fear of me is a commandment of men which hath been learned by rote:[1] therefore, behold, I will proceed to do a marvelous work among this people, even a marvelous work and a wonder: and the wisdom of their wise men shall perish, and the understanding of their prudent men shall be hid." Is not this the very portrait of the men whose well-conned wisdom was so riddled by the honest doubts of Job?

Isaiah xxix. 13, 14.

It seems to me, therefore, that we have found an eminently probable date for our poem. What so natural as that, just about at the time when the men of Hezekiah, perhaps in response to a kind of popular vogue, were giving enlarged currency to the old Solomonic lore, some unknown country poet, speaking not for a rich and thrifty class but for man

The Book of Job, dating probably from the time of Hezekiah.

See Proverbs, xxv. 1.

---

[1] So the margin of the Revised Version.

as man, should have shown wherein that lore was lacking, and by sifting it with doubt should have fitted his times with a greater truth? Such, I am not reluctant to think, was the origin of the Book of Job. And in so concluding, we see in many significant points how the age and its needed lesson are met together.

With this conjecture agrees very well the one seemingly clear recognition of contemporary history which the Book of Job contains. In the speech wherein Job concedes to his friends what he holds in common with them concerning God's ways, he says:— *Job's allusion to contemporary history.*

"With Him are wisdom and might;
  To Him belong counsel and understanding.
  Behold, He teareth down, and it shall not be
    builded;
  He shutteth up a man, and there shall be no opening.
  Behold, He restraineth the waters, and they dry up;
  He letteth them forth, and they lay waste the earth.
  With Him are strength and truth;
  The erring one and he that causeth to err are His.
  Who leadeth counselors away captive;
  And judges He maketh fools.
  The bond of kings He looseth,
  And bindeth a cord upon their loins.
  Who leadeth priests away captive;
  And the long established He overthroweth.
  Who removeth the speech of trusted ones;
  And the discernment of the aged He taketh away.
  Who poureth contempt on princes;

Section viii. 27-53.

> And the girdle of the strong He looseth.
> Who revealeth deep things out of darkness,
> And bringeth forth to light the shadow of death.
> Who maketh nations great,—and destroyeth them;
> Who spreadeth nations out,—and leadeth them away.
> Who disheartenth the leaders of the people of the land,
> And maketh them wander in a waste, where there is no path.
> They grope in darkness without light;
> And He maketh them wander like a drunken man."

Here there is such insistence on the idea of captivity — counselors, priests, and whole nations being pictured as led away, kings as dethroned and bound with cords, princes as treated with contempt, strong leaders as trudging in despair over the pathless desert — that we most reasonably conclude some world-filling event, or series of events, observed in the author's lifetime,[1] and still recent enough to point a solemn moral, had made a deep impression on his mind. He talks about such history, whatever it was, much as we would talk about the well-remembered events of the Civil War; only, according to the devout Hebrew custom, he interprets the work of human agents *Historical characteristics of this period.* as the permitted and appointed judgment of God. Now the period of which we are speaking was just the time when the Assyrians were vigorously en-

---

[1] The two lines immediately succeeding the above are:—
> "Behold, all this hath mine eye seen;
> Mine ear hath heard and understood it well."

gaged in prosecuting their conquests in the countries around Judæa; of which conquests the most striking and peculiar feature was deportation of whole tribes and cities across the deserts to Assyria. The northern kingdom fell in 722 B. C., seven years before Hezekiah came to the throne of Judah. *Certain dates of Assyrian conquests.* Arpad had been taken by Tiglath-Pileser in 740; Damascus by the same, in 732. Sargon, who became king of Assyria in the same year in which Samaria fell, took Hamath in 720, and not long after advanced almost to the borders of Egypt in a war with the king of Gaza. In 712 the embassy from Merodach-Baladan, of Babylon, came to congratulate King Hezekiah, and obtained, as was doubtless their secret purpose, a sight of his treasures. In 711 Sargon captured the Philistine city of Ashdod, and carried its inhabitants away into captivity. It was not until 701, when Sennacherib's invasion of Judæa was checked by a sudden and mysterious calamity, that the Assyrians ceased to threaten Judæa and its surrounding nations.[1] *Date of the passage above cited.* May it not have been while these events were still fresh in memory, yet long

---

[1] These dates, which are the ones authenticated by the Assyrian inscriptions, are taken from Professor Driver's excellent *Life and Times of Isaiah*, in the Men of the Bible Series.

enough thereafter for the nation to have learned its lesson and settled down to a prosperous peace, that the author of the Book of Job wrote the passage I have cited above?

Objections to putting it later.
That it was much later than Hezekiah, say when Manasseh was disquieting the kingdom by his wholesale experiments in idolatry, does not seem to me so naturally borne out by the general complexion of the book. Still less natural would it seem, especially in view of the other characteristics of the book that I have traced, to make the above passage refer, as some do, to the captivity of Judah, which began in 588. A second captivity would have been too trite a story to be expounded thus freshly and vividly; and it would more reasonably have been employed to teach a national lesson, instead of the individual or rather universal one of our book. Besides, we cannot well imagine the tranquil settled surroundings which, as we have seen, evidently filled the writer's consciousness, to have entered the work either of a captive exile or of a lone survivor in a desolated land; one of which, if the writer lived in the Judæan captivity, he must have been.

Comparison with other literary works.
It is in no unfitting place in the Hebrew literature if we thus regard the Book of Job as contemporary

with the great Isaiah. At what period could we find language or thought in greater vigor or beauty? Nor does it thus disagree with whatever literature may, for likeness of style or thought, be compared with it. At about that time, as we have seen, the men of Hezekiah were making their supplement to the Book of Proverbs; and the part that they added, chapters xxv. to xxix., shows the same tendency to extend the *mashal* from a detached couplet to a continuous passage that we have noted in the Book of Job. Not yet was the section written that introduces the Book of Proverbs (chapters i. to ix.); that was the addition of the latest compiler, who lived perhaps during the reign of Josiah or a little before.[1] When

With Proverbs xxv.–xxix.

With Proverbs i.–ix.

[1] "For my own part, I incline to connect the 'Praise of Wisdom' with the age of Deuteronomy. Apart from the details to be mentioned elsewhere, it is clear (I speak now of Prov. i.–ix.), that the tone of the exhortations, and the view of religion as 'having the promise of the life that now is,' correspond to similar characteristics of the Book of Deuteronomy. And if we turn from the contents to the form of this choice little book, the same hypothesis seems equally suitable. The prophets had long since seen the necessity of increasing their influence by committing the main points of their discourses to writing; some rhetorical passages indeed were evidently composed to be read and not to be heard. It was natural that the moralists should follow this example, not only (as in the anthologies) by remodeling their wise sayings for publication, but also by venturing on long and

we compare its praise of Wisdom, chapters viii. and ix., with Job xxviii. (section xix.), it is not difficult to estimate which is the earlier. The Wisdom that is praised in Job as the most precious thing in the world is still the literal austere virtue toward which the early sages directed their eyes; while in Proverbs, though no less glowingly portrayed, it has passed into the feebler and less sincere artistic refinements of personification and allegory. In the same way of greater refinement, less simplicity and directness, the following passage from Jeremiah bears the marks of a copy, or a later echo, as compared with the passage where Job opens his mouth and curses his day:

Jeremiah xx. 14–18; compare Job, section ii.
"Cursed be the day wherein I was born: let not the day wherein my mother bare me be blessed. Cursed be the man who brought tidings to my father, saying, A man child is born unto thee; making him very glad. And let that man be as the cities which the LORD overthrew, and repented not: and let him hear a cry in the morning, and shouting at noontide; because he slew me not from the womb; and so my mother should have been my grave, and her womb always great. Wherefore came I forth out of the womb to see labor and sorrow, that my days should be consumed with shame?"

Jeremiah began to prophesy about 618 B. C., in the reign of Josiah. The way in which he echoes the passage in Job seems to indicate

animated quasi-oratorical recommendations of great moral truths." — Cheyne, *Job and Solomon*, p. 157.

that the latter, which then, as now, must have been, of all the book, the words most easily and universally recalled, had existed so long as to have become a household word. In modeling his complaint after the words of the sufferer of Uz, the prophet was making the most vivid portrayal of his own woes, connecting them as he thus did with a woe that had become historic and sacred.

Several of the psalms, notably Psalms xxxvii., xlix., and lxxiii., touch upon one of Job's perplexing problems, the prosperity and apparent impunity of the wicked. They seem to present a rather later phase of the thought than is apparent in the Book of Job: later, in this respect, that what Job works out as a discovery and makes good against the prevailing view is in these psalms taken as an assured tenet of thought. Job is the pioneer; and these psalms, whenever they were written, follow in the path that his sturdy faith has blazed out. *Job compared with certain psalms.*

For the great ideals which the Book of Job contains, there is no other book, as Professor Cheyne has pointed out, which affords so striking a parallel as the Book of the Servant of Jehovah, Isaiah xl. to lxvi. Pervading them both is the idea of a servant of God pure and upright yet suffering, *Comparison of Job with Isaiah xl.-lxvi.*

a servant so afflicted that men turn their faces from him, seeing in him the stroke of God's wrath. Job is the man of every-day life, who proves by his unconquerable integrity what it is to serve God for His own holy sake. The Servant of Jehovah is the idealized, mediatorial man, moving in some mysterious sphere above us and making intercession for sin, even while he dwells on earth with us. Job reaches by faith to the idea of a Heavenly Friend, in consequence of whose intercession he will some day see God a stranger no more. In the Servant of Jehovah is portrayed, not only a friend of humanity, but a somewhat developed plan of vicarious atonement. The ideal in the second Isaiah, which adapts itself [1] confessedly to the national needs of the Babylonian Captivity, seems to represent a considerably later and more matured stage of theological thought.

Conclusion. Who was the author of the Book of Job it is idle to inquire. He represents, whoever he was, the ripest thinking and culture of an age which, just because it could environ such a book, we cannot forbear to pronounce great; and with a self-abnegation

[1] Whether by anticipation or actual composition, I leave to the interpreters of Isaiah to decide among themselves.

which to our modern literary ambitions seems marvelous, he has committed his book to the care of the ages without a name. Nor is it unfitting so. The book is ours, all men's; the thankful world will always care for it reverently, for it will never cease to be young. And as we look back toward its origin, we shall be glad to cherish this our priceless heritage, not in the narrow human copyright due to name or definite date, but as beholding therein a large divine Idea, shaping itself out of the nebulous confusion of a far distant period, and orbing into a perfect star, in whose unchanging light we, with the patriarchs, may walk.

II

THE POEM

"*The spirit of man is an instrument which cannot give out its deepest, finest tones, except under the immediate hand of the Divine Harmonist.*" — PRINCIPAL SHAIRP.

> "*He seems to hear a Heavenly Friend,
> And thro' thick veils to apprehend
> A labor working to an end.*"
> TENNYSON.

PERSONS

The LORD (JEHOVAH).
JOB, *a wealthy landholder of Uz; a man perfect and upright.*
ELIPHAZ, *of Teman, in Idumæa; a venerable and devout wise man.*
BILDAD, *of Shuah; a disciple of tradition.* } *Friends of Job.*
ZOPHAR, *of Naamah; a dogmatist, eloquent and impetuous.*
ELIHU, *son of Barachel the Buzite; a young Aramæan, full of zeal and self-confidence.*
The SATAN, *or Accuser; the spirit that denies.*
Job's Wife.
 Sons of God, Friends, Messengers, and Spectators.

 PLACE: *Uz, a country lying eastward of Palestine, between Idumæa and Chaldæa.*
 TIME: *The patriarchal age.*

THE ARGUMENT

I. PROLOGUE. — I. Job's prosperous estate and his piety. II. His first trial determined in heaven, and inflicted on him in the loss of family and possessions. III. His second trial determined in heaven, and inflicted on his body in sore disease. IV. His three friends, Eliphaz, Bildad, and Zophar, visit him, and are silent at his affliction. (Chapters i., ii.)

II. JOB. — Opens his mouth, and I. Curses the day of his birth. II. Laments that he ever was born. III. Longs for death, being in darkness and bewilderment as to the meaning of his life. (Chapter iii.)

III. ELIPHAZ. — Addressing Job courteously, I. Reminds him of the faith in which he had formerly found comfort. II. Recounts a vision of his own, that revealed to him God's unapproachable holiness. III. Warns Job of the danger of anger against God's ways. IV. Directs Job to return to God and be blest. V. Gives sweet promise to him who accepts God's chastening. VI. Concludes. (Chapters iv., v.)

IV. JOB. — I. Justifies his anger, and finds Eliphaz's words insipid. II. Passionately desires death to release him, while his integrity yet remains. III. Bewails the treachery of his friends, and urges return of friendship. IV. Describes the greatness and hopelessness of his anguish. V. Resolves to speak out and seek explanation of God. (Chapters vi., vii.)

V. BILDAD. — Reproaching Job for his rash words, I. Maintains that God has dealt justly, yet promises restoration to Job on condition of repentance and confession. II. From the sayings of the ancients describes the precarious existence of the wicked. III. But holds out promise to Job. (Chapter viii.)

VI. JOB. — I. Acknowledging the truth of Bildad's words,

yet doubts how man can be just with God. II. Complains that God is so inaccessible, and on Bildad's data finds the world's government out of joint. III. In his forlorn state, so hopeless of maintaining his cause, longs for a Daysman, whom yet he does not believe in. IV. In the boldness of despair arraigns God for His seeming hardness toward the work of His hands. V. Implores a little rest before he goes hence. (Chapters ix., x.).

VII. ZOPHAR. — In great heat affirming that God is punishing Job less than he deserves, I. Reproaches Job for desiring to find out God's hidden ways. II. Promises, as did Bildad, restoration on condition of repentance and confession of sin. (Chapter xi.)

VIII. JOB. — Perceiving that the friends, after all, have not the real secret of God, and cutting loose accordingly from their doctrine, I. Describes what he, in common with them, may hold of God's mysterious dealings. II. Accuses them of asserting what is wrong, in order to propitiate God. III. Commits himself to the firm faith that his own way of honest integrity will issue in salvation, in spite of the present seeming verdict of divine wrath. IV. Faces the stern prospect of death, and longs for return of life after the grave. V. Yet acknowledges how groundless is such longing in any analogies that we can here see or experience. (Chapters xii., xiii., xiv.)

IX. ELIPHAZ. — Accusing Job, out of his own mouth, of impiety, I. Repeats his before-asserted doctrine of God's holiness and man's uncleanness. II. Describes, in the words of ancient wise men, the lifelong terror of the wicked man, and his inevitable doom in this world. (Chapter xv.)

X. JOB. — Reminding his friends how easy it is for the unafflicted to make theories, I. Describes anew the ravages of his disease. II. Affirms his certain belief that he has an Advocate in heaven, in which belief he is able to meet their reproaches calmly. III. Perceives the spiritual blindness of his friends, and his own truer insight. IV. In this consciousness draws resignedly near the grave. (Chapters xvi., xvii.)

XI. BILDAD.—Incensed that Job accounts him and his fellows blind, I. Describes, largely in terms of Job's affliction, the sudden and terrible doom of the wicked. II. Seals it with an affirmation. (Chapter xviii.)

XII. JOB.—Recognizing to the full but not yet answering the friends' reproaches, I. Affirms anew that God is the Author of his wrong, which then he describes at length as God's inveterate enmity. II. Bewails his loneliness, being deserted of all his friends; and implores pity. III. Breaks out into the solemn affirmation that because his Redeemer liveth he shall, beyond death, see God as his Friend. IV. In this confidence warns his friends against misjudging him. (Chapter xix.)

XIII. ZOPHAR.—Replying in passionate haste, I. Describes how short-lived and unsubstantial is the triumph of the wicked. II. How the sweetness of sin turns to a bitter curse, till an outraged God sweeps away the wicked in darkness. III. Concludes. (Chapter xx.)

XIV. JOB.—Calling for attention to his answer, I. Describes his shuddering dismay at what he sees in the world, and shows, in contradiction to what the friends have asserted, how prosperously the wicked live, and how securely they die. II. Yet disclaims sympathy with their ways. III. Challenges his friends to gainsay the apparent equality of righteous and wicked before God. IV. Denies their assertion that the wicked are swept away by an earthly doom. V. Concludes by branding their answers as falsehood. (Chapter xxi.)

XV. ELIPHAZ.—I. Accuses Job directly of sinning and trusting that God regards it not. II. Counts him as cherishing wicked ways. III. Gives him a final exhortation to put away iniquity and return to God and renewed prosperity. (Chapter xxii.)

XVI. JOB.—Yielding to the strenuous impulse of his complaint, I. Replies to the accusation of cherishing wickedness by asserting his longing to find God and present his cause. II. Bewails God's hidden face and inscrutable ways. III. Describes in detail the ways in which wicked men, all around him, are sinning with impunity. IV. Denies at length the common idea that the wicked are especially marked out for earthly doom. V. Concludes by challenging disproof of his words. (Chapters xxiii., xxiv.)

XVII. BILDAD. — Describes, in lofty terms, God's unapproachable holiness and man's necessary impurity before Him. (Chapter xxv.)

XVIII. JOB. — Ridiculing with scorn the inapplicableness of Bildad's words, I. Continues, in similar strain, the description of God's greatness and mystery. II. Yet avers that this description touches but the outskirts, not the secret, of His ways. (Chapter xxvi.)

XIX. JOB. — The friends having exhausted their arguments, Job, resuming his discourse, I. Affirms anew, with a solemn oath, the essential righteousness and truthfulness of his life. II. Describes, in correction of his friends' intemperate and one-sided portrayals, the real state of the wicked, as insecure, without delight in God or hope of a blessed future. III. Sets over against this the true Wisdom of life, which is to fear God and shun evil. (Chapters xxvii., xxviii.)

XX. JOB. — Pursuing his discourse further, I. Looks back on the days of his former prosperity and honor, and describes his life therein. II. Contrasts the woe and obloquy of the present, wherein even the most degraded despise him. III. Solemnly calls down judgment on himself if he have sinned against righteousness and goodness, and with this noble record stands ready to meet God. (Chapters xxix., xxx., xxxi.)

THE WORDS OF JOB ARE ENDED.

XXI. TRANSITION. — Elihu, a young speaker hitherto silent, perceiving ou the one hand Job's stout justification of his ways, and on the other the friends' inability to answer, takes upon himself to set both parties right, his wrath being kindled. (Chapter xxxii. 1–5.)

XXII. ELIHU. — I. Volubly describes his youth, his hesitation, and his final resolve to speak, being impelled by fullness of words. II. Takes upon himself, as a Daysman, to represent to Job the cause of God. III. Censures Job for his complaint that God answers not, and shows how God answers both by vision and by affliction. IV. But maintains, moreover, that these are to be interpreted by a messenger from God, such as he evidently regards himself, that the afflicted may penitently and joyfully return. V. Concludes, by demanding either reply or further hearing. (Chapters xxxii. 6-22, xxxiii.)

XXIII. ELIHU. — Turning to the friends and requesting a candid hearing, I. Condemns Job in that his defense of himself censures God, whereas God will not pervert judgment. II. Shows what it is to condemn the Just and Mighty One, in whose hands are the destinies of all. III. Counsels for Job rather humility and confession of having sinned in ignorance, than such arrogance as his. (Chapter xxxiv.)

XXIV. ELIHU. — Addressing Job and the friends together, I. Shows the folly of which Job is guilty in virtually making his justice more than that of God, who is so high above our conceptions. II. Explains that oppression comes upon the poor because in their distress they turn not to God, who is always ready to deliver. (Chapter xxxv.)

XXV. ELIHU. — Calling yet for hearing, and identifying his notions with God's hidden knowledge, I. Shows how by affliction God draws the soul in discipline to Himself, and applies this in Job's case. II. Describes, by occasion of a distant storm, the mighty works of God, which are beyond us to comprehend. III. As the storm approaches and bursts upon them, he becomes confused, incoherent in speech, and finally breaks off abruptly in terror and abject confession of ignorance. (Chapters xxxvi., xxxvii.)

XXVI. THE LORD. — From the whirlwind dismissing Elihu with a word, and calling on Job to answer, I. Passes in review before Job His great creative works, — earth, sea, and light. II. Mentions the great things of common nature, — snow, rain, and the influence of the stars. III. Describes the wonderful animal life, which displays varied wisdom in its creation and adaptation to its place. IV. Calls anew on Job bidding him answer his own censurings of God. (Chapters xxxviii., xxxix., xl. 1, 2.)

XXVII. JOB. — Is overwhelmed with the sense of his littleness, and declines to answer. (Chapter xl. 3-5.)

XXVIII. THE LORD. — Calling again for answer, I. Bids Job exert God's power, as he has presumed on God's judgment. II. Describes Behemoth, which, though so powerful, is inoffensive and submissive to man. III. Describes Leviathan, which in overwhelming strength sets at nought all that man can do; how much more exalted, then, Leviathan's Creator. (Chapter xl. 6-24, xli.)

XXIX. JOB. — Having now the sight of God for which he has longed, and no more hearsay, is content not to know all and to abide in penitent humility. (Chapter xlii. 1-6.)

XXX. EPILOGUE. — I. Job is commended before the friends, because he has spoken concerning God the thing that is right; and at the LORD's behest he prays for them, who are forgiven at his intercession. II. He is restored to double his former prosperity. III. His subsequent happy life, and his death in a ripe old age. (Chapter xlii. 7-17.)

JOB

I

PROLOGUE

I.

THERE was a man in the land of Uz, whose name was Job; and that man was perfect and upright, one who feared God

CHAP. I. 1.

The narrative portions of the Book of Job, which comprise the Prologue (section i.), the introduction of Elihu (section xxi.), and the Epilogue (section xxx.), are written in prose; the rest (except the section headings) in poetry. To the English reader the difference in tone, character of subject-matter, and diction, are so plainly discernible that the distinction between the two kinds of discourse cannot easily be mistaken. The adoption of the paragraph form for the one, and of the parallelistic form for the other, is as natural, and as fitting to the thought, in a translation as in the original. It is this fact which makes Hebrew poetry, as poetry, so susceptible of reproduction in another language: the poetic form depends, for the most part, on principles essential to the thought, as passion, imagery, and elevation, rather than on rules of quantity and assonance. The rhythm is such as our impassioned prose makes to itself,— fashioned, that is, by the impelling spirit within the thought to a regularity of flow and accent, though not a strictly measured regularity like that of our

and shunned evil. And there were born to
him seven sons and three daughters. And
his property was seven thousand sheep, and
three thousand camels, and five hundred
yoke of oxen, and five hundred she-asses,
and a very great household; and this man
was the greatest of all the sons of the East.
And his sons used to go and make a feast

CHAP. I. 2-4.

metre. Its manifestation, the parallelism, is a thought-measure rather than a form-measure.

LINE 1. The most probable location of the land of Uz, which at best is matter of conjecture, is indicated in the table of persons prefixed to the poem. What is of chief importance to note here is, that the poet has laid his scene in a land outside of Palestine, with its national traditions of law and ritual; and thus he has chosen a fitting place for an action that deals with the pure essentials of religion and morals.

3. Job's character, too, exemplifies that devout righteousness which is well-pleasing to God, whatever the external form of service; compare Acts x. 35. In the life of Job the poet evidently intends to portray the plain and universal ideal of a good life, such as every one can understand. The word *perfect* is not to be complicated with modern dogmatic subtilties; it corresponds not inaptly to Horace's *integer vitæ*, being the adjective of which *integrity* is the substantive.

6. The word translated *sheep* designates in Hebrew both sheep and goats, corresponding to the German *kleinvieh*, "small cattle."

9. The household included family, servants, and dependents.

10. The term *sons of the East* is a general designation for all who lived in the regions eastward and southeastward of Palestine.

I.　　　*PROLOGUE*　　　133

at the house of each on his day; and they would send and invite their three sisters to eat and drink with them. And so it was, that whenever the feast-days came round, Job sent and sanctified them; and he rose early in the morning and offered burnt offerings according to the number of them all; for Job said, "Haply my sons have sinned and blasphemed God in their hearts." Thus did Job continually.

II.

Now there was a day when the sons of

CHAP. I. 4-6.

12. It would appear from the expression in section ii. 2, that the day observed by each of the sons was his birthday. Seven times a year, therefore, such a feast-day would come round.

16. Job sanctified his children by some simple ceremony of washing and change of garments, probably, such as is inculcated in Genesis xxxv. 2.

17. The form of sacrifice here mentioned was not such as is laid down in the ceremonial law of Moses, but the simple patriarchal form, such as from earliest times expressed the primitive impulse to worship.

20. The word translated *blasphemed*, which occurs again in lines 43 and 109, where it is translated *renounce*, and in line 119, where it is translated *curse*, primarily means *bless*. It probably got its secondary meaning from the idea of giving the good-by blessing, hence bidding farewell, renouncing.

22. *Sons of God* is an ancient term — see Genesis vi. 2 — designating the spirits who attend Him and work His will.

God came to present themselves before the LORD; and among them came also Satan.

And the LORD said to Satan, "Whence comest thou?" 25

And Satan answered the LORD and said, "From roaming to and fro in the earth, and from walking up and down in it."

And the LORD said to Satan, "Hast thou 30 considered my servant Job, that there is none like him in the earth, a man perfect

CHAP. I. 6-8.

24. The word here translated the LORD is the Hebrew name Jehovah. Outside of the Prologue and Epilogue the name occurs only in section viii. 20. As the interlocutors are all dwellers in lands outside of Palestine, it is natural that they should apply to the Deity designations more general than that of the national God of the Hebrews; the writer, however, being a Hebrew, has no such reason for avoiding that name in the Prologue and Epilogue.

The Hebrew word Satan is literally *the* Satan, that is, the Accuser; being at the time this Prologue contemplates, a designation rather than a name.

28. Satan's first account of himself betrays that lack of dignity and stability which Goethe has taken as the basis for his portrayal of Mephistopheles. He is a wandering spirit, unattached to any allegiance, unsteadied by any principle; his only occupation being, apparently, to appease the restlessness of an active mind, as well as he can, by incessantly roaming over the earth and observing its affairs; see Introductory Study, p. 33. From this trait of unrest, the unrest of a spirit who has lost his moorings, all other traits of Satan's character, as here brought to light, are naturally traceable.

31. Not the author alone, but the LORD Himself ac-

and upright, who feareth God and shunneth evil?"

And Satan answered the LORD and said, "Doth Job fear God for nought? Hast Thou not Thyself set a hedge about him, and about his house, and about all that is his, on every side? Thou hast blessed the work of his hands, and his property is spread out in the land. But put forth now Thy hand, and touch all that he hath, — and

CHAP. I. 8-11.

knowledges Job's good life; nor does Satan deny it. That Job is a true and upright man is to be accepted as an unquestionable element, so to say, in the hypothesis with which we set out. And yet it is just this element which Job's friends, merely on the ground of his affliction, deny.

36. Satan's question opens the whole argument, or problem, of the poem. It discloses, for one thing, the weak point of the current Wisdom philosophy, which, associating as by an unfailing law of nature prosperity with righteousness and destruction with wickedness, opens the way for a merely selfish barter of religious service for worldly wages; and thus the question says, in effect, why not be righteous when righteousness pays so well? But for another thing, the question reveals Satan's character, which, as the sequel shows, is in polar contrast to that of Job. A half wondering, half sneering, wholly selfish question, the question of one who, having no allegiance outside of self, has no ability to understand unselfishness, it says in effect, Is there such a thing as disinterested integrity, goodness without thought of reward, possible in the world? See Introductory Study, p. 19.

42. *And see if he will not renounce Thee.* This is virtually a wager, as if he had said, "My word for it, he will re-

see if he will not renounce Thee, to Thy face."

And the LORD said to Satan, "Behold all that he hath is in thy power; only, on himself put not forth thy hand."

And Satan went forth from the presence of the LORD.

. . . .

And it was the day when his sons and his daughters were eating and drinking wine in the house of their brother the first-born.

And there came a messenger to Job, and said, "The oxen were ploughing, and the she-

CHAP. I. 11-14.

nounce Thee." The disposition to wager, to try experiments with the future, is quite in accord with the author's conception of Satan's character. Having neither fixed principle in himself nor connection with the Source of order outside, Satan has not prophetic ability. He can appeal to chance, but he cannot foresee. Goethe attributes, by a fine insight, this same wagering disposition to his Mephistopheles:—

> "*The Lord.* — Though still confused his service unto Me,
> I soon shall lead him to a clearer morning.
> Sees not the gardener, even while buds his tree,
> Both flower and fruit the future years adorning?
>   *Mephistopheles.* — What will you bet? There's still a chance
>   to gain him,
> If unto me full leave you give,
> Gently upon *my* road to train him!"

On *renounce*, see note, line 20.

50. *The day*, — namely, the birthday of the eldest brother; see note on line 12.

asses feeding beside them; and the Sabæans fell upon them and took them away; and the youths they killed with the edge of the sword; and I, only I alone, am escaped to tell thee."

While this one was yet speaking, another came and said, "Fire of God fell from heaven, and burned the sheep and the youths, and consumed them; and I, only I alone, am escaped to tell thee."

While this one was yet speaking, another came and said, "The Chaldæans made three bands, and rushed upon the camels, and took them away; and the youths they killed with the edge of the sword; and I, only I alone, am escaped to tell thee."

While this one was yet speaking, another came and said, "Thy sons and thy daugh-

CHAP. I. 14-18.

55. *Sabæans*,— predatory hordes from the mountainous regions southwest of Uz. In section iv. 39, the same people are represented as traveling in caravans.

56. *The youths*,— that is, the servants who attended the flocks.

61. The expression *fire of God* is probably meant to designate lightning, though there is something surprising, not to say preternatural, in its destroying seven thousand sheep. The storm in which it came we may regard as identical with the hurricane reported by the fourth messenger.

66. *Chaldæans*,— marauding bands from the region north and northeast of Uz.

ters were eating and drinking wine in the house of their brother the first-born; and behold, a great wind came from beyond the wilderness, and smote the four corners of the house, and it fell upon the young men, and they are dead; and I, only I alone, am escaped to tell thee."

Then Job arose, and rent his mantle, and shaved his head, and fell upon the ground and worshiped, and said, "Naked came I out of my mother's womb, and naked shall I return thither. The LORD gave, and the LORD hath taken away: blessed be the name of the LORD!"

In all this Job sinned not, nor attributed aught unbeseeming to God.

CHAP. I. 18–22.

75. Great winds from beyond the desert lying east and northeast of Uz are still a much dreaded and not unusual phenomenon of that region.

78. To report the four messages in identical words is not so much a crudeness as a *naïveté* of the ancient narrative method, which is not at all reluctant to repeat the same words, and perhaps looks upon such repetition as a grace, when the words are applicable to the same situation.

82. Job's attitude in this first trial is that of firm, almost proud loyalty to God. He regards the stroke, indeed, as directly from God; but he has not yet begun to realize the depth and the involvement of his visitation.

88. *Aught unbeseeming*, — that is, unworthy or ungodlike. The word so translated means literally *insipidity* or *folly*, and,

III.

Again it was the day when the sons of God came to present themselves before the Lord; and among them came also Satan, to present himself before the Lord.

And the Lord said to Satan, "Whence comest thou?"

And Satan answered the Lord and said, "From roaming to and fro in the earth, and from walking up and down in it."

And the Lord said to Satan, "Hast thou considered my servant Job, that there is none like him in the earth, a man perfect and upright, who feareth God and shunneth evil? and he still holdeth fast his integrity,

CHAP. II. 1-3.

as applied to man, is a not unfrequent term for wickedness. It is the quality in God's dealings concerning which Job begins to question, as soon as the greatness of his affliction has become fully evident to him; see section vi. 75, "Is it beseeming to Thee that Thou shouldst oppress?" As yet, however, he views his stroke as only the right of God to take away what He has given.

102. The question whether Job would hold fast his integrity was the point at issue between the Lord and Satan. It is worth while to note the simplicity and sufficingness of the old conception, which the world does not well to outgrow, that integrity or wholeness of the man is identical with loyalty to God. The man who renounces God goes to wreck as a man.

though thou didst move me against him, to destroy him causelessly."

And Satan answered the LORD and said, "Skin for skin: all that a man hath will he give for his life. But put forth now Thy hand, and touch his bone and his flesh, — and see if he will not renounce Thee, to Thy face."

And the LORD said to Satan, "Behold, he is in thy hand; but spare his life."

And Satan went forth from the presence of the LORD, and smote Job with grievous boils, from the sole of his foot to his crown.

CHAP. II. 3-7.

104. It will be serviceable, in estimating the justice of Job's complaint, to bear in mind that God Himself is represented as acknowledging that the visitation was causeless, that is, not just to Job's deserts. In estimating himself as unjustly punished, Job sees as God sees.

106. *Skin for skin,*—presumably a proverbial expression. Its uncouthness, as used in such majestic Presence, accords with the mocking, detracting, impudent character of Satan, and perhaps furnishes the suggestion of Goethe's conception of Mephistopheles as incapable of lofty and dignified speech, "Verzeih', ich kann nicht hohe Worte machen." Nowhere in the Prologue to Faust is the genius of Goethe more exquisitely displayed than in the shrewd, cutting, yet essentially low language and imagery in which Mephistopheles' thoughts are everywhere conveyed. It is of sarcasm and impudence all compact.

114. These *grievous boils,* with the signs mentioned by Job subsequently, indicate that the disease with which Satan

And Job took him a potsherd to scrape himself with, and sat among the ashes.

And his wife said to him, "Dost thou still hold fast thine integrity? Curse God, and die." 120

And he said to her, "Thou speakest as one of the foolish women speaketh. What! shall we receive good from God, and shall we not receive evil?"

In all this Job sinned not with his lips. 125

CHAP. II. 8-10.

afflicted him was black leprosy, or elephantiasis, which, of all diseases, was universally regarded as the most indubitable sign of God's direct stroke. It is the cruel irony of Satan to work as if he were God. Blake, in his picture of this scene, represents Satan as wielding God's natural agencies.

117. *The ashes,* — that is, the heap of ashes and refuse, outside the gates of the city, to which in Oriental lands the leper is banished.

118. With true feminine tendency to think in the concrete and leap straight to conclusions, Job's wife traces his affliction directly to its personal cause, having no disposition to philosophize, or to leave matters in abeyance.

119. *Curse God,* — the same word elsewhere translated *blaspheme* or *renounce;* see note on line 20. The abrupt imperative here and the evident resentment that fills her words seem to call for the translation *curse* as best representing the animus of her suggestion.

122. The word *foolish* was the common Hebrew word for vile or wicked.

123. As when God removed His gifts, so now when He sends positive afflictions, Job's first attitude is strong and undoubting loyalty. Browning, in "Ferishtah's Fancies" (The Melon-Seller), has thus drawn the lesson of this reply of Job: —

IV.

Now three friends of Job heard of all this evil that had befallen him, and came, each from his place: Eliphaz the Temanite, and Bildad the Shuhite, and Zophar the Naamathite. And they made an appointment to- 130

CHAP. II. 11.

"'How
Enormous thy abjection, — hell from heaven,
Made tenfold hell by contrast! Whisper me!
Dost thou curse God for granting twelve years' bliss
Only to prove this day's the direr lot?'
" Whereon the beggar raised a brow, once more
Luminous and imperial, from the rags.
'Fool, does thy folly think my foolishness
Dwells rather on the fact that God appoints
A day of woe to the unworthy one,
Than that the unworthy one, by God's award,
Tasted joy twelve years long?'"

It is the every-day monotony of pain, here just beginning, and with this the friends' hard reports of God, that rouses by degrees an agony of inquiry and doubt.

127. *And came;* but owing to the distance, and the leisurely modes of travel and of sending reports in the East, very likely the " months of wretchedness," of which Job speaks in section iv. 66, intervened before the friends reached him.

Each from his place. Teman, in Idumæa, was noted, as would appear from Jeremiah xlix. 7, for the wisdom of its inhabitants, — a distinction which Eliphaz well bears out. We may perhaps regard Teman as the renowned seat of a kind of university, if we may use so modern a term, where Wisdom was especially cultivated. Of the dwelling-places of Bildad and Zophar nothing positive is known.

gether to come and mourn with him and comfort him. And when they raised their eyes from afar and knew him not, they lifted up their voice and wept. And they rent every man his mantle, and they sprinkled dust on their heads toward heaven. And they sat with him on the ground seven days and seven nights; and none spake word to him; for they saw that his affliction was very great.

CHAP. II. 11–13.

132. *Knew him not,* — that is, so disfigured was he already with the ravages of disease, that they did not recognize the countenance they had so familiarly known in the past.

138. *None spake word to him.* The friends' shock of surprise was also a shock of disappointment. They had arranged to go and comfort him; but when they found him stricken with elephantiasis, the special scourge of God, how could they comfort whom God had afflicted? So the silent days gradually become ominous; from sympathizers the friends are changed to spectators, as they see that God's favor is withdrawn. It is like what Isaiah describes, liii. 3, 4, of our treatment of the servant of Jehovah: "He is despised and rejected of men, a man of sorrows and acquainted with grief; *and we hid as it were our faces from him.*" The reason, too, is the same: "We did esteem him stricken, smitten of God, and afflicted."

At this point the view into heaven is withdrawn, and the scene is left with its two principal elements, their attitudes already indicated: Job, ignorant of the Satanic origin of his affliction, plunged into an abyss of punishment which, even by the confession of God, is wholly without ground in justice; and the friends, who, judging by the outer sight of Job's disease instead of the inner recognition of Job's unshaken integrity, are already withdrawing sympathy and becoming estranged. It is a supreme test alike of the loyalty of Job to God, and of the current philosophy of life. Will Job prove that his service of God is not for reward, but because of his deep hunger for divine righteousness and communion? And if so, will he not reach a higher point than has been found in that philosophy which counts on prosperity, or shuns destruction, as its terms of allegiance?

II

JOB

AFTER this Job opened his mouth and cursed his day. And Job answered and said:

1.

" Perish the day wherein I was born,
And the night which said, A man-child is conceived.
That day — let it be darkness;

CHAP. III. 1-4.

The opening of Job's first speech reveals something of the obscure march of his soul during those silent days. From being proudly trustful in God his musing spirit has sunk back into passionate despair and blank bewilderment. It seems to be the poet's intention to portray him as thrown for the moment out of his orbit into a condition too elementary for hope; back of trust, back of religion, into that crude necromantic superstition which curses days and deals in the obscure mysteries of materialism. From this deep starting-point he is to find his way upward to light and God again.

LINE 1. *Cursed*, — not the word used by Job's wife, section i. 119, but the usual word for imprecation on what is base and worthless.

2. *Job answered*. In the Hebrew conception an answer could be made, not only to the words of another, but to any experience or state of things with which the soul was confronted. Hence Job meets his affliction with an answer.

Let not God inquire after it from above,
And let not light shine upon it.
Let darkness and shadow of death reclaim it;
Let cloud rest upon it;
Let darkenings of the day terrify it.   10
That night — thick darkness seize upon it;
Let it not rejoice among the days of the year;
Let it not come into the number of the months.
Lo! that night — let it be barren;
Let no joyful voice come therein.   15
Let them curse it who curse days,
Who are skilled to rouse up leviathan.

CHAP. III. 4-8.

6. *Inquire after it,* — that is, so as to take account of it as a day of history. It is to have no office in the sum of things, and hence no record.

8. *Reclaim it,* — that is, let that day revert to the chaos that belonged to time before the creation.

10. *Darkenings of the day,* — eclipses, which in unscientific times and lands have always been regarded with terror as of mysterious and sinister portent.

11. *Thick darkness,* — that is, let it be plunged into a deeper than natural night, the night, as it were, of night.

14. *Barren,* — that is, of births. The *joyful voice,* in the next line, means the voice of gladness over new-begun lives.

16. *Who curse days,* — magicians who were supposed by their spells and incantations to make days unlucky.

17. *Rouse up leviathan,* — according to an ancient solar myth, the storm-dragon that swallows up the sun in cloud. Perhaps the same myth is alluded to in the "monster of the deep," section iv. 86, and in the "flying serpent," section xviii. 25. See also Isaiah li. 9, and Jeremiah li. 34.

Let the stars of its dawning be darkened;
Let it look for light and there be none;
And let it not see the eyelids of the morning. 20
Because it shut not the doors of the womb that bare me,
Nor hid sorrow from mine eyes.

II.

"Wherefore did I not die from the womb, —
Come forth from the belly, and breathe my last?
Why were knees ready to meet me, 25
And why the breasts, that I might suck?

CHAP. III. 9-12.

20. *The eyelids of the morning.* This beautiful figure, which is used again in section xxviii. 73, has been transplanted into English by Milton, Lycidas, 26: —

> "Under the opening eyelids of the Morn
> We drove afield."

21. *The womb that bare me,* — literally, "*my* womb." In this and the next line this strophe reaches its first definite goal of feeling. So far Job's plaint has been only the spontaneous overflow of anguish, venting itself blindly on the day of birth, but as yet evolving no meaning out of the stroke. Job is almost "stunned from his power to think;" but even in his wild and aimless expression, being unchecked, there is a use, as an assuager of pain and a means of bringing the calmer mind. Compare Tennyson's In Memoriam, v. 2; xvi. 4. The first eighteen sections of In Memoriam are strikingly parallel in spirit to sections ii. and iv. of this Book of Job, as portraying the slow emergence of a soul out of the chaos of despair, and into a definite conception of its evil case.

For then had I lain down and been quiet;
I had slept, — then would there be rest for me, —
With kings and counselors of the earth,
Who built themselves ruins; 30
Or with princes who had gold,
Who filled their houses with silver;
Or as a hidden untimely birth I had not been, —
As infants that never saw light.
There the wicked cease from troubling, 35
And there the weary are at rest.
The prisoners are at ease together;
They hear not the voice of the taskmaster.
Small and great — both are there;
And the servant is free from his lord. 40

CHAP. III. 13-19.

27. In this thought of rest and oblivion, which is the keynote of this second strophe, Job's plaint begins to gather to its focus, though as yet he has formed no theory of his affliction.

30. *Built themselves ruins*, — that is, palaces that decayed and passed away, became ruins, after their builders' death. Job is thinking of the kings and counselors of so long ago that not only themselves but their works have passed into oblivion; it is for such intensified oblivion that he longs.

35. *There.* It is a state rather than a place that Job is contemplating, — a state of utter nothingness, which, by contrast with the present, seems to have all the sweetness of quiet, peace, and freedom. His thoughts go no farther than the phenomenal aspect of death: —

"There is no other thing express'd
But long disquiet merged in rest."

III.

"Wherefore giveth He light to the wretched,
And life to the bitter in soul?—
Who long for death, and it cometh not,
And dig for it, more than for hid treasures,
Who are glad, even to exulting,   45
And leap for joy, when they find the grave,—
To a man whose way is hid,
And whom God hath hedged in?
For instead of my food cometh my sighing,

CHAP. III. 20-24.

41. So at last Job's obscure meditations concentrate themselves into a *wherefore*. In this depth of suffering, life has become an insoluble problem.

47. The construction of this line is joined on to that of line 41: "Wherefore giveth He light ... and life ... to a man whose way is hid." In this and the next line Job reaches his defining-point, the real secret of his anguish of soul. He has lost the clue to God and God's ways, being plunged into an abyss of punishment for which he can find no cause. The way that he has hitherto taken, with its consciousness of divine companionship and friendship (compare section xx. 7), is suddenly closed; there is no longer any outlook. From this point he must grope his way, a long and weary road, before he can say, "He knoweth the way that is mine;" see section xvi. 18, and compare xx. 122.

49. *Instead of my food.* The word translated "instead of" may also mean "before." The exact expression is obscure, but the general meaning is that sighing fills as prominent a place in life as food once did, giving woe as food used to give pleasure and nourishment.

And poured out like water are my groans.　　50
For I feared a fear, and it hath overtaken me,
And what I dreaded is come upon me.
I was not heedless, nor was I at ease,
Nor was I at rest, — yet trouble came."

CHAP. III. 24-26.

51-54. *I feared a fear.* It is a common Hebrew idiom to use a verb thus with a cognate noun. These lines, while they reveal the genuineness of Job's piety, also betray the comparatively crude nature of it hitherto. A touch of the same quality has already been shown in his solicitude for his sons, section i. 19, his fear lest some unsuspected sin, like a grain of sand in the machinery, may have destroyed the delicate adjustment of their souls to God. Here, too, his piety has been largely an uncertain, uncomfortable fear. It has been negative rather than positive, a prophylactic against evil rather than an unruffled confidence in God, an anxious endeavor to avoid some blow in the dark rather than going on to triumphs in light. One important result of Job's trial will be to change his piety from negative to positive, from fear to love; so that what Satan intended for his destruction will not only confirm his integrity, but exalt and refine his whole relation to God. It is in this sense that Satan's tearing-down may work also to building-up, — that, as Goethe says (Prologue to Faust) " er muss, als Teufel, schaffen."

III

ELIPHAZ

THEN answered Eliphaz the Temanite, and
    said:

"If one essay a word with thee, wilt thou be
    offended? —
Yet who can forbear speaking?

1.

" Behold, thou hast admonished many,
And thou hast strengthened feeble hands;   5

CHAP. IV. 1–3.

  Eliphaz, being the oldest and wisest of the friends, is in some sense their spokesman, and strikes the keynote for all. His present speech goes over nearly the whole ground of the friends' argument.

  LINE 2. Job has paused in the expectation of sympathy; he has counted on this consolation at least that friends are around him, and that they will comfort him. Instead of sympathy, however, he meets a courteous word deprecating offense, which of course implies that the speaker must as a disagreeable duty use rebuke and admonition.

  4. *Behold, thou hast admonished many.* This is true. Job has heretofore been not only a believer but a teacher of the very same doctrine that Eliphaz now brings before him; Eliphaz is passing in review before Job the latter's own philosophy of life.

Thy words have confirmed the faltering,
And bowing knees hast thou made strong;
But now it is come upon thee, — and thou faintest;
It toucheth thee, and thou art confounded.
  Is not thy piety thy confidence?   10
Thy hope — is it not the integrity of thy ways?
  Bethink thee now: who that was guiltless hath perished,
And where have the upright been cut off?
As I have seen, — they that plough iniquity,

Chap. IV. 4–8.

8. The ground of Eliphaz's reproach is that Job fails to apply his own key of life when the real difficulty comes, has shown himself lacking in one of the acknowledged tests of the philosophic mind, see Proverbs xxiv. 10. As yet Job has uttered no rebellious word; his offense consists in being bewildered, in not being certain what it all means, — a real offense in the eyes of such a sage as Eliphaz, for it is a virtual impeachment of the adequacy of the current Wisdom.

10. The word translated *piety* is the same that is elsewhere translated *fear*. Fear of God and integrity, Job's standard of life heretofore, ought to be his ground of confidence now; he ought to rest in them, and believe that they will receive their natural reward in God's favor.

12–15. As the basis of his argument, Eliphaz lays down the universal law of sowing and reaping, making no applications, but leaving Job to get what comfort or warning he can from it. If Job is really upright, there is a gleam of comfort: the word *perished*, which is the strongest Hebrew word for destruction, may leave the implication open that at some time his suffering will be turned, and not end in death. On the other hand, the most natural implication is clearly oppo-

III.   *ELIPHAZ*   153

And that sow wickedness, reap the same. 15
By the breath of God they perish,
And by the blast of His anger they are consumed.
The lion's cry, and the voice of the roaring lion,
And the teeth of the young lions, are broken.
The strong lion perisheth for lack of prey, 20
And the lioness's whelps are scattered abroad.

II.

" To me once a word came stealthily,
And mine ear caught the whisper of it.

CHAP. IV. 8–12.

site to this; for if a man reaps what he sows, then the fact that he is reaping misery is a *prima facie* indication that he has somehow sown evil. Eliphaz and his friends err, not in their general assertions, which are true enough, but in taking too readily for granted that Job's affliction is a reaping. Their theory of the world is not broad enough to make it anything else, nor are they humble enough to own ignorance of its cause.

18–21. Under the figure of vanquished lions, Eliphaz represents that the wicked, however strong and fierce, must some time meet their overthrow. It is a rhetorical amplification which spreads out far beyond Job's case; his wickedness, if he has any, is by no means lionlike.

22. Seemingly aware that he has left the implication too violent, and that indeed he must needs explain how it is possible that there can be an equivalent in sin for so much affliction as Job's, Eliphaz relates a vision that he once had, which revealed to him the innate and inevitable sinfulness of the

In wandering thoughts from visions of the
    night,
When deep sleep falleth upon men,   25
Fear came upon me, and trembling,
Which made all my bones to shake.
Then a spirit glided before my face, —
The hair of my flesh rose up, —

CHAP. IV. 13-15.

creature. On this vision the author of "Mark Rutherford" comments: "Eliphaz is partly a rhetorician, and, like all persons with that gift, he is frequently carried off his feet and ceases to touch the firm earth. His famous vision in the night, which caused the hair of his flesh to stand up, is an exaggeration, and does nothing but declare what might as well have been declared without it, that man is not just in the eyes of perfect purity."

24. *Wandering thoughts.* These two words are necessary to represent a single Hebrew word. It means the mingled and confused thoughts that come without direction or control of the will. Delitzsch translates *gedankengewirr*.

26. The vision, far from involving Eliphaz's real communion with the supernatural, was evidently neither sought, nor expected, nor enjoyed. It came and went, wholly beyond his will or desire; and simply left him proud of having received such a communication, as if he were a specially favored repository of hidden truth. With this compare how Job meets the theophany at the end of the book, and how reverent and humble it leaves him.

28. Nor did the vision in any sense bring God near. It was only a spirit that Eliphaz saw, an intermediate agency; and even the spirit's words but serve to remove God to an inaccessible distance. The God here contemplated is the God of the cool theorizer, not the God of palpitating human life.

It stood still, but its form I could not discern, 30
A figure before mine eyes ;
— Silence — and I heard a voice :
' Shall mortal man be just before God ?
Shall the strong man, before his Maker, be pure?
Behold, in His servants He putteth no trust, 35
And He imputeth error unto His angels ;
How much more them that dwell in houses of clay,
Whose foundation is in the dust ;

CHAP. IV. 16–19.

30. "There is no such weird passage," says Professor Cheyne of this description, " in the rest of the Old Testament. It did not escape the attention of Milton, whose description of death alludes to it : —

> ' If shape it could be called that shape had none,
> Distinguishable in member, joint, or limb ;
> Or substance might be called that shadow seemed '
> (Par. Lost, ii. 266.) "

37. The implication is, that however a man may seem righteous by his own standard, by the standard of God's unapproachable purity he must necessarily be corrupt. Thus the conception of justice and purity is so sublimated in degree as to become practically different in kind; so unattainable that man cannot choose but err, and that any punishment inflicted upon him cannot be other than right. This is the beginning of that wholesale justification of God at the expense of facts and consciousness, that Job afterward detects and reproves (section viii. 63–76), and that Eliphaz finally reduces to an absurdity (section xv. 6–21).

Who are crushed like the moth;
Who are beaten in pieces from morning to evening, 40
Who, for lack of one that regardeth, perish for ever.
Is not their tent-cord within them plucked away?
They die, and not in wisdom.'

III.

"Call now: is there that answereth thee?

CHAP. IV. 19 — V. 1.

42. *Their tent-cord.* A metaphor familiar enough in Oriental countries, where life is passed in tents, and where the plucking away of the cord that supports the frail structure lays the slight tenement in ruins at once. A striking image of the precarious human life.

43. *They die, and not in wisdom;* a euphemism for dying in misery and woe. To a student of Hebrew philosophy, who identifies goodness with wisdom, and wickedness with folly, the expression would be suggestive.

The oracle of Eliphaz's vision condemns all men alike, not because they are sinners merely, but because they are creatures, and especially, mortal creatures. Job's consciousness of rectitude has no word to say in the matter; under such a judgment his only recourse would be to call himself a sinner, and to call his punishment just, and this his honesty with himself will not let him do.

44. Eliphaz thinks a good deal of his vision; for the fact that he is the recipient of supernatural communications is to him evidence that he is in the way of true insight into the deeps of life. To this happy condition he now contrasts Job's forlorn case, by challenging the latter to obtain a similar

And unto whom, of the holy, wilt thou
   turn? 45
Nay, rather, anger destroyeth the foolish man,

CHAP. V. 1, 2.

oracle; implying that Job, not being, so to speak, in the circuit of mystic communication, is therefore not in the way of God's favor. Eliphaz attributes this, as line 46 implies, to Job's anger at God's dealings, which shuts his heart to celestial visitants; his idea being evidently somewhat like Tennyson's, in In Memoriam, xciv.: —

> "In vain shalt thou, or any, call
>   The spirits from their golden day,
>   Except, like them, thou too canst say,
> My spirit is at peace with all. . . .
>
> "But when the heart is full of din,
>   And doubt beside the portal waits,
>   They can but listen at the gates,
> And hear the household jar within."

45. *The holy*, — that is, probably, angelic spirits, sons of God, such as are mentioned, section i. 22, 89; for there is no evidence that Eliphaz had any conception of spirits of departed saints.

46 Still carefully avoiding any direct accusation of Job, Eliphaz deprecates that anger which not only closes the spiritual ear, but, so to say, burns out the life, disintegrates the inner man. It is as a diligent student of spiritual things, who has reached the secret of life in calm, that Eliphaz speaks. At the same time it is evident that his soul has never been ploughed by affliction, as Job's is; for if it had been, he would not speak so dispassionately, almost lightly, of Job's profound disturbance, as if it were mere vexation or fretfulness, which he should school himself to avoid. Eliphaz's use of the word *anger* evidently stings Job; it is the only word that Job takes up and answers, section iv. 2, when he speaks again.

And the simple are slain by passion.
I myself saw a foolish man taking root,
But straightway I cursed his habitation.
His children are far from succor ;
And they are crushed in the gate,
And there is none to deliver.
Whose harvest the hungry man devoureth,
And taketh it even from the thorns,
And the snare gapeth for their substance.
  For evil goeth not forth from the dust,

CHAP. V. 2-6.

48. *Taking root,* — that is, becoming settled in life and prosperity, in seeming exception to the rule that anger and passion are disintegrating forces.

49. *I cursed his habitation ;* — that is, his dwelling-place was desolated so suddenly that I recognized it as blasted by the judgment of God. These words seem to refer to some old custom of cursing where God has evidently set the marks of His wrath ; and indeed, does not the friends' whole treatment of Job (compare section i. 138, note) illustrate the same spirit ?

51. The gate of an Eastern city was the place where justice was administered, or counsel obtained; but to these whom Eliphaz describes it is no refuge, because their oppressors, or perhaps their rightful accusers, are so numerous and overwhelming.

54. In his greedy hunger he gleans even the last stray ears of the harvest from the thorn-hedges that surround the fields.

56-59. Drawing a lesson from the seemingly hard fate of the "foolish" man, but with a strong implication for Job, Eliphaz maintains that the cause of our evils and afflictions is to be sought, not in the world outside of us, nor in the accidents of time, but in our own nature, in antecedents as rigid

III.

Nor is it from the ground that trouble springeth;
For man is born to trouble,
As the sons of the flame fly aloft.

IV.

"But I, I would seek unto God,

CHAP. v. 6–8.

as birth and heredity. The assertion that man is born to trouble, as to an inevitable fate, does not hang together very logically with Eliphaz's other doctrines, nor with his glowing promises to Job. The author of "Mark Rutherford" says, "A certain want of connection and pertinence is observable in him. A man who is made up of what he hears or reads always lacks unity and directness. Confronted by any difficulty or by any event which calls upon him, he answers, not by an operation of his intellect on what is immediately before him, but by detached remarks which he has collected, and which are never a fused homogeneous whole. In conversation he is the same, and will first propound one irrelevant principle and then another, — the one, however, not leading to the other, and sometimes contradicting it." It is this lack of relevance and sequence, possibly, which Job has in mind in his reply (section iv. 50, 51) when he calls for "forthright words."

59. *Sons of the flame*, — that is, sparks. This fine Hebrew metaphor is worth perpetuating in a literal translation.

60 sqq. In directing Job to God, Eliphaz leaves his rather rhetorical remarks so vague and general in their application that Job takes up the same line of truth in a subsequent speech (section vi. 2–35), and turns it in a quite different direction. The couplet lines 62, 63 Job quotes almost verbatim in section vi. 18, 19, where see note.

And unto the Mightiest would I commit my
  cause;
Who doeth great things, and unsearchable,
Marvelous things, and that without number.
Who giveth rain upon the face of the earth, 64
And sendeth water upon the face of the fields;
To set the lowly in a high place,
And mourners are exalted to safety.
He bringeth to nought the devices of the
  crafty,
That their hands can accomplish nothing real.
He ensnareth the wise in their own cunning, 70
And the counsel of the subtile overreacheth
  itself.
They meet with darkness in the daytime,

CHAP. v. 8-14.

61. The common Hebrew word for God, Elohim, is derived from a root meaning *mighty*. As the word in line 61 is the plural of the word for God in the previous line, it would seem to be intended both as a variation and as a climax on the other name; hence the translation adopted here.

69. A recognition of the logic of events, which makes all endeavors not in the current of truth and righteousness, however for a time they may seem to prosper, to pass away into unreality, being annulled or overruled for good.

The word translated [no] "thing real" is one of the most abstract words in Hebrew, and seems to have been a philosophical term evolved by the Hebrew Wisdom. It is sometimes equivalent to *truth*, sometimes to *reality*. The evolution of this term indicates considerable age and maturity in the Wisdom philosophy when this book was written.

And at noontide they grope as in the night.
So from the sword, from their mouth,
And from the hand of the strong, — He rescu-
    eth the needy. 75
So there is hope for the weak,
And iniquity shutteth her mouth.

v.

"Behold, blessed is the man whom God cor-
    recteth;
Therefore despise not thou the chastening of
    the Almighty.
For He it is that woundeth and bindeth up; 80
He bruiseth, and His hands make whole.
In six troubles shall He deliver thee,
And in seven shall no evil touch thee.
In famine He shall redeem thee from death,
And in war from the power of the sword. 85

CHAP. V. 14–20.

78. In this strophe, in which the present section reaches its most rhetorical and beautiful expression, Eliphaz anticipates the doctrine of God's chastening, which Elihu afterwards carries out to greater length. True as it is in the abstract, it errs in presupposing Job as needing to be restored and corrected by chastisement. Here is the sticking-point with Job. He is not conscious of a sinfulness that merits such extremity of punishment, and he is too honest with himself to acknowledge such sin. So the chastisement does not chasten; and Eliphaz's words are in effect urging Job to purchase God's favor by an insincere confession.

When the tongue scourgeth thou shalt be hid,
Nor shalt thou be afraid of devastation when
    it cometh.
At devastation and dearth thou shalt laugh;
Nor hast thou aught to fear from the beast of
    the earth.
For thou hast a league with the stones of the
    field,   90
And the beasts of the field shall be at peace
    with thee.
And thou shalt know that thy tent is peace,
Shalt review thy household, and miss nothing.
Thou shalt know also that thy seed is numer-
    ous,
And thine offspring as the grass of the earth. 95
Thou shalt go to the grave in a ripe old age,
As the sheaf is garnered in, in its season.

CHAP. V. 21-26.

89–91. Eliphaz has a profound idea of the harmony of man with nature; all things animate and inanimate strike hands in the covenant of the righteous with God.

92 sqq. It will be observed that the supreme blessing here contemplated by Eliphaz is essentially the restoration of Job's former state, the blessing of prosperity and peace and long life and numerous offspring. After such blessings Job does not seem to seek; one result of his suffering is that all other desires give way in time to the supreme longing for God's presence. It is in this longing that Job disappoints Satan and leaves his friends far behind; such pure aspiration they neither cherish nor appreciate.

96, 97. In these lines Eliphaz promises Job what actually

VI.

"Lo, this; we have searched it out; so it is;
Hear it, and know thou; it is for thee."

CHAP. V. 27.

comes to pass. Other promises, too, made by the friends on the condition of Job's confession of sin (see, for instance, section v. 11-14; vii. 31-33; xv. 52, 58, 59), and fulfilled though he continues to assert his righteousness, demonstrate the poetic justice of his restoration, as recorded in the Epilogue.

98. *Lo, this; we have searched it out.* Eliphaz speaks doubtless for all the students of wisdom; and this speech of his, so strangely lacking in application, and seeming to contain so many presuppositions of Job's case, may be so merely as being a review of the Wisdom philosophy. In it we find men's highest interpretation of life, as held in Job's day, an interpretation heretofore shared by the patriarch himself, until his very affliction, with its passionate discoveries of faith, carried men's thoughts to a reach higher still.

IV

JOB

AND Job answered, and said:

1.

"Oh that mine 'anger' were weighed, were weighed,
And, laid in the balances against it, my wretchedness!
For so it would be heavier than the sand of the seas;
Therefore it is, my words have been rash.
For the arrows of Shaddai are within me,

CHAP. VI. 1-4.

LINE 2. The "anger" that Eliphaz has deprecated, section iii. 46 (see note there), Job justifies, by referring to the unexplained visitation that compels it. Looking into his affliction honestly, and interpreting it according to the only data he has, as God's especial displeasure, he sees only too much reason for being profoundly disturbed and embittered in soul. He is slow, however, to push his misery to its personal Source; it is not until line 83 that he can gird himself up to brave his reverential piety and address a remonstrance to God Himself.

6. *Shaddai*,— the word elsewhere translated " the Al-

Whose poison my spirit drinketh up;
God's terrors are in war-array against me.
  Doth the wild ass bray over the fresh grass?
Or loweth the ox over his fodder?   10
Can it be eaten — what is tasteless, unsalted?

CHAP. VI. 4–6.

mighty;" a semi-poetic name of God, used more frequently in Job than in other books of the Bible. Job seems thrown back for the time, by his affliction, to the conception of God as mere power; he cannot trace motive or design in such a visitation; to him God is the Almighty One, who without giving a reason does with mortal man as He will.

  8. *In war-array.* This is Job's most frequent figure of God's attitude toward him; see section vi. 107; xii. 22–24. He feels himself besieged by mysterious thronging hosts.

  9 sqq. The trenchant interrogations fit well with the intensity of Job's emotion, quite in contrast to the leisurely amplifying rhetoric of Eliphaz. See note, section iii. 56–59. "The sixth and seventh chapters," says the author of "Mark Rutherford," "are molten from end to end, and run in one burning stream."

  9. Job is not crying out for nothing; if things were as they should be, or even as explicable as Eliphaz would make out, he would not complain. There is a mystery in his affliction that no interpretation has touched.

  11. The thought of the rich, toothsome food over which the beasts are content rouses by contrast the thought of the spiritual food that is set before Job. Eliphaz has passed in review the Wisdom philosophy before him, and here is his judgment upon it: it is insipid, like tasteless, unsalted food. Not that Eliphaz's words are untrue: they simply do not reach Job's case, do not find him, —

> "And common is the commonplace,
> And vacant chaff well meant for grain."

Job's new experience needs some new view of truth to ex-

Or is there savor in the white of an egg?
My soul refuseth to touch!
They are as loathsome food to me.

II.

"Oh that my request might come, 15
And that God would grant my longing!
That it would please God to crush me,
That He would loose His hand and cut me off.
For then it would still be my comfort, —
Yea, I should exult in pain, though He spare not, — 20
That I have not denied the words of the Holy One.
What is my strength, that I should endure?
And what mine end, that I should be patient?

CHAP. VI. 6-11.

plain it, some vitalized interpretation to which his awakened soul can answer.

17. Job's anguish, spiritual and physical, is suggestively indicated in that strong word *crush*. What a wish!

19-21. In these words we read the strength of Job's loyalty. The allegiance to what is godlike is the root even of his longing for death; he wishes to be cut off before temptation has overcome him, to preserve his integrity intact even at the expense of life. This, after his wife has exhorted him to "curse God and die."

22. This note of self-distrust, as Job looks forward to a life of pain, deepens our sense of his heroic loyalty. To be patient without any outlook, to endure without divine support, — Job does not promise it, and he trembles at the prospect; but none the less he sets his feet on the toilsome way.

IV. JOB 167

Is my strength the strength of stones?
Is my flesh of brass?
Nay, is not my help within me gone,
And well-being driven away from me?

III.

"Kindness from his friend is due to the despairing,
Who is losing hold of the fear of the Almighty.
My brethren are deceitful, like a brook,
Like the channel of brooks that pass away;
Which are turbid by reason of ice;

CHAP. VI. 12-16.

27. *Well-being,* — the word elsewhere translated "reality" or "truth;" see note, section iii. 69. Does Job mean that he has lost the clue to the truth, the reality of things, so that even patience and endurance may have no significance?

28. It is from this view of friendship that the way begins to diverge by which Job arrives in time to a point wholly opposite to theirs, where he is fully fixed by faith on God; see section x. 45, 46; xii. 25-56. That God has afflicted him is no reason why friendship should be withdrawn; rather he needs friends the more as he feels himself slipping away from his old moorings in God. He desires simply that their natural affection remain undisturbed by what they see of his disease, and be kept faithful to his essential righteousness.

30. But they are not to be trusted to keep friendship in such adversity as this. *Like a brook;* the simile derives its suggestiveness from the Oriental brooks, or *wadies,* which in a rainy season suddenly become torrents, and in the dry season disappear utterly. In the time of thirst, when they are most needed, they are least trustworthy.

Whereon the snow falling hideth itself.
What time heat toucheth them, they vanish;
When it is hot, they are dried up out of their place. .35
The wayfarers along their course are turned aside;
They go up into the wastes, and perish.
The caravans of Tema looked;
The companies of Sheba set their hope upon them;
They were ashamed because they had trusted;
They reached the spot, and were dismayed. 41
See now, — ye are just like that;
Ye have seen a terror, and are confounded.
Is it because I have said, Give to me?

CHAP. VI. 16–22.

33. One is reminded of Burns's familiar lines, —

" Or like the snow falls in the river,
A moment white — then melts for ever."

39. *The companies of Sheba,* — the same people is referred to as the Sabæans, mentioned in section i. 55.

43. *The terror* that the friends have seen is the awful spectacle of God's hand working His wrath in Job's leprosy; and it confounds them because they suppose they must put their condemnation where God has put His displeasure; compare note, section iii. 49. Recall also how they were taken aback when they saw Job's affliction, section i. 138; see note there. Their friendship, instead of being spontaneous and natural, as Job desires, is at the mercy of their theology.

44. Job's plea for sympathy is the more reasonable because kindness costs them nothing; it is simply following nature.

Or, Bestow of your wealth for my sake? 45
Or, Deliver me from the hand of the enemy,
And from the oppressor's hand redeem me?
   Teach me, and I will hold my tongue;
And make me understand wherein I have erred.
How cogent are forthright words! 50
But your upbraiding — what doth it prove?
Do ye think to censure words,
When they are a despairing man's words to the wind?
Nay, ye would even cast lots for the orphan,
And make traffic over your friend. 55
   But now, be pleased to look upon me,

CHAP. VI. 22–28.

50. *Forthright words*, words that go straight to their mark, without evasion or covered meaning, are what Job, true to the universal experience of affliction, longs for; and against such he contrasts what to his sick sensitiveness seems their "upbraiding," or perhaps we might render it their "insinuations." He is irritated because they speak in vague and general terms, begging the question of his guilt, and yet making nothing pointed and clear; see note, section iii. 56–59.

53. Job feels that the words pressed from him by pain are no conclusive index of his true self. They are but "words to the wind;" and to found a reproof on such indications is to him the extremity of heartlessness.

55. In his anguish Job states his friends' hardness with cutting strength, and doubtless hyperbolically; yet is not their ignoring of truth for the sake of a theory, and their haste to sacrifice friendship in order to get on the right side of God, equivalent in a sense to "making traffic" over their friend?

And surely I will not lie to your face.
Return, I pray ; let there be no hardness ;
Yea, return ; — I am still righteous therein.
Is there perverseness in my tongue ? 60
Cannot my taste discern what is wicked ?

CHAP. VI. 28–30.

57. *Will not lie*, — that is, he will not represent himself before them as he is not ; his sin and his integrity will alike be open and manifest, to be recognized as they are. Their conduct toward him virtually assumes that all his professions of righteousness are lying, — disproved, that is, by his leprosy.

58. *Return*, — that is, from their coldness and suspicion to the confidence that they had in him before his affliction ; be just to the facts that they have always seen. It is a plea to be held innocent until he is proved guilty.

Hardness, — the same word translated *perverseness* in l. 60. It seems to refer to that warped, twisted, perverted mind due to prejudice and bigotry ; and Job's plea is a plea for candor.

61. *My taste*, literally *my palate*, meaning here, not the æsthetic sense that we associate with taste, but spiritual sense and insight. Job avers that his spiritual sense is not blunted ; that when he says he is righteous it is from a real discernment, as keen and true as it ever was, of good and evil. Both Job and the friends recognize that one's spiritual discernment of truth may be impaired or destroyed, so that evil and good may cease to appear in their real guise ; and Job is evidently solicitous to keep this fine sense intact in all his affliction ; see section viii. 23, 24 ; x. 40 ; xix. 4, 5. He comes to see clearly after a while that the friends' spiritual insight is not true ; see section x. 59, 60, 70 ; and Eliphaz likewise seems to think that *Job* has blinded himself by sin, — see section xv. 20. Which party has the real " perverseness " will appear in the final event.

IV.

"Hath not man a hard service on the earth?
And are not his days as the days of a hireling?
As the servant, who panteth for the shadow, 64
And as the hireling, who longeth for his wages,
So I am made heir to months of wretchedness,
And nights of distress are doled out to me.
When I lie down I say, How long till I arise!
And the evening stretcheth itself out,
And I am wearied with tossings till the dawn.
My flesh is clothed with worms and crusts of earth; 71

CHAP. VII. 1–5.

62. Job's affliction opens his heart to sympathize with all who suffer, and with mankind in general, whose lot is a hard one; and thus he feels himself a representative of humanity. We are reminded of Tennyson's similar use of his sorrow to broaden his sympathy in In Memoriam, xcix.: —

> "O wheresoever those may be,
> Betwixt the slumber of the poles,
> To-day they count as kindred souls;
> They know me not, but mourn with me."

A hard service; — the Hebrew word refers to such a service as a soldier has to fulfill; a war-fare, war-service.

64. *For the shadow,* — that is, on the sun-dial, the shadow that indicates the time to cease work.

66. This would seem to imply, what is likely enough, that a considerable time had elapsed from the beginning of his affliction to the coming of the friends. See note, section i. 127.

67. *Doled out,* slowly and reluctantly, as it were, every one counting for its utmost in pain.

My skin closeth up, and breaketh out afresh.
My days are swifter than a weaver's shuttle;
And they are consumed away, without any hope.
Remember Thou, that my life is a breath; 75
Never again shall mine eye see good.
The eye of him that looketh after me shall not espy me;
Thine eyes will seek me, — and I am not.
The cloud vanisheth away, and is gone;
So he that goeth down to Sheol shall not come up again; 80

CHAP. VII. 5-9.

71, 72. These lines describe what are said to be veritable characteristics of elephantiasis, or black leprosy. The "crusts of earth" refer to the hardened ash-colored scab that forms over the sores.

73. To look back upon, and in comparison with their fruitlessness of result, his hopeless days seem very short, however irksome in the passing. Perhaps they seem so short because he has "taken wings of foresight" and can look upon them as it were from a distance, or in the large view which we apply to the sum total of human life in general. He identifies himself with the race.

75. The thought of his brief life and its hopelessness gives him the first impulse to address himself directly to God, though not at first with remonstrance. It is his first approach to that mystery of death, the idea of which plays such a large part in the achievements of his faith throughout the poem. See Introductory Study, p. 56.

80. *Sheol*, — the Hebrew word designating the unseen abode of the dead; a neutral word presupposing neither mis-

Never again shall he return to his house,
Nor shall his place know him any more.

V.

"So therefore I, I will not restrain my mouth;
I will speak in the anguish of my spirit;
I will complain in the bitterness of my soul. 85
   Am I a sea, or a monster of the deep,
That Thou settest a watch over me?
When I say, My bed shall comfort me,
My couch shall help me bear my complaints, —

CHAP. VII. 10-13.

ery nor happiness, and not infrequently used much as we use the words "the grave," to denote the final undefined resting-place of all.

83. Face to face with death, as the utmost that suffering can do, Job resolves to speak out what is in him. "It is stated by Dr. Livingstone, the celebrated explorer of Africa, that the blow of a lion's paw upon his shoulder, which was so severe as to break his arm, completely annihilated fear." Job's trembling solicitude lest he should "lose hold of the fear of the Almighty" (compare section ii. 51-54; iv. 29) is passing away as he faces death, and in its place is rising a boldness before God which mounts in his next speech to the amazing height of his everlasting No; see section vi. 70-85, and note thereon. It is a time for nothing but utter honesty with self and with God.

86. *Am I a sea?* — that is, one of the great objects or forces of nature, on which supposably God must exert transcendent power, to tame or restrain it. His suffering, which of course he has to refer to God, seems out of all proportion to his own importance; why such attention to a creature so insignificant?

Then Thou scarest me with dreams, 90
And with visions dost Thou terrify me.
So that my soul chooseth strangling,
Yea, death, rather than these my bones.
I am filled with loathing; let me not live alway;
Cease from me; for my days are a breath. 95
  What is mortal man, that Thou magnifiest him,
And that Thou settest Thy thought upon him?
That Thou visitest him every morning,
And every moment dost try him?
How long wilt Thou not look away from me, 100
Nor let me alone till I swallow my spittle?
If I have sinned, what could I do unto Thee?

CHAP. VII. 14–20.

90. Even sleep, filled as it is with the vivid and distressing dreams of sickness, fails to bring oblivion of pain. Blake illustrates this verse by a figure of Satan hovering in the guise of God over Job's couch.

93. *These my bones*, — referring to his emaciation, one of the marks of his disease, which left him a skeleton.

96. A reminiscence of Psalm viii. 4, in a kind of "bitter parody," as it has been called. For whereas in the psalm the feeling is grateful wonder that God, the Creator of the worlds, should condescend to such a lowly creature as man, here the feeling is perplexity that the same great God should be so relentless in pursuing man with affliction.

101. *Till I swallow my spittle*, — that is, the smallest appreciable time. Probably an expression in common use.

102. The greatness of Job's punishment, so far beyond what natural and spiritual law can explain or demand, gives

Watcher of men, wherefore hast Thou set me
    as Thy mark?
So that I am become a burden to myself?
And why wilt Thou not pardon my transgres-
    sion,   105
And take away mine iniquity?
For now I shall sleep in the dust,
And Thou wilt seek for me, — and I am not."

CHAP. VII. 20, 21.

this visitation the look of vindictiveness, as if God were making some conduct of Job a personal matter; so the question what Job could possibly do to injure God is not unnaturally suggested. A question that in the abstract men had pondered and answered; see section xv. 2–5; xxiv. 8–15, and compare Psalm xvi. 2, 3. The distance between God and men is so vast that neither can sin injure nor righteousness benefit Him, —

> "For merit lives from man to man,
> And not from man, O Lord, to Thee."

In this idea of God, as throned high above the creature's merits and sins, Job and the friends are not as yet at issue; but the latter acquiesce in it as a necessity of the creature's lowliness and impurity (see section iii. 35, 36; ix. 26–31; xvii. 6, 7), while they make sin a natural, self-punishing thing (compare section iii. 14, 15): Job, on the other hand, turns straight to God, seeking for light, interpretation, communion, while he mourns over His remoteness (section ii. 47, 48), and cannot rest until he has come to see God as He is (xxix. 10).

105. Job seems to claim pardon almost indignantly, as if it were a right. Even the God who will by no means acquit (see Exodus xxxiv. 7) may be called on for pardon; and much more, when the sin is below consciousness, not to be merciful is not to be just.

107. *For now I shall sleep in the dust;* — this, after all, is

what makes Job's inquiries and expostulations so natural. So near death as he is, the logic of his case demands pardon; for what is the significance of torturing by pain a life so soon to go out? The thought of a life beyond has not risen to Job's mind out of this enigma.

V

BILDAD

Then answered Bildad the Shuhite, and said:

" How long wilt thou speak such things ?
For the words of thy mouth are a mighty wind.

I.

" Will God pervert the right?
Or will the Almighty pervert justice?
If thy children have sinned against Him,
So hath He given them over into the hand of their transgression.

Chap. VIII. 1-4.

Line 2. Bildad replies with considerably more heat than Eliphaz; Job's words have irritated and disquieted him, having roused him to indignation, as a strong wind makes a man shelter and defend himself.

4. The mere fact that Job is bewildered and asks God for explanation of his affliction astonishes Bildad, for it seems to impugn God's justice, the fundamental thing in Bildad's creed. His philosophy is not so broad as Eliphaz's, but perhaps all the more clear; and with a kind of brutal directness he blurts out what is in his mind; though with some remnants of courtesy he applies his explanation to the children who were so mysteriously slain, and forbears to accuse Job, except by implication.

But thou — if thou wilt seek earnestly unto God,
And to the Almighty make supplication, —
So be that thou art pure and upright, —   10
Verily then He will awake for thee,
And will restore the habitation of thy righteousness.
Then, though thy beginning be small,
Thine end shall increase exceedingly.

II.

" For inquire now of the generation gone,   15

CHAP. VIII. 5–8.

8–14. This very accurately describes both Job's attitude toward God and what afterward befell him; only it contemplates Job's approach to God as a return from sin and rebellion rather than as the hunger of an unselfishly righteous heart. We see through it all the irreconcilable difference between the friends' point of view and Job's; the friends reasoning that Job is a leper, and therefore, of course, a sinner; Job asserting, I am a righteous man, and my leprosy is a mystery that I cannot penetrate.

10. This is put in slyly, as a delicate implication that Job is not all that he should be in purity and uprightness.

12. Observe that Bildad, like Eliphaz, sets before Job merely a promise of reinstatement, restoration to worldly prosperity; compare note on section iii. 92 sqq. This is all that the friends contemplate, and is their measure of blessing. Job's ideal is much higher, being measured by nothing short of God's presence.

15. Bildad is a disciple of tradition, drawing his philosophy of life from the sayings and precepts of the ancients, the well-

And give heed to the research of their fathers, —
For of yesterday are we, and know nothing;
For our days are a shadow on the earth; —
Will they not teach thee, speak to thee,
And from their heart bring forth sayings? — 20
' Doth the rush grow tall without mire?
Doth the marsh-grass thrive without water?
While yet in its greenness it is uncut,
Yet sooner than all herbs it drieth up.
So are the ways of all that forget God; 25
And the hope of the unholy shall perish.
Whose confidence is cut asunder,
And whose trust is but the spider's house.
He leaneth upon his house, and it standeth not;
He graspeth it fast, and it abideth not. 30

CHAP. VIII. 8-15.

tested wisdom of the ages. It is worthy of remark that the wisdom that he represents is already regarded as venerable, and as having reached ripened and irrefragable results.

21. Here the sayings of the fathers begin, and they are not without great beauty and impressiveness. Nor is exception to be taken to them. Job assents to them at once (section vi. 2), and when he comes to sum up the significance of the world his result is nearly the same as Bildad's (section xix. 14-19). In fact, these sayings embody truths that have become truisms; they are perhaps the oldest statement of what we call the logic of events. It was a great discovery of man, and fresher in Job's days than now, to know that the powers of history and the world were with good, and against wicked-

Green he is, in the sunshine,
And his sprouts shoot forth over his garden;
Over heaps of stone his roots are entwined;
He looketh upon a house of stone.
If he be destroyed from his place, 35
It straightway disowneth him — I never saw
    thee.
Behold, this is the joy of his way;
And out of the dust shall others spring up.'

III.

" Behold, God will not despise the perfect man,
Nor will He grasp the hand of the wicked. 40
While He filleth thy mouth with laughter,
And thy lips with a song of joy,
They that hate thee shall be clothed with
    shame,
And the tent of the wicked shall be no more."

CHAP. VIII. 16–22.

ness. Our book takes this idea, the law of spiritual gravitation, so to say, in the tenacity of its prime vigor, before the exceptions, as exemplified in Job's life, came to be recognized; and it is apparently one object of the author to submit this spiritual law to its needed regulative of doubt.

   39. *God will not despise the perfect man;* but apparently God despises Job, for Job is suffering God's distinctive scourge. The ending of Bildad's speech, courteous though it is, comes weighted with this implication, and conditions its promise on his being pure and upright (l. 10). The courtesy is thus only a clumsy disguise to what is really cutting and harsh.

VI.

JOB

And Job answered, and said:

I.

"Of a truth I know it is so;
And yet — how shall a mortal be just with God?

Chap. ix. 1, 2.

The vague and aimless questioning which Eliphaz's lecture roused in Job is in the present section precipitated, so to say, by the influence of Bildad's rigid assertion of divine justice, into sharp doubt and despair. There is no other section of the poem in which the tide of passion and remonstrance rises so high. It retraverses in the main the field of thought that was opened in section iv., only with more assurance and definiteness; being, as it were, a higher sweep of the wave of Job's meditations toward the culmination of his problem, and with negative beginnings of a solution.

Lines 2, 3. To Bildad's assertion that God is just, and that He gives to righteous and wicked their deserts, Job accords undoubting assent. That is not his difficulty; the real question regards man's relation to God, man's justice, which from Job's point of view of a just man suffering unmerited punishment is wholly obscure. The question asks in effect, What does justice mean?

3. Both Eliphaz (section iii. 34) and Bildad (xvii. 6, 7) ask the same question, but with a different setting and involvement. They contemplate God as so unapproachably pure

Should he desire to contend with Him,
He could not answer Him one of a thousand. 5
Wise in heart, and mighty in strength, —
Who hath defied Him, and remained secure?
Who removeth mountains, and they know not
That He hath overturned them in His anger.
Who maketh the earth to tremble from its place,
And the pillars thereof are shaken. 11
Who speaketh to the sun, and it shineth not;
And setteth a seal round about the stars.
Who stretcheth out the heavens alone,
And walketh upon the heights of the sea. 15
Who maketh the Bear, Orion, and the Pleiades,
And the secret chambers of the south.

CHAP. IX. 3–9.

that man's utmost righteousness can be only a far-away reflection, a broken light. Job's question, on the other hand, implies that man cannot be just because he cannot be sure of the standard of justice. This undeserved and apparently unmotived suffering of his confuses all known standards; it makes God seem to wanton in power for the mere power's sake.

4. *To contend*, — that is, on equal terms, as men contend in law. A legal term.

8 sqq. In these descriptions Job has in mind merely God's power, so vast as to be wholly beyond human explanation, in motive or principle.

12. A description of eclipse, which in unscientific nations is always one of the most impressive and mysterious phenomena of nature.

17. *The secret chambers of the south* are the supposed quarter whence the rain comes.

Who doeth great things, past searching out,
And marvelous things, past numbering.

II.

"Lo! He goeth by me, and I see Him not; 20
He passeth along, and I perceive Him not.
Lo! He snatcheth away, and who will restrain
    Him?
Who will say to Him, What doest Thou?
God will not turn away His wrath;—
Beneath it bowed the helpers of Rahab; 25
How much less shall I answer Him,—
Choosing out my words against Him!

CHAP. IX. 10–14.

18, 19. These lines are quoted almost verbatim from Eliphaz, section iii. 62, 63, though with a somewhat different connection and implication.

20. *I. see Him not*,—this is the source of Job's deepest trouble; compare section ii. 47, 48. He has lost the standard of life, the means of tracing God; to what there is in man, in his ideals and definitions, God no longer corresponds. Tennyson's address to his dead friend,

"But thou art turn'd to something strange,
  And I have lost the links that bound
  Thy changes,"

comes to mind as a parallel to Job's feeling as he mourns over God's withdrawn friendship. God is simply a vast Power working in the dark, inscrutable, unrestrainable.

25. *Rahab*,—literally *the proud one*. There is here an allusion to some legend, now lost, of some Titanic war against God, such as is apparently alluded to in Genesis vi. 4. Perhaps Bildad's words, section xvii. 3, refer to the same event.

Whom, though I were righteous, I could not
    answer;
I must supplicate Him that judgeth me.
If I should call, and He should answer me,   30
I would not believe that He listened to my
    voice,—
He — who overwhelmeth me with tempest,
And multiplieth my wounds without cause.
Who suffereth me not to recover my breath,
For He surfeiteth me with bitternesses.   35
  Is the question of strength, — behold, the
    Mighty One He!

CHAP. IX. 15-19.

29. Job's righteous cause ought to give him the right to answer as defendant; instead of that he must entreat as culprit. The Accuser is also the Judge, setting His own standard of judgment, and accountable to none. This consideration ploughs deeply; in fact, does it not strike the rock against which all interpretations of the world on the mere score of human justice and desert must be shattered?

31. *I would not believe;* the next line tells why, — because deeds, louder than words, disprove all that his words could say.

33. *Without cause,* — this consideration defines Job's issue with the friends; and we, who know the Prologue, know that Job, on God's own confession (section i. 104), has pronounced truly. This is no plea of sinlessness; Job would not make such a plea; but a complaint of *multiplied* wounds, — punishment far beyond its desert. All sense of proportion between desert and punishment is lost in this experience.

36-47. In these lines Job reaches his most agonized height of doubt, and his words evince, from the human point of

Of judgment, — 'Who will set Me a day?'
Were I righteous, mine own mouth would condemn me;
Perfect were I, yet would He prove me perverse.
Perfect I *am*, — I value not my soul — I despise my life —   40
It is all one — therefore I say,
Perfect and wicked He consumeth alike.
If the scourge destroyeth suddenly,

CHAP. IX. 19-23.

view, how insoluble is the world-problem on the lines of human righteousness and reward, work and wages. The same truth is recognized, from the divine side, by the address from the whirlwind; see section xxvi. 145, 146.

37. *Who will set Me a day?* — that is, to come into judgment with Me. This is God's supposed answer, implying His transcendence, so great that no one will venture to approach Him with a plea.

38. *Mine own mouth*, being so infinitely crude and unskilled in speech, as compared with God, could only demonstrate inferiority in argument.

40, 41. With full view of its awful boldness, and of its possible utter futility, Job yet ventures to assert himself, to bring his integrity into the field with God. It is an amazing conception, — the mortal thus in strife with the Creator. The beginning of this bold resolve we have already seen, in section iv. 83-85, in Job's determination to speak out; see note there.

41. *It is all one*, — that is, whether Job be crushed now or writhe in anguish a little longer. While he has voice, therefore, he will lay open the thoughts of his honest soul.

He mocketh at the dismay of the innocent.
The earth is given over into the hands of the
    wicked;   45
The face of its judges He veileth;—
If it is not He, who then is it?

III.

"My days are swifter than a courier,
Are fled away, and have seen no good.

CHAP. IX. 23-25.

44. *He mocketh,*—hard words these, but on the principle by which Job is judging God, not beyond the data of actual experience and observation. Indeed, from the Hebrew point of view, which attributes natural events directly to God, Job is saying no more than do the moderns when they call Nature "red in tooth and claw." Nor can we well escape Job's conclusion, if we judge merely by the standard that his friends press upon him.

45. Job speaks bitterly and too strongly here; but he is looking at a real fact, which later he expands in calmer mood; see sections xiv. 12-69; xvi. 34-93.

46. *The face of its judges He veileth,*—that is, so that absolute truth and right are matter of uncertainty, to be established, if at all, by dialectics, and not seen face to face. And this is true if, as the friends maintain, God is afflicting Job in order to define sin and righteousness.

47. Job has of course no means of tracing Satan's agency; but the asking of this question betrays what a pain it is to him, as well as what a dark problem it raises, to attribute such things to God.

48 sqq. In more plaintive mood Job recurs to the thought of the brevity and fruitlessness of life, a thought already broached in section iv. 73, 74. "The complaint of Job is not

They have swept by, like the ships of reed, 50
As the eagle swoopeth upon its prey.
If my thought be — I will forget my plaint,
Change my aspect, and be cheerful,
Yet I shudder at all my pains;
I know that Thou wilt not hold me innocent; 55
I, I must be counted guilty; —
Wherefore then this bootless labor?
If I should wash myself in snow,
And cleanse my hands with lye,
Even then Thou wouldst plunge me into the ditch, 60

CHAP. IX. 26, 31.

merely of the brevity of human life; it is that he can see no reason for that brevity; it is that it seems cruel that it should last only long enough to cease; it is that he has no light to show him life and immortality beyond the grave. It is of mystery that he complains, — of mystery which, unexplained, makes God seem cruel or capricious."

50. *The ships of reed*, — presumably such as he, or the author of the book, may have seen in Egypt, light and swift. But the word is uncertain, being found only here.

55, 56. Job has in mind, doubtless, Eliphaz's theory, which may have been his own formerly, of man's innate and necessary corruptness; see section iii. 33-43. He has not learned to question this yet; though the mystery presses hard upon him here, that he should in his own consciousness be innocent, yet be *held* guilty.

60. It comes to the idea of arbitrary power: God is so great that He can compel Job to be what He holds him to be. A bitter extremity of logic, that God, who has all the power, simply works His own inscrutable will, and man has neither knowledge nor resource.

So that my garments would abhor me.
For He is not a man, like me, that I should
    answer Him,
That we should come together in judgment;
Nor is there any Daysman between us,
Who might lay his hand on both of us,   65
Who might remove His rod from upon me,
That the dread of Him should not unman me.
Then would I speak, and would not fear Him;
For as I am now, I am not myself.

Chap. ix. 31-35.

62. *He is not a man, like me ;* — this characteristic of God, removing Him from all human standards and conceptions, and making justice and mercy as between God and man mere empty names, is the ultimate root of Job's problem. His deeply felt need, which his unexplained punishment makes palpable, is that God should be like man, — that there should be some common ground of understanding between them. Thus his outreach from the depths is Messianic.

64. *Nor is there any Daysman,* — only a negative assertion this, but noteworthy as suggesting what would solve his problem if only it were true, and especially noteworthy as originating with the human, with Job. And though only negative, yet it is to him such a fascinating idea that he broods upon it, and turns it over in his mind, and finally comes to believe and assert it; see sections x. 43-48; xii. 50-56; and Introductory Study, p. 54.

66, 67. With these two lines compare section viii. 91-94. These are the two immediate things that Job desires to have done, and he images the Daysman as the ideal agency to do them.

69. Of this line I take the view of Dr. Tayler Lewis, and translate somewhat freely, in order to make the expression

IV.

"My soul is weary of my life;
I will let loose my plaint over myself;
I will speak in the bitterness of my soul.
I will say unto God, Hold me not guilty;
Make me know wherefore Thou contendest
 with me.

CHAP. X. 1, 2.

plain in English. "The word *imadi* (with myself) denotes something *nearer, more familiar*, than *im* (another word for *with*) would have done; . . . *lo kēn imadi, not so with me*, would seem to give us the idea of *de-rangement* or *being not one's self — out of himself.*"

70 sqq. The stormy passages of the book, and especially those passages in which a special reach of faith and insight is attained, are followed by passages of more calm character, in which the comfort of the suggestion infuses itself into his further thought and comes to be taken for granted. This is true whether the suggestion is negative, or conjectural, or positive; for indeed Job's reaches of faith pass through all these stages before they are thoroughly wrought out into expression. In this section the stormy passage that defines the chaos of the moral world is followed by the suggestion of the Daysman, which would solve the problem from Job's point of view. This idea, negative though it is, calms him. The succeeding verses in this calmer mood do not take the Daysman for granted indeed, but attempt in the absence of a Daysman to present the remonstrance directly to God.

71. *I will let loose my plaint;* — as if it were a flood, to be let gush forth with risk of devastation and drowning. With these lines compare section iv. 83-85, and note there. The coming passage, lines 75-107, wherein Job so boldly arraigns

Is it beseeming to Thee that Thou shouldst oppress, 75
That Thou shouldst despise the labor of Thy hands,
Whilst Thou shinest on the counsel of the wicked?
Do eyes of flesh belong to Thee?
Or seest Thou as a mortal seeth?
Are Thy days like a mortal's days, 80
Or Thy years like the days of a man,

CHAP. X. 3-5.

God to His face, we may call, in Carlyle's phrase, Job's Everlasting No; see Introductory Study, p. 45, and footnote.

75. *Is it beseeming*, — that is, worthy of God as God. At the outset of his misery Job would not "attribute aught unbeseeming to God" (section i. 87). Neither does he here; he does rather what is more honest and open, goes straight to God with his difficulty and seeks explanation by some principle that he can understand. It is like Abraham's question, Genesis xviii. 25: "Shall not the Judge of all the earth do right?"

That Thou shouldst oppress; — notice that Job uses the word presupposing his innocence; not *punish*, as if he were guilty.

76. The creature reading the Creator a lesson. Job is giving deep expression to his own creative consciousness; and such consciousness demands love in the world.

"Who trusted God was love indeed,
And love creation's final law."

This is enlarged upon, in Job's peculiar meditative way, lines 86-95 below.

78-83. To search narrowly after hidden sin, as if it were a

That Thou searchest after mine iniquity,
And makest inquisition for my sin?
Though Thou knowest that I am not guilty,
And there is no deliverer out of Thy hand. 85
  Thy hands have fashioned me and finished me,
Together, all round; — yet Thou wouldst destroy me!
Remember now that Thou hast moulded me as in clay;
And wilt Thou turn me unto dust again?
Didst Thou not pour me out like milk, 90
And curdle me like cheese, —
Clothe me with skin and flesh,
And with bones and sinews weave me together?
Life and favor hast Thou granted unto me, 94
And Thy providence hath preserved my spirit.

Chap. x. 6–12.

matter of uncertainty, is like man, not like God; it is not calmly wise, it is not consistent with omniscience or omnipotence. For omniscience should know Job's integrity without such elaborate inquisition; and omnipotence can crush without giving account to any one.

86–95. The vividness with which God's process of creation is conceived and portrayed is an indication of the keenness with which Job realizes the awful inconsistency that confronts him. The wantonness of the destruction heightens his sense of the wonderfulness of creation.

And yet in Thy heart Thou hast hid these things,
I know that this was in Thy mind:
If I sin, Thou takest account of me,
Nor wilt Thou absolve me from mine iniquity.
If I am wicked, woe unto me! 100
And if righteous, yet may I not lift up my head, —
Filled as I am with shame, and seeing my misery, —
And should it lift itself, like a lion wouldst Thou hunt me,
And show anew Thy wonders upon me.
Thou renewest Thy witnesses against me, 105
And Thou multipliest Thy displeasure toward me,
With changing host on host opposing me.

CHAP. X. 13–17.

97. *This was in Thy mind*, — namely, what follows, that God should hunt out every sin and pursue it relentlessly. This, then, is what creation and preservation mean! Just about what the friends' doctrine involves, only reduced to a somewhat sharper antithesis, and viewed from Job's standing-point. There is a bitter irony in this passage. Although Job says "I know," yet we cannot read these words as his real and settled conviction; he cannot rest in it any time at all. It is merely the awful *reductio ad absurdum* to which the friends' views and his own former philosophy lead.

104–107. At the ends of these lines there is a wealth of Hebrew prepositions which can be rendered only approximately in idiomatic English.

107. Literally, *changes and a host*. Job's most frequently recurring image to describe his afflictions; see section iv. 8.

ie. besieged.

v.

"Wherefore then didst Thou bring me forth
    from the womb?
I might have breathed my last, and eye had
    not seen me;
As though I had never been might I be, —   110
Carried forth from the belly to the tomb.
    Are not my days few?
Let Him cease then; let Him leave me alone,
That I may be cheerful a little while,
Before I go hence, and return not,   115
To the land of darkness and shadow of death,
A land of blackness, like midnight,

CHAP. X. 18–22.

108. *Wherefore then?* Job's question of section ii. 23, 41 repeated, with the added significance imparted to it by all the steps and involvements through which his thought has passed. After all that the friends have urged, after all the aspects in which the case may be viewed, it remains true that there is no satisfactory solution of life. This may be regarded as the summing-up of the present section, comprising the dreary outcome of the friends' philosophy.

112 sqq. Compare section iv. 75–95.

116. *To the land of darkness.* By the side of his present misery the darkest aspect of death makes a picture on which Job's imagination dwells fondly. Of course he is using merely the language of phenomena, a language not conclusive for or against a belief in immortality. To such language he holds himself strictly; nor will he commit himself to a solution beyond, except as a rational faith can accept it.

Of the shadow of death, and without order,
And where the shining is like midnight."

CHAP. X. 22.

119. It is the superlative of darkness when even *the shining* — what light there supposably is — is like midnight.

VII

ZOPHAR

THEN answered Zophar the Naamathite, and
    said:

" Shall a throng of words go unanswered,
And a man of lips be counted in the right?
Shall thy babblings put men to silence,
That thou mayest mock, with none to shame
    thee,   5
And say, My doctrine is pure,
And clean am I in Thy sight?

        CHAP. XI. 1-4.

  Zophar's indignation rises still higher than that of the others; being a narrower man, his views are correspondingly more intense and dogmatic. With no pretense of courtesy, he characterizes Job as a "man of lips," whose words are mere babbling and mocking.

  LINE 4. The word *men* means men of full growth, mature men; and there seems to be an implication in the word *babblings* that Job is childish. Perhaps the fact that Job's words reach no resting-point, but remain gyrating in uncertainty, is what makes them seem so barren and childish. The complacency of a cut-and-dried theory!

  7. *Clean am I*,— this is the sticking-point with the friends. Job's words seem presumptuous insistence on what all ortho-

But oh, that God would indeed speak,
And open His lips against thee,
And show thee the hidden things of wisdom, — 10
For there is fold on fold to truth, —
Then know thou, that God abateth to thee, of thine iniquity.

CHAP. XI. 5, 6.

dox thinking has disclaimed. That no mortal can be clean in God's sight is perhaps the most unquestionable article of their philosophy; see sections iii. 33-37; ix. 26-31; xvii. 6-11. And Zophar is just the man to be bitter and bigoted over it.

8. *Would indeed speak,* — probably an allusion to what Job says, section vi. 4-7, 26-33; and to Job's general demand for explanation of his misery.

11. *For there is fold on fold to truth,* — literally, *truth is twofold.* The word translated *truth* is elsewhere translated *reality;* see note, section iii. 69. This theory of a twofold and mystical sense in truth is a significant indication of the refinement that the Hebrew Wisdom had reached by feeding on its speculations.

12. *God abateth to thee,* — that is, even in this punishment does not take account of all the evil Job has done. To say this is not personal spite; it is merely the extreme to which the theory of man's necessary depravity, unchecked by sober sense, may lead, — an extreme that requires a twofold interpretation of things to substantiate.

Observe how the friends have gathered heat as they proceeded. Eliphaz was courteous and indirect, exhorting merely to repentance; Bildad spoke of the sons' calamity as just; Zophar finds Job's punishment less than his desert.

VII.   *ZOPHAR*   197

I.

"Canst thou find out the secret of God?
Canst thou find out the Almighty unto perfection?
Heights of heaven, — what canst thou do?   15
Deeper than Sheol, — what canst thou know?
Longer than the earth its measure,
And broader than the sea.
If He pass by, and apprehend, and call to judgment,
Who then shall prevent Him?   20
For He, He knoweth false men;
And He seeth wickedness, though He seemeth not to heed.
But the witless will never become wise,
Till the wild-ass' foal be born a man.

CHAP. XI. 7–12.

13-18. Nothing can be more beautiful or true than these words, abstractly considered; and it is only Zophar's point of view that makes them convict Job of presumption. Job has been trying to find merely what concerns him as a responsible being, something that he feels he has a right to know if he is judged on grounds of mere justice; but Zophar identifies this with presumptuous curiosity about God's hidden ways.

21, 22. Zophar and the others have an intellectual delight in God's inscrutableness; as they are not hurt by it, they like to note the sudden stroke that overtakes the sinner. Suffering has changed all that in Job; see section iv. 62, and note.

23, 24. Literally, *the witless will become wise when* (*and*)

II.

"But thou, if thou wilt direct thy heart,   25
And spread forth thy hands unto Him, —
If iniquity be in thy hand, put it far away,
And let not perverseness dwell in thy tents, —
Then surely shalt thou lift up thy face without spot,
And thou shalt be steadfast and not fear.   30
For thou shalt forget misery,
Shalt remember it as waters that have passed away;
And brighter than noonday shall the future arise;
And be it never so dark, it shall be as the morning.

CHAP. XI. 13–17.

the wild-ass' foal will be born a man, — that is, never; presumably a proverb. Does not the use of this proverb indicate that Wisdom culture was becoming intolerant, — as the Pharisees came afterward to say, "This people that knoweth not the law are cursed"?

25. The same call to repentance that Eliphaz (section iii. 60 sqq.) and Bildad (section v. 8–14) have given. It is in more courteous tone than the foregoing lines; but its animus is still evident, in the fact that it traverses Job's presupposition entirely and exhorts to what Job can do only as a confessed sinner.

27, 28. Zophar puts in the same kind of saving clause that Bildad has done (section v. 10), but not quite so delicately.

And thou shalt be confident because there is hope, 35
And shalt look around thee and lie down securely.
Thou shalt lie down and none shall make thee afraid;
And great ones shall pay court unto thee.
But the eyes of the wicked shall waste away,
And refuge vanisheth from them; 40
And their hope is — to breathe forth their life."

CHAP. XI. 18–20.

39. A tag about the wicked, to give a bite to the end of his speech.

41. *Their hope is*, etc., — a contrast to what he has just said (l. 35) about the repentant righteous man, and possibly a little hint against Job's rash desire to die. The paradox of the expression is like Bildad's "This is the joy of his way," section v. 37, and is probably one of the aphoristic crystallizations of the Wisdom philosophy.

VIII

JOB

AND Job answered, and said:

"Of a truth, ye are the people,
And wisdom will die with you!
I also have understanding, as well as you;
I am not inferior to you;
And who knoweth not things like these?

CHAP. XII. 1–3.

Hitherto Job's attitude toward his friends has been that of unquestioning assent. Agreeing with all their assertions, he has endeavored, but wholly without result, to make their philosophy explain these perplexing facts. Now that all three have spoken, however, and revealed their uniform drift, the barrenness of their generalizations flashes upon him, and he sees that they have not touched the difficulties of the case at all. They have urged no more than he has always known. From this point his attitude toward them changes. They no longer stand to him as representatives of wisdom; and this section, ceasing to arraign God, arraigns the friends instead.

LINE 6. The friends' words are the veriest commonplace; strangely insipid as they seemed from the first — see section iv. 11, note — they have become but more evidently so as they multiplied.

A laughing-stock to his friend — such must I
 be, —
I who call upon God, and whom He answer-
 eth, —
A laughing-stock I, the just, the upright.
For woe there is contempt in the thought of
 the secure;   10
It awaiteth them whose feet stumble.
The tents of spoilers are at peace;
And there is full security to them that provoke
 God,
To him that carrieth his God in his hand.

I.

"Nay, ask now the beasts, and they will teach
 thee,   15

CHAP. XII. 4-7.

7. *A laughing-stock*, — because his perplexities are ignored and contemned, while his fundamental righteousness is coolly denied.

10. The friends are secure; they do not look at suffering through sufferers' eyes; they can contemn a woe that they do not feel.

12-15. These lines are the logical sequence of the previous. Those who live in high-handed wickedness, whose spear or sword is all the God and deliverer they desire, have the same unfeeling security; like the friends, they have the arrogance of the upper hand. This consideration carries on the thought first broached in section vi. 45, advancing it one step toward that view of the wicked and their ways which Job carries out in sections xiv. 12-67; xvi. 34-91.

15 sqq. In these lines, as far as l. 56, Job takes up and iter-

And the bird of the heaven, and it will tell
    thee;
Or direct thy thought to the earth, and it will
    teach thee,
And the fishes of the sea will recount unto
    thee.
Who knoweth not, by all these,
That the hand of Jehovah worketh thus?   20
In whose hand is the soul of every living thing,
And the spirit of all human flesh.

    Doth not the ear try words,
As the palate tasteth meat for itself?
Doth wisdom dwell with hoary heads,   25
And is length of days understanding?
    With Him are wisdom and might;

Chap. XII. 7-13.

ates what is true in the views of the friends, at the same time broadening its application. Everything, both good and evil, is in God's hands; no Eliphaz's vision, or Bildad's traditional wisdom, or Zophar's occult philosophy, is needed to prove that; the commonest things teach it.

    20. *The hand of Jehovah*, — this is the only place in the poem, aside from the Prologue and the Epilogue, where the name Jehovah occurs; see note, section i. 24. Jehovah, the God of the Hebrews, is here recognized as the universal God.

    23-26. The wisdom of which the friends think so much is not the gift or prerogative of years; it is revealed to a native insight as natural as taste or hearing; hence Job can trust his own conclusions as well as those of the friends. In this confidence he leaves their philosophy, and sets out for himself.

    27 sqq. In these lines Job gives the results of his observa-

To Him belong counsel and understanding.
Behold, He teareth down, and it shall not be builded;
He shutteth up a man, and there shall be no opening. 30
Behold, He restraineth the waters, and they dry up;
He letteth them forth, and they lay waste the earth.
With Him are strength and truth;
The erring one and he that causeth to err are His.
Who leadeth counselors away captive; 35
And judges He maketh fools.

CHAP. XII. 13-17.

tion in nature and history. In the main it is in the same line as the friends' philosophy, possibly drawn from the great body of Wisdom literature, but differing from it (see especially l. 34) in making God's dealings irrespective of human sin and desert. So far as the moral character of God herein involved is concerned, He might be an irresponsible and arbitrary tyrant, giving no reasons and caring for no justifications. This is an important step in advance of the friends' wisdom; it clears the ground, so to say, of their narrow moral considerations, and forms a clean basis on which to build anew.

35. So much is said here of captivity, and of removal (see ll. 35, 39, 48), and with such apparent marks of an eye-witness (see l. 53), that we naturally conclude some great national upheaval was fresh in memory, the writer putting his own memories into the mouth of the patriarch. To me this event seems most probably to have been the fall of the Northern Kingdom; see Introductory Study, pp. 111-114.

The bond of kings He looseth,
And bindeth a cord upon their loins.
Who leadeth priests away captive;
And the long established He overthroweth. 40
Who removeth the speech of trusted ones;
And the discernment of the aged He taketh away.
Who poureth contempt on princes;
And the girdle of the strong He looseth.
Who revealeth deep things out of darkness, 45
And bringeth forth to light the shadow of death.
Who maketh nations great,—and destroyeth them;
Who spreadeth nations out, and leadeth them away.
Who dishearteneth the leaders of the people of the land,
And maketh them wander in a waste where there is no path. 50
They grope in darkness without light;
And He maketh them wander like a drunken man.
  Behold, all this hath mine eye seen;
Mine ear hath heard and understood it well.

CHAP. XII. 18 — XIII. 1.

53-56. Job has thus accurately defined how far he and the friends are at one; they agree in ascribing all events to God. But from this point their paths diverge.

What ye know, that know I also; 55
I am not inferior to you.

II.

" But I, — to the Almighty would I speak;
I long to make plea unto God.
But ye too, — forgers of lies are ye;
Patchers-up of nothings are ye all. 60
Would that ye were silent altogether!
And it would be to you for wisdom.
 Hear ye now my rebuke,
And listen to the charges of my lips.
Will ye speak *what is wrong*, for God? 65
And will ye, for Him, utter deceit?

CHAP. XIII. 2-7.

57, 58. Taking Zophar at his word (see section vii. 8) Job would invite God's answer by making plea to Him. In the absence of a Daysman to represent his cause (section vi. 62-69), Job approaches God directly, as indeed he has approached Him before (vi. 70-107), but in much better spirit now.

59. *Forgers of lies.* What the friends have said, true though it is, is only the half-truth, which in their application of it has all the effect of a lie. Two essential elements they have ignored: the fact, illustrated by Job's affliction, that man may be punished though righteous; and the converse, taught by obvious facts, that man may be wicked and prosper. Hence their philosophizings are of no worth at all; see ll. 75, 76.

65 sqq. At this sublime point the utter honesty of Job's heart comes in conflict with what he must recognize as dishonesty

Will ye respect His person?
Or will ye be special pleaders for God?
Would it be well, if He should search you
 out?
Or will ye mock Him, as man mocketh man? 70
He will surely convict you utterly,
If in secret ye are respecters of persons.
Shall not His majesty make you afraid,
And the dread of Him fall upon you?
Your wise maxims are proverbs of ashes; 75
Your bulwarks turn to bulwarks of clay.

III.

"Be silent; let me alone; and speak will I,
Let come upon me what will.
Wherefore do I take my flesh in my teeth,
And put my life in my hand? 80

CHAP. XIII. 8-14.

on the part of the friends. In denying facts in order to justify God they are simply currying favor with God, respecting His person in opposition to candid conviction.

69-74. Job takes his stand on God's truth; dark though the divine ways are, Job is afraid to be dishonest to conviction before Him. Thus his philosophy comes home at last to personal character.

75. It was in the maxim or aphoristic form that the utterances of Hebrew Wisdom were formulated; this remark of Job is in effect the condemnation of their whole philosophy.

77, 78. This emphatic preface is Job's hint of the importance and significance of what he is going to say. He is going to make a declaration on which life and death hangs.

Behold — He may slay me; I may not hope;
But my ways will I maintain, to His face.
Nay, that shall be to me also for salvation,
For no false one shall come into His presence.
Hear, oh hear my speech, 85
And let my declaration sound in your ears.
Behold, now have I set in order my cause;
I know that I shall be justified.
Who is he that will contend with me? —
For then would I be silent and give up my life. 90

CHAP. XIII. 15-19.

81. A more authentic reading, as well as the homogeneity of the context, seems to make it necessary that the much-loved text "Though He slay me, yet will I trust in Him" shall yield to the translation here given.

82. *My ways will I maintain.* This is not foolhardy presumption on Job's part; from ll. 69-74 it is apparent that he is afraid to do otherwise. This declaration we call Job's everlasting Yea, in which he definitely leaves his friends, who are trying to have him forsake his ways and repent, and commits the event of his life, as he has hitherto lived it, to God; see Introductory Study, p. 52, footnote.

83. But at the same time he does this in faith, that only on the issue of truth can salvation be found. To maintain the ways that he sees to be right will be, must be, his salvation.

85. Another call to attention, indicating Job's confidence in the importance of his declaration.

87, 88. Job regards himself throughout as a defendant bringing a righteous cause to God.

89, 90. These lines indicate how deeply Job's avowal has taken hold of his life. So sure is he of its truth that if it were possible for one to make good the opposite, then life would have no more significance for him; his whole being is committed to this position of his.

Only these two things do not Thou unto me, —
Then will I not hide myself from Thy face:
Remove Thou Thy hand from upon me,
And let not Thy terror unman me;
Then call Thou, and I will answer Thee,   95
Or I will speak, and return Thou answer to me.
   How many are mine iniquities and my sins?
My transgressions and my sins make Thou
    known to me.
Wherefore hidest Thou Thy face,
And countest me for Thine enemy?   100
Wilt Thou chase away a driven leaf,
And pursue after the dry stubble?
For Thou writest bitter things against me,
And makest me inherit the sins of my youth.
And Thou puttest my feet in the stocks,   105
And keepest watch on all my paths.

CHAP. XIII. 20-27.

91. Comparing this passage with section vi. 64-69, we see that the two things for which Job asks here are just the boons that he associates with a Daysman. Note, then, the place of this plea. As soon as Job, committing life and destiny to his integrity, feels that he has reached a point where God and he may stand together, and where, believing that God will hear and heed, he may set in order his cause, he makes his plea for that which a Daysman would secure.

97, 99. *How many?* and *Wherefore?* These are the problems that have all along perplexed Job; but he now urges them as part of the cause which he has "set in order."

103. *Writest bitter things*, — as it were an indictment, which Job has to answer.

On the soles of my feet hast Thou set Thy
    mark;
On one who as a rotten thing consumeth away,
As a garment that is moth-eaten.

IV.

"Man, born of woman, 110
Scant of days, and full of unrest,
Cometh forth, like a flower, and withereth,
Fleeth like the shadow, and abideth not.
Yet on such a one dost Thou open Thine eyes,
And me bringest Thou into judgment with
    Thee. 115

CHAP. XIII. 27 — XIV. 3.

107. *Hast Thou set Thy mark*, — as a driver marks a camel so that he can trace it. "The grievance that Job complains of, in this case, would be like putting such a mark upon an old worn-out camel, which, instead of straying, was unable to stand up." — *Tayler Lewis.*

110. The thought of his diseased and exhausted condition brings anew the thought of death, round which his mind has already eddied; here, however, he begins to work toward a solution of the perplexing fact, though, as in the case of the Daysman, only negatively at first.

115. By this skillful transition to the first person Job identifies himself with the race, and reveals his consciousness that his case is a lesson for all humanity. A similar manner of expression is used in Tennyson's In Memoriam, cix. 6: —

"All these have been, and thee mine eyes
Have look'd on."

Oh that a pure could come from an impure!
— Not one!
If his days are determined,
The number of his months with Thee,
His bounds if Thou hast set, that he may not pass them, 120
Then look away from him, that he may rest,
Until he shall enjoy, as a hireling, his day.
    For there is yet hope for a tree;
If it is cut down, it will shoot up again,
And its tender sprout will not fail. 125
Though its root should grow old in the earth,
And in the dust its trunk should die,
Yet through the scent of water it sprouteth again,

CHAP. XIV. 4-9.

116, 117. Job's thought, in this ejaculation, seems to be, Oh, that all these pains and diseases, all this frailty and suffering of humanity, might issue in completion rather than in corruption; that they had some result corresponding to their severity; but in the present outlook they seem wholly fruitless of their due. It is this longing that apparently supplies the impulse for his further conjectures on death and renewed life.

120. *His bounds*, — the human soul of Job is too large for its dwelling-place; it beats blindly against its earthly limitations, longing to pass them.

122. *As a hireling*, — a doubtful enjoyment, merely making the best of a hard matter; see section iv. 62-67.

123. An analogy occurs to Job, which is full of suggestion for better things and rouses great thoughts of what ought to be.

And putteth forth boughs like a young plant.
But man dieth, and is fallen prostrate; 130
But man gaspeth out his breath, — and where
   is he?
Waters fail from the sea,
And the river wasteth and drieth up:
So man lieth down, and riseth not;
Till the heavens be no more they will not
   awake, 135
Nor be roused out of their sleep.
   Oh that Thou wouldst hide me in the grave,
Wouldst keep me secret until Thy wrath is
   past,
Wouldst set me a time, and remember me!
If a man die — might he live again? 140

CHAP. XIV. 9–14.

130–133. Yet Job sternly represses the application of the figure, and makes it yield to the counter-analogy of the failing waters. Throughout this passage, to the end of the section, there is a conflict between intellect and imagination, reason and fancy, the seen and the longed-for. And altogether we have here such a picture of faith struggling to get free from the inexorable suggestions of this phenomenal life and find a free standing-point in the unseen beyond, as can hardly be paralleled elsewhere in literature.

137. This longing, which surges up unsubdued by the previous analogy, seems to be suggested by the last clause about sleep. "If sleep and death be truly one," — then, there may be a waking! For a parallel passage, read Tennyson's In Memoriam, xliii.

140. *Might he live again?* The whole context indicates that Job asks this question with the thought — provisionally,

All the days of my service would I wait,
Until my renewal came;
Thou wouldst call, and I would answer;
Thou wouldst yearn after the work of Thy hands!
For then wouldst Thou number my steps,   145
Nor wouldst Thou watch upon my sin;
Sealed up in a bag would my transgression be,
And Thou wouldst sew up mine iniquity.

CHAP. XIV. 14-17.

of course — of the affirmative answer in mind. Hence the translation "*might* he live." The translation "*shall* he live" would be the oratorical interrogation suggesting a negative answer, which would be quite out of place here. It is this affirmative answer which Job uses as an implied basis for the succeeding lines, 141-148.

141. *My service,* — the same war-fare, or war-service, which Job attributes to himself, as representative of humanity, in section iv. 62.

142. *My renewal,* — Job uses this word apparently in reminiscence of his analogy of the tree, l. 124, where the word " will shoot up " has the same Hebrew root. *If* man should live again, then he would be renewed like the tree, and could wait in hope.

144. How persistently Job presupposes in God a love like that of a father! — see section vi. 75, 76; 86, 87. In this respect he is in contrast to the hard theology of his friends; and it is on this line of affection — Creator for creature, friend for friend, an affection which in his relations here on earth has failed — that he reaches his greatest achievements in faith.

145-148. A contrast to God's present treatment of him; see ll. 103-109. If Job were to live again, his steps would be

V.

"And yet — the mountain falling crumbleth away,
And the rock removeth out of its place. 150
Water weareth down the stones;
Its floods sweep away the dust of the earth;
And the hope of mortal man Thou makest perish.
Thou overpowerest him for ever, and he passeth;
Thou changest his countenance, and sendest him away. 155
His sons come to honor, and he knoweth it not;
They are brought to shame, and he doth not regard it.
Only his flesh upon him suffereth pain;
And his soul within him mourneth."

CHAP. XIV. 18–22.

all numbered, his account made up and sealed, ready for the final award.

> "So that still garden of the souls
> In many a figured leaf enrolls
> The total world since life began."

149. *And yet,* — Job is not quite ready to commit himself to the fancy that he has indulged; he makes his way cautiously, inductively. The mountains, the most permanent objects that we see, gradually crumble down to dust. Job cannot ignore this analogy; and so for the time he seems to be left where he began; but his thought is only germinating, and when we meet it again it will have grown perceptibly.

IX

ELIPHAZ

AND Eliphaz the Temanite answered, and said:

" Shall a wise man answer windy knowledge,
And fill his belly with the east wind, —
Reasoning with a word that availeth not,
And with speeches wherein is no profit?
Nay, and thou bringest piety to nought,
And lessenest devotion before God;
For thine iniquity teacheth thy mouth,

CHAP. XV. 1-5.

LINE 2. *A wise man.* Eliphaz, who comes from Teman, a place famed for its wisdom, evidently prides himself on belonging to the guild of wise men; which guild he regards Job, hitherto an eminent member thereof, as dishonoring by his strange ideas, which to Eliphaz are " windy knowledge."

6. To the friends' conception of God, which demands a hushed, subdued, unreasoning worship, Job has been very irreverent, not to say rebellious. They cannot reconcile his wild remonstrances with piety.

8. *Thine iniquity.* Eliphaz can attribute Job's bold words only to high-handed defiance of God; there is no room in his system for honest doubt and inquiry. Even Job's assumption of honesty, as would seem from the next line, looks to him like craft.

And thou choosest the tongue of the crafty.
Thine own mouth condemneth thee, and not I;
And thy lips testify against thee. 11

I.

"Wast thou born the first man?
And wast thou brought forth before the hills?
Didst thou listen in the council of God?
And didst thou draw wisdom to thyself? 15
What knowest thou that we know not?
What understandest thou, and the same is not
    in us?
Yea, the grey-haired, yea, the aged man, is
    amongst us,
Fuller of days than thy father.
    Are the consolations of God too small for
    thee, 20
And a word spoken unto thee kindly?

CHAP. XV. 5-11.

16. Job's ideas so strike out from the beaten path that he talks like one with a new source of knowledge. His assertion that he knows all that they have told him (section viii. 6, 55), and his contempt of their philosophy, is galling to Eliphaz.

18. *The aged man*, — not only the old men who are actually alive, but those who live still in their words of wisdom; see next clause, and section v. 15 sq., as well as this present section, ll. 32-35.

20. *Consolations of God*, — such is the name that Eliphaz gives to his admonitions, a name that evidently rankles in Job's mind; see section xiv. 3.

Why hath thy heart carried thee away,
And why quiver thine eyes, —
That thou turnest thy spirit against God,
And lettest forth such words out of thy mouth?
What is mortal man, that he should be clean,
And that the woman-born should be right-
    cous?
Behold, in His holy ones He putteth no trust,
And the heavens are not clean in His eyes;
How much less the abominable and corrupt, —
Man, that drinketh in perverseness as water!

II.

" I will show thee; listen thou to me;
And that which I have seen will I declare;
Which wise men tell, and have not hidden, —
Things heard from their fathers,

CHAP. XV. 12-18.

24. Job *has* turned his spirit against the friends' conception of God, a Being without affection, and dealing only according to iron justice.

26-31. Eliphaz here repeats, with some tendency to intensification, what his vision revealed to him, section iii. 33-39. It is the Old Testament doctrine of total depravity; and how far the wise men's speculations had emphasized it is apparent from ll. 30, 31.

34-37. These lines indicate that the guild of Wise Men, of whom we first hear in connection with Solomon, was already ancient enough to have established a philosophy which was an implicit oracle. The Wisdom had become an orthodoxy, priding itself on its antiquity, and on the fact that no inter-

Unto whom alone the land was given,
And no stranger hath passed among them: —
  'All his days the wicked is in torment,
And the number of his years reserved to the oppressor.
A voice of terrors is in his ears;   40
In peace the spoiler cometh upon him.
He hath no hope of returning out of darkness,
And he is marked out for the sword.
He wandereth about for bread — where is it?
He knoweth that just at hand is a day of darkness,   45
Trouble and anguish make him afraid, —
Overcome him, as a king ready for onset.

Chap. xv. 19-24.

mixture of strange doctrine had ever been permitted. An international philosophy too; for Eliphaz is of Teman, and none of his auditors are represented as of Palestine. All this is proof of the ripened age of the Hebrew Wisdom at the time when the Book of Job was written.

38. Here begin the words of the fathers. Eliphaz brings up this lurid picture of the wicked in order to counteract Job's intimations that the wicked are prospered while the righteous suffer. Such intimations, in direct contradiction to the conclusions of wisdom, seem to open the door to all kinds of violence and infidelity; it lets down the barriers of doubt and admits indefinable riotings of extravagant doctrine. So Eliphaz, who gives the tone to the others, desires to put himself strongly on record for God; hence this purely theoretical picture of the wicked, drawn not for truth, but for theological consistency, and erring grossly by exaggeration; see, for instance, ll. 57, 58, which Job will show to be palpably untrue.

Because he stretcheth out his hand against God,
And against the Almighty maketh himself strong, —
Runneth against Him with hardened neck, 50
With the thick bosses of his bucklers; —
Because he covereth his face with his fat,
And gathereth suet upon his loins,
And dwelleth in desolated cities,
In houses that no man would inhabit, 55
Which are doomed to be heaps of stones; —
Therefore he shall not be rich, nor shall his substance endure;
Neither shall their possessions spread out in the earth.
He shall not escape out of darkness;

CHAP. XV. 25-30.

48. This line is perhaps a covert warning to Job who seems dangerously near doing the same thing. The second clause, or apodosis, of the sentence begins at l. 57.

50. *With hardened neck,* — like a bull, which rushes blindly against whatever rouses its wrath.

52. His prosperity makes him obtuse and unspiritual; indifferent to divine things. Eliphaz has exalted ideas of spiritual insight and keenness; compare sections iii. 44-47; xv. 18-21.

54. *Desolated cities,* — perhaps cities that he himself, as conqueror or as heartless rich man, has desolated in order to make them his own residence; or it may be cities that, as dwelling-places of the cursed and godless, are viewed in anticipation as desolated; compare section iii. 49, "I cursed his habitation."

A flame shall dry up his tender shoots, 60
And by the breath of His mouth shall he pass away.
Let him not trust in vanity; he is deceived;
For vanity shall be his recompense.
While yet his time is not, it shall be paid in full;
And his palm-branch is no longer green. 65
He shall cast off, like a vine, his unripe grapes;
And shall scatter his blossoms, like the olive.
For the company of the profane is barren,
And fire devoureth the tents of bribery.
They conceive mischief, and bring forth iniquity, 70
And their womb matureth deceit.'"

CHAP. XV. 30–35.

61. Compare Eliphaz's earlier words, section iii. 16.

62-67. As Eliphaz has apparently no conception of a future state of retribution, his words seem to assert that the wicked will have their fearful recompense in this life; Proverbs xi. 31 may be taken as the key to his and the friends' philosophy; a position that Job, when the time comes, will controvert with vigor.

In the above speech of Eliphaz it seems to be the writer's intention to make him overstate his doctrine and make it obviously untrue to fact; see Introductory Study, p. 63.

X

JOB

And Job answered, and said:

"I have heard many things like these!
Tormenting comforters are ye all.
Is there any end to words of wind?
Or what hath provoked *thee*, that thou answerest thus?
I also could speak as ye do,
Were your soul in my soul's stead;
I could compose words against you;

Chap. XVI. 1-4.

Line 3. Eliphaz has just blamed Job (section ix. 20) for despising the "consolations of God." Job retorts that the friends are administering just the reverse of consolation; they are tormenting comforters.

5. Job seems to recognize in Eliphaz's answer a heat and violence of assertion so much beyond the demands of the subject that it has the look of personal vindictiveness. He cannot understand how such honest doubt as his own should rouse such *odium theologicum*.

8. *Compose words,* — this expression contains a double sarcasm. It implies that their minds are so calm, so untouched by deep affliction, that they can have leisure to put together pleasing and faultless rhetoric. At the same time it implies

And I could shake my head over you;
I could strengthen you — with my mouth,   10
And my lip-sympathy could sustain you.

1.

"If I speak, my anguish is not assuaged;
And if I forbear, what am I eased?
Nay — now hath He wearied me out;
Thou hast desolated all my household,   15

CHAP. XVI. 4-7.

that their rhetoric is unreal, unfaithful to fact, being merely words, intellectual performance, not the outflow of the heart.

9. Job is not slow to recognize what their general pictures of the fate of the wicked mean; they are shaking their head over *him*.

12. Leaving here what Eliphaz has said, Job returns to his own line of thinking, which he laid down at the end of section viii. with the unsolved problem of death. It is the thought of his suffering that he now takes up, and especially with reference to the author of it.

14. The notable thing of this whole passage is that Job hardly knows how to identify the author of his misery. He speaks here of "He," without naming God; in the next breath he turns directly to God and says "Thou" (l. 15); again it is "His anger" (l. 19), as if Job were reluctant to tax God directly with it; then it is "mine enemy" (l. 21), as if it were some fell power whom he dared not name. Anon it is "they" (l. 22), as if it were an army of foes, or as if his friends were combined with the unseen powers. Clearly Job is hesitating to ascribe to God such hatred as he must recognize in his punishment; he is groping after the God of love, and unwittingly drawing near to Him.

And Thou hast shriveled me up, till it is be-
    come a witness;
Yea, my leanness riseth up against me;
It beareth witness to my face.
His anger teareth and hateth me;
He gnasheth upon me with his teeth;   20
Mine enemy whetteth his eyes against me.
They gape upon me with their mouth;
With scorn they smite me on the cheek;
As one man they combine themselves against
    me.
God delivereth me to the perverse,   25
And into the hands of wicked ones He casteth
    me headlong.

CHAP. XVI. 8-11.

16, 17. Extreme emaciation is one accompaniment of elephantiasis.

19. An exaggerated picture this, charged with the bitterness of long anguish. The hatred that is portrayed in it is its estranging feature; such hatred is so opposite to Job's conception of the Godlike (compare sections vi. 75, 76; 86-89; viii. 144) that he is wholly bewildered by it.

22. Who are "they?" Certainly not the friends. I think the word is Job's undefined term for the powers of evil; perhaps he uses the plural as typical of the manifold wickedness that opposes the good.

25, 26. The *perverse, wicked ones,* seem to be left undefined, whether men or unseen powers. Or perhaps it may also mean that this punishment, being due to the wicked, identifies him with them, compels him to be counted in their company.

I was at ease, — and He hath shattered me,
Yea, hath seized me by the neck and dashed
    me down;
And He hath set me up for His mark.
His arrows beset me round about;   30
He cleaveth asunder my reins, and spareth not;
He poureth out my gall upon the earth;
He breaketh me through, breach on breach;
He runneth upon me as a mighty man of war.

    I have sewed sackcloth upon my skin,   35
And have thrust my horn into the dust.
My face is burning red from weeping,
And on mine eyelids is the shadow of death;
Yet not for any violence in my hands;
And my prayer too is pure.   40

CHAP. XVI. 12–17.

27 sqq. Job describes his suffering in such strong terms that it is most natural to take it as typical, and Job himself as a type of the suffering righteous. There is veritable Messianic language here (see especially ll. 20–26), such as we find in Second Isaiah, though not yet so idealized into the suffering Servant of Jehovah. See Introductory Study, p. 117.

29. The same image that is employed in section iv. 103.

30–34. Job habitually uses this image of war and siege to describe God's treatment of him; see sections iv. 8; vi. 107; xii. 22–24.

40. A profound yet very practical test this of one's integrity before God. One is reminded of Coleridge's Ancient Mariner, who relates that as soon as he could look on God's creatures with love instead of hatred, "that self-same moment I could pray."

II.

"Earth, cover not thou my blood,
And let my cry have no resting-place!
Even now, behold, in heaven is my witness,
And mine advocate is on high.
My friends are my scorners,   45
But unto God mine eye poureth tears,
That HE would plead for man with God,
And as the son of man for his neighbor.
 For a few years will pass,
And I shall go the way whence I shall not
 return.   50

CHAP. XVI. 18–22.

42. The old idea, expressed in the Cain incident (Genesis iv. 10), that a murdered man's blood cries out for vengeance. Of course this puts in the strongest terms Job's sense of injustice.

43. Yet in the next breath Job turns for vindication to the very quarter whence he has supposed the injustice comes. In his thought he seems to divide the God who oppresses him from a God who loves him and represents his cause; at least he commits himself by a mighty reach of faith to an Advocate on high, though he does not clearly identify such an Advocate fully with God.

47. Job evidently thinks of the Advocate as the Daysman whom he so longed for (section vi. 62–69); and we see the advance he has made in faith by the fact that the being whose existence he despairingly denied then he now acknowledges with passionate assertion.

48. It is Job's hunger for love, his longing for friendship, that works especially to drive him to the Advocate; see l. 45.

50. Yet here his idea of the Advocate stops; it must take

My breath is spent ; my days are quenched ;
For me are left only the graves.
Were it not that mockery is with me,
Mine eye could rest calmly on their taunts.

III.

"Give now the pledge ; be Thou surety for me
    with Thyself ; — 55
Who is he that striketh hands with me?
For *their* heart hast Thou hid from understanding ;
Therefore wilt Thou not exalt them.

CHAP. XVII. 1-4.

another surge of faith before he connects his immortality therewith.

52. *The graves,* — a curious plural. Perhaps the word was used to designate the cemetery, the place of graves.

53, 54. Job's thought of the Advocate has so calmed his mind in the contemplation of death that he speaks as if content to go, — see, also, ll. 72-83 ; the only drawback to his calmness is that he has "mockery" to meet and set right. His friends are saying things that demand answer ; Job refers doubtless to their intemperate assertions about the wicked, which he will soon address himself to refute.

55, 56. Full of the idea of an Advocate, Job turns spontaneously to God as if to make a covenant ; then he seems to pause, as if uncertain whether to identify the Advocate with God or not.

57. The insight that Job's faith has given him makes him see also that the friends are spiritually blind ; he has mistrusted this before (see section viii. 2, 3) ; now he knows it. From this point on he is their open antagonist.

'He betrayeth friends for a prey,
And the eyes of his children fail.' 60
And He hath made me a by-word of peoples;
And I am become as one to be spit upon in the face.
Dim too, from sorrow, is mine eye,
And my members are as a shadow, all of them.
   For this shall the upright be amazed, 65
And the pure shall be roused to anger against the profane;
But the righteous shall hold on his way,
And the clean of hands shall wax stronger and stronger.
   But you — all of you — return ye! and come now!
For I shall not find a wise man among you. 70

CHAP. XVII. 5-10.

59, 60. Presumably an aphorism or proverbial expression which Job here quotes as applicable to his friends. Whoever betrays friends incurs a spiritual blindness which descends to his posterity. He has already said bitterly of them that they would make traffic over their friend (section iv. 55); he has convicted them also of speaking what is wrong, for God (section viii. 65). Hence the pertinence of the proverb, now that he is fully aware of their spiritual blindness.

61. Job seems to take up typical language again, and to look upon himself as an object-lesson to the ages.

65-68. This passage seems to prophesy that the bounds and definitions of righteousness are to be henceforth more clear by reason of his affliction; his trial is to be the crucible in which great truths are wrought out.

69, 70. To emphasize how far his thought has borne him

IV.

"My days are past;
My plans are broken off, —
The treasures of my heart.
Night they put for day;
The light draweth near the face of darkness. 75
If I have any hope, the grave is my house;
I have spread out my bed in the darkness.
Tó corruption I have said, 'My father thou!'
'My mother, and my sister!' — to the worm.
And where is now my hope? 80
Yea, my hope — who shall discover it?
Will the bars of Sheol fall down,
When together there is rest in the dust?"

CHAP. XVII. 11–16.

beyond them, he calls ironically to his friends, and throws despite on their wisdom.

71 sqq. Job accepts the near doom of death, and draws consciously towards it, but with much more calmness than heretofore, as if, whether explicable or not, it were surely right. This is certainly a step gained.

76. *The grave*, — literally, *Sheol;* but the word was often used as we use the word *grave;* see note, section iv. 80.

XI

BILDAD

AND Bildad the Shuhite answered, and said:

"How long will ye hunt for words?
Consider well, — and afterward will we speak.
Wherefore are we accounted as the brute —
Are regarded as vile in your eyes?
Thou that tearest thyself in thy rage,
Shall the earth be forsaken for thy sake,
And the rock be removed from its place?

CHAP. XVIII. 1-4.

LINE 2. Addressed to the other friends; alluding to Job's reproach in the foregoing section (l. 8), that their pleas were only words, and implying that deeper arguments, founded more on the laboriously sought truth of things, must be adduced.

4. *Accounted as the brute*, — this is merely the coarser and bitterer language in which Bildad interprets Job's assertion, "Their heart hast Thou hid from understanding" (section x. 57).

6. Job's profound disturbance of soul seems to Bildad like rage, and to oppose the well-established conclusions of Wisdom seems to him like the childish madness which would attempt to overthrow mountains.

"Verily, the light of the wicked shall go out,
And the flame of his fire shall not shine.   10
Light darkeneth in his tent,
And his lamp above him goeth out.
Straitened are the strides of his might;
And his own counsel casteth him down.
For he is cast into a net by his own feet;   15
And he chooseth his way over a pitfall.
The trap seizeth his heel;
The snare layeth fast hold upon him;
Hidden in the ground for him is a cord,
And a noose for him in the pathway.   20

CHAP. XVIII. 5-10.

9. Bildad takes up the same theme that Eliphaz has laid down, — the fate of the wicked; but he carries out his promise (l. 3) to ground it more carefully in truth by hinting continually at Job's condition, as a case in point.

Line 9 is a stock assertion of Wisdom (see Proverbs xxiv. 20), which Job submits, in section xiv. 32, to the test of observed fact.

11. Perhaps an allusion to Job's complaint that God had "desolated his household," section x. 15; and the obverse of Eliphaz's assertion, section iii. 92.

12. *His lamp above him,* — the great lamp suspended in the top of the tent.

13. The wicked is represented as a wealthy and powerful man, in just such a condition as Job's has been.

15-22. A kind of exaggeration of Eliphaz's words, section ix. 38-43, and making the wicked man's fate more definitely the consequence of his own foolish counsel and infatuation.

Round about him terrors make him afraid,
And chase him away at his heels.
His might standeth hunger-bitten;
And ruin is ready at his side.
It shall devour the parts of his skin; 25
It shall devour his members — the firstborn of death.
He is torn out of his tent wherein he trusted,
And he is led away to the king of terrors.
There shall dwell in his tent that which is none of his;
Brimstone shall be showered on his habitation.
Underneath, his roots dry up; 31
And from above, his branch withereth.
His memory perisheth out of the earth;
And no longer hath he a name on the face of the fields.
They drive him out from light into darkness, 35

CHAP. XVIII. 11–18.

21, 22. Bildad apparently alludes here, as Eliphaz has already alluded, section ix. 40, to Job's description of his terrifying visions, section iv. 90, 91.

23-26. An allusion to Job's emaciation and disfigured condition; see sections x. 16-18, 64; iv. 71, 72.

27. Is not this a heartless allusion to Job as a leper, cast out of his tent to the ash-heap outside of the city, with an ill-concealed threat of death added thereto?

30. Apparently an allusion to the inhabitants of Sodom, Genesis xix. 24, who were historical types of extreme wickedness requited.

35. *They,*—perhaps the mysterious unseen powers of Ne-

And chase him from the world.
Offspring and descendant hath he none among his people;
Nor is there an escaped one in his dwelling-places.
At his day shall they of later time be astonished,
As they that were before were seized with terror. 40

II.

"Verily, such are the dwellings of the wicked;
And this is the place of him that knoweth not God."

CHAP. XVIII. 18–21.

mesis and vengeance, whom Job has already referred to as pursuing him, section x. 22.

37. Job's children, it will be remembered, have perished in his calamity.

39, 40. Job conceives that the righteous shall be amazed at his case, section x. 65–68; Bildad makes the astonishment due to his wickedness. This same astonishment the friends have already shown, section i. 134–140; see also section iv. 43, and note.

XII

JOB

AND Job answered, and said :

" How long will ye vex my soul,
And break me in pieces with words?
These ten times do ye reproach me ;
Ye are not ashamed to act as strangers to me. 5

" And be it of a truth that I have erred,
With me remaineth mine error.

CHAP. XIX. 1-4.

LINE 2. Bildad's speech has been, as we have seen, an exasperating series of allusions to Job's diseased condition, as illustrating the punishment of the wicked and as prophesying worse things. Job does not yet answer these insinuations; but they are not lost on him — only delayed.

5. *As strangers*, — this idea furnishes the cue to the present section. They have ceased to be friends to him; they coolly doom him to an awful fate, as if they had never had bonds of sympathy with him. To one like Job, who yearns for affection and sympathy (see section iv. 56-61), this fact is the bitterest drop in his cup.

7. That is, Job's error, even supposing it real, is not a mat-

If in sooth ye magnify yourselves against me,
And prove against me my reproach,
Know then that God hath wronged me,   10
And hath encompassed me with His net.
    Behold, I cry out — violence ! — and am not heard;
I shriek for help, and there is no judgment.
He hath fenced up my way, and I cannot pass;
And over my paths hath He set darkness.   15
My glory hath He stripped off from me,
And He hath taken the crown from my head.
He breaketh me down on every side, — and I am gone;
And He uprooteth, like a tree, my hope.
He maketh His anger burn against me,   20
And counteth me as He doth His enemies.

Chap. XIX. 5–11.

ter that concerns them, or that should operate to estrange them from him; it is wholly between him and God.

8–11. In these words Job makes his final defiant answer to his friends' insinuations; they are fastening his "reproach" upon him as the deserving cause; Job maintains unalterably that God has wronged him. If that be wickedness, let them make the most of it.

12 sqq. As in burning indignation Job has portrayed his affliction before God, section x. 12–40, so now before his friends, in calmer and more pensive mood, he enlarges on his evil case. It is merely an amplification and summary of what he has said before.

14, 15. Compare section ii. 47, 48.

18. Compare section x. 80–83.

Together come His troops;
And they cast up their way against me,
And encamp round about my tent.

II.

" My brethren hath He removed far from me; 25
And mine acquaintance are wholly estranged
    from me.
My kinsfolk stand aloof;
And my familiar friends have forgotten me.
Dwellers in my house, and my maids, —
As a stranger they account me; 30
I am become an alien in their eyes.
I call to my servant, and he answereth not;
I have to entreat him with my mouth.
My breath is strange to my wife,
And I am loathsome to the sons of my body. 35
Even the boys despise me;

CHAP. XIX. 12-18.

22-24. The recurring figure of a siege; compare section x. 30-34, and note there.

25 sqq. Job now enlarges on what he suggested, l. 5. As in section x. 12-40 he approached his belief in an Advocate through the thought of God's enmity to him, so here he approaches his belief in a Redeemer, a next of kin, through the thought of the friendship that fails on earth, which thought he here sets forth in its strongest expression. It is in this thought of his loneliness that Job reaches here the profoundest depth of his trial; here also we are brought nearest to the yearning human heart of the man.

I try to rise, and they speak jeeringly against
  me.
All mine inward friends abhor me;
And those I love have turned against me.
My bone cleaveth to my skin and to my flesh, 40
And shrunk away is the covering of my teeth.
  Have pity on me, have pity on me, O ye my
    friends!
For the hand of God hath touched me!
Why do ye persecute me as God,
And are not satisfied with my flesh? 45

III.

" Oh that now my words were written!
Oh that they were inscribed in a book!

CHAP. XIX. 18-23.

38. *Mine inward friends*,—literally, *men of my secret intercourse*, or *counsel*. The same word is used for the friendship of God, section xx. 7.

41. Of this line, whose expression is very obscure in the original, I take the view of Dr. Tayler Lewis. It seems to describe that corpse-like appearance of the leper, wherein the face seems like a half-covered skull, with teeth protruding and hollow eyes.

44, 45. That is, why take God's prerogative in hand, and give reproach merely because He has inflicted suffering. It is a plea to let natural feelings of compassion have free course, and not to bestow their regards and reproaches theoretically.

46. The extreme depth of woe to which Job has just reached is immediately followed by a height of conviction so great and significant that Job would make the expression of

That, with iron pen, and with lead,
They were graven in the rock, for ever!
    I know that my redeemer liveth;   50
That he will stand, survivor, over the dust;
And after my skin is gone, they will rend this
    body,

Chap. xix. 24–26.

it monumental, permanent. In the same way Job has called solemn attention before to assertions that in his view are especially important; see section viii. 63, 77, 85. This, however, as being his supreme confession, reached by long struggle through darkness, is prefaced by the most emphatic note of attention.

48. A reference to the ancient manner of engraving inscriptions on the rocks. After being cut in, the lines were filled with molten lead, and thus made more legible and permanent.

50. *My redeemer*, — so it seems best to translate here, rather than disturb the associations of the passage; because not enough would be gained by the more accurate term *Avenger* to pay for the change. The word denotes the next of kin, whose duty it was to avenge the blood of a murdered man (see Numbers xxxv. 19), and to succor the bereaved and needy (see Ruth iii. 9–13; iv. 1–8). With wonderful skill Job chooses the word that gathers into itself all that he has longed for; it means one who will befriend him, avenge his wrong, be his Daysman, make God his friend again. Note too that it is the word to which he was led through the thought of failing earthly friendship, just as the word *Advocate* was the term to which he was led through the thought of God's injustice and enmity; section x. 44.

52. *They will rend*, — the mysterious *they* again (see sections x. 22; xi. 35); unnamable powers of destiny. — *This body;* only the word *this* is expressed in the original; and Job may be thought of as indicating by a gesture his wasted frame, too loathsome and disfigured to be named.

And I, from my flesh, shall see God;
Whom I shall see, I, for myself;
Whom mine eyes shall behold, a stranger no
    more.   55
Oh, for this my reins consume within me!

IV.

"If ye say, 'How we will persecute him!'"

CHAP. XIX. 26–28.

53. *From my flesh*, — in this translation I have preserved exactly the same ambiguity that exists in the original: it may mean either being in the flesh and looking out, or being out of the flesh. The context favors the latter meaning; but nothing positive can be gathered, nor do I believe the discrimination was in the author's mind between disembodied immortality and resurrection of the body. I am inclined to think it is an emphatic way of saying "in my truest self," the word *flesh* being used somewhat as the word for *bone* is used in a common Hebrew idiom; e. g., "as the *bone* of heaven," for "as the heaven itself," Exodus xxiv. 10.

55. Even yet Job does not clearly identify the Redeemer with God; he merely says that in consequence of the Redeemer's living and representing his cause he shall see God, and God will be his friend. Still the remarkable Messianic idea lingers, which we have noticed in other passages; and we hardly know whether the author is thinking of one being or two. But there is a great advance beyond the idea of section x. 43-48; for there God had not ceased to be an enemy who was to be conciliated through an Advocate; here God is "a stranger no more."

57-61. It is quite in accordance with Job's custom elsewhere (see sections x. 69, 70; xiv. 68, 69; xvi. 92, 93) to follow one of his passages of deep and true insight by a note of warning in which the friends' purblindness is recognized.

And that the root of the matter is found in me, —
Be ye afraid of the sword;
For there is wrath against the sins of the sword, 60
That ye may know there is a judgment."

CHAP. XIX. 28, 29.

This is the most solemn passage of the kind, as befits the lofty reach of faith that precedes it.

58. That is, if ye still maintain (compare ll. 8, 9) that I am the culprit, that the cause of this punishment lies in my guilt. Job seems to think, what also has been intimated before (see sections iii. 44, note; iv. 61, note; see also xix. 4-7), that his spiritual insight achieving this revelation of a vindication after death proves his heart and conduct also pure. Both he and the friends would deny true insight to a wicked man.

59. That is, the sword of God's wrath, of which they are in danger if they set themselves against a conviction so pure as this of his.

From this point onward, Job no more struggles with the problem of déath; a fact which indicates that the immortality here recognized is henceforth taken for granted. Nor is God any more regarded as an enemy; note rather the different attitude in section xvi. 4-13.

XIII

ZOPHAR

AND Zophar the Naamathite answered, and said:

"Therefore do my thoughts give me answer,
And for such cause is this my haste within me, —
Chiding, to my reproof, must I hear!
And the spirit out of mine understanding replieth. 5

CHAP. XX. 1–3.

LINE 2. *Therefore*, — referring forward to line 4. Zophar replies with headlong haste, being incensed at Job's insinuation that they who have preached repentance to him are themselves in imminent danger of sin. — *My thoughts*, — the same word that is used of the "wandering thoughts" of Eliphaz's vision; see section iii. 24, note. It may indicate here the tumultuous emotions that have been roused by his indignation, a rush and confusion of thought.

5. *Spirit*, — in the sense of *zeal*. In section xi. Bildad professed to give a well-considered speech (l. 3), and made it a series of undisguised allusions to the various features of Job's calamity, which he employed as a portrayal of the wicked; Zophar, impelled by hot zeal and indignation, draws a picture that is declamatory, intemperate, and largely fanciful, having little if any traceable connection with sober fact.

1.

"What! thou surely knowest this, from of old,
Since Adam was placed upon the earth,
That the triumph of the wicked is short-lived,
And the joy of the ungodly but for a moment.
Though his summit mount up to heaven,   10
And his head reach unto the clouds,
Yet like his own dung shall he perish utterly;
They that see him shall say, Where is he?
Like a dream he flitteth, and is no more found,
And he is chased away, as a spectre of the night.   15
Eye hath looked upon him, — it looketh not again;

CHAP. XX. 4-9.

6. *From of old*, — what Zophar says, though exaggerated by passion and rhetoric, is really one of the long-settled results of Wisdom, which he is astonished to hear traversed.

8. *The triumph of the wicked*, — perhaps an allusion to Job's solemn exaltation in his discovery of a Redeemer, section xii. 50-56. Strange blindness, that would view such a triumph as the triumph of the wicked!

10. The rhetorical tendency of Zophar's speech is manifest especially in his labored amplification of each picture that he brings up, with the evident attempt to make everything as vivid and intense as possible; note this in ll. 10-15; 22-31; 33; 36-40; 47-51. He lets his imagination riot in terrific images.

16. *Hath looked*, — the original word means a mere momentary glance, as if he had vanished in a twinkling.

And no more shall his place behold him.
His sons shall seek the favor of the poor;
And his hands shall restore his wealth.
His bones are full of his youth, 20
But it shall lie down with him in the dust.

II.

"Though evil is sweet in his mouth,
And he hideth it under his tongue,
Spareth it, and is loath to let it go,
And holdeth it back in his palate, 25
Yet in his bowels his bread is changed,
It is the gall of asps within him.
He hath swallowed down riches, and must
    vomit them up;
Out of his belly God will cast them forth.
It is the poison of asps that he sucketh in; 30
The tongue of the adder shall slay him.
Never more shall he gaze upon the streams,
The floods, the brooks of honey and cream.

CHAP. XX. 9-17.

20. *His youth*, — the strength, the vigor, of youth.

22 sqq. Another rhetorical tendency is manifest here, in Zophar's evident desire to trace the wicked man's fate as a history, from the height of his prosperity to the fearful disaster at death.

26. It is to this that Zophar reduces the prosperity of the wicked, — the wicked seeming to enjoy, perhaps really enjoying, the first taste of evil, but finding it unreal and bitter to his soul. A picture not without basis, but conceived here in mere fancy.

He must restore the fruit of toil, and not devour it;
As borrowed wealth it is, and he hath no joy therein; 35
Because he oppressed, he abandoned the poor,
Seized upon a house that he would not build, —
Because he knew not rest in his belly,
In his greed would let nothing escape, —
No, not a shred that he could devour, — 40
Therefore his prosperity shall not endure;
In the fullness of his abundance shall he be straitened;
Upon him shall come every hand of the wretched.
So shall it be, until his belly is filled:
He shall cast upon him the fire of His wrath, 45
And shall rain it upon him with his food.
Fleeth he from the iron armor,
The bow of brass pierceth him through;
He draweth it out, — and it cometh forth from his body,
The gleaming shaft, from his gall, — 50
Terrors come upon him!
All darkness is laid up for his hid treasures;

CHAP. XX. 18-26.

37. Compare section ix. 54-56. The friends seem to have in mind some notorious evil of rich men seizing houses by violence and turning them to their own use.

A fire not blown shall consume him ;
It shall feed upon the last remnant in his tent.
Heaven shall reveal his iniquity, 55
And earth shall rise up against him.
The increase of his house shall depart,
Shall flow away in the day of His wrath.

III.

"Such is the portion of the wicked man, from God,
And the heritage decreed from the Mighty One." 60

CHAP. XX. 26-29.

53. *A fire not blown,* — self-enkindled, so eager is it to burn.

59, 60. It seems to be the author's intention in this speech to run the friends' threefold portrayal of the fate of the wicked into mere froth and declamation, which soon Job's honest sense will sweep away. The whole, though the most violent and vivid of the three, is after all vague: the horrible woes it denounces on the wicked are not referred to cause and ground, nor are they easily verifiable in fact.

XIV

JOB

AND Job answered, and said:

"Hear, oh hear ye my word,
And be this the 'consolations' ye give.
Suffer me, and I will speak;
And after I have spoken, — then mock thou. 5

I.

"As for me, is my complaint unto man?

CHAP. XXI. 1-4.

The three friends have all spoken in the same strain, portraying in violent and exaggerated terms the doom of the wicked; but to their arguments Job has deigned no answer until now. The present speech, however, squarely traverses what they have said, and indicates that he has merely waited for what all had to urge, that he might answer all of them at once.

LINE 3. *Consolations,* — an allusion to "the consolations of God" (section ix. 20), with which Eliphaz has plied him.

6. Zophar's heat and haste arose from the "chiding" that he must hear (section xiii. 4), as if it were a personal matter; Job's complaint is directed not against man, but against what he must see in the world.

And wherefore should not my spirit be short-
    ened?
Turn ye unto me, and be amazed,
And lay hand upon mouth.
Even as I think thereon, I am dismayed,   10
And shuddering seizeth on my flesh.
  Wherefore do the wicked live,
Become old, yea, wax mighty in power?
Their seed is established around them, in their
    sight,
And their offspring before their eyes.   15
Their houses are peace, far from fear;
And no rod of God is upon them.
Their bull gendereth, and doth not fail;

CHAP. XXI. 4-10.

7. Alluding, perhaps, to what Eliphaz has said to him, section ix. 22-25, and Bildad, section xi. 6.

8-11. The friends have so reveled in their highly colored descriptions that they have almost exulted over the fate of the wicked; Job, on the other hand, full of sympathy with right and truth, must view with amazement the confused order of things: it is not what he wishes to see.

12 sqq. This is the appeal to plain and palpable fact which Job sets over against the friends' theory. It is essentially the expansion of what he has touched upon before; see sections vi. 45, 77; viii. 12-14.

14 sqq. Of course Job does not mean to say that they have all this material welfare *because* they are wicked; that is not the issue. His point, made against the whole tenor of the friends' arguments, is simply that, being wicked, they are not treated according to their wickedness. Contrary to the law of Hebrew Wisdom they are prospered in the earth; they

Lightly calveth their cow, and casteth not her
 calf.
They send forth their little ones like a flock, 20
And their children dance.
They sing to timbrel and harp,
And rejoice at the sound of the pipe.
They fill out their days in weal;
And in a moment they sink down to the
 grave. 25
And yet they said unto God, 'Depart from us;
The knowledge of Thy ways we desire not.
What is the Almighty, that we should serve
 Him?
And what gain we, if we pray unto Him?'

Chap. XXI. 10–15.

have the pleasures of sin and the good of life too; so that on the mere scale of justice, if that is all that governs the universe, in a very true sense "the earth is given over into the hands of the wicked" (section vi. 45).

24, 25. That is, not a moment is left, so far as we can see, for the fearful doom that has been ascribed to them. This is a square contradiction of what all the friends have maintained; see especially sections ix. 38–47; 59–61; xi. 27, 28, 35, 36; and most recklessly stated of all, xiii. 44–58.

28. Observe how the wicked speak of God as *what*, a neuter, a thing, to be taken advantage of; all their thought is pitched in the key of selfishness and gain. This is Job's portrayal of the exact opposite of his own feeling; to him such a spirit is the centre of all wickedness.

II.

"Behold, not in *their* hand is their weal.　　30
The counsel of the wicked — be it far from me!

III.

"*How often* doth the lamp of the wicked go
　　out,
And their destruction come upon them,
Or He distribute woes in His anger?
How often are they as straw before the wind,　35
And as chaff which the storm snatcheth
　　away?
'God layeth up his iniquity for his children'? —

CHAP. XXI. 16-19.

30. Yet Job does not say this, as the friends assert afterward (see sections xv. 28, 29; xxiii. 12-17, 76-80), because he is in sympathy with wicked ways; it is mere loyalty to fact that compels the admission. Nor does he maintain that they are the authors of their own weal; it is still, in some mysterious way which none have found out, in the hands of God.

32. *How often?* A challenge as to the truth of Bildad's assertion, section xi. 9-12. The friends ought to specify how universal a fact their theory contemplates; it is in truth not universal enough, not distinctive enough, to be a fact at all.

35. Job quotes the substance of his friends' assertions here, though not in the same imagery; compare sections xi. 21, 22; 35, 36; xiii. 14, 15.

37. This question is a fair representation, in more condensed form, of what the friends have maintained; see sections iii. 50-52; xiii. 18-21.

On *him* let Him requite, and he shall feel it;
Let his own eyes see his ruin,
And let himself drink from the wrath of the
    Almighty.   40
For what careth he for his house after him,
When the number of his months is cut off?

    Shall any teach knowledge unto God, —
Him — who judgeth them that are high?
One dieth in the fullness of his strength,   45
All at ease and quiet, —
His vessels full of milk,
And the marrow of his bones well moistened;
And another dieth with a bitter soul,
And hath never tasted of good.   50

Chap. XXI. 19–25.

38 sq. Out of Job's strong sense of justice rises this demand for the individual punishment of the wicked. It is the earliest remonstrance against the old Hebrew idea that posterity suffers for ancestral sins; a remonstrance that becomes incorporated in revealed prophetic word, in Ezekiel xviii. See also Jeremiah xxxi. 29, 30. The human, out of its own needs and insight, makes the discovery, and in due time the divine comes to define and sanction it.

41. *What careth he?* It is from the depth of Job's unselfish love that the foregoing demand comes; for he sees that in the cold selfishness of the wicked punishment reserved for posterity does not touch his soul at all, — it does not punish sin of that kind.

45–52. These lines describe the accurate fact, so far as we can see; namely, that righteous and wicked fare alike; moral desert, at least on this earth, having apparently nothing to do with their doom.

Together they lie down, in the dust,
And the worm spreadeth a covering over them.

IV.

" Behold, I know your thoughts,
And the devices whereby ye wrong me.
For ye say, ' Where is the tyrant's house, 55
And where the tent, wherein the wicked
 dwelt ? '
Have ye not inquired of the wayfarers ?
And do ye not know their tokens, —
That in the day of destruction the wicked is
 spared,
That in the day of wrath they are led away ? 60
Who then will declare his way to his face ?
And hath he done aught, who will requite it
 unto him ?
For he — he is carried to his grave,

CHAP. XXI. 26–32.

53, 54. Job divines the answer that is in their mind, a kind of manufactured answer urged out of spite, and meets it.

55. They are supposably asking him to adduce cases that prove their wholesale assertions untrue.

57. And Job replies that the prosperity of the wicked, which he proceeds again to enlarge upon, is so notorious that all who travel abroad, who look about them at all, cannot fail to observe it.

59 sqq. We are still to bear in mind here what has been said in the note to l. 14 sqq. It is a portrayal of what is as likely to befall the wicked as the righteous.

And watch is kept over his tomb;
Sweetly lie upon him the clods of the valley; 65
And after him draw all men,
As there were numberless before him.

V.

" How then comfort ye me with vanity,
Since your answers remain falsehood?"

CHAP. XXI. 32–34.

66. Men follow and imitate the wicked, just as they do the good; it is the rule of the world to imitate *success*, apart from moral considerations. Compare Ecclesiastes iv. 15, 16.

69. *Falsehood,*—that is, untrue to obvious fact.

XV

ELIPHAZ

AND Eliphaz the Temanite answered, and said:

I.

"Can a man be profitable unto God,
As the prudent getteth profit unto himself?
Is it a pleasure to the Almighty that thou art righteous,
Or is it a gain, that thou makest thy ways perfect? 5
Is it for thy piety that He reproveth thee, —

CHAP. XXII. 1–4.

LINES 2, 3. The expression here is a little obscure on account of the turning around of the comparison. It means, "Is man's righteousness a thing out of which God gets profit, as a prudent man turns things to his advantage."

4, 5. This question merely embodies the logical sequence of Eliphaz's favorite doctrine, expressed in sections iii. 33–37; ix. 26–31. The doctrine removes God to such an inaccessible distance that He is really unaffected by either righteousness or wickedness: He rewards and punishes in an abstract, mechanical way, merely because He has made it the law of a universe which He is sitting outside of and seeing go.

6. Eliphaz's syllogism is very simple. God is evidently

That He cometh with thee into judgment?
May not thy wickedness be great,
And no end to thine iniquities?
For thou hast taken a pledge from thy brother
    causelessly,   10
And stripped off the clothes of the naked;
Thou hast given no water to the faint,
And from the hungry hast withholden bread;
While the man of the strong arm — his was
    the land,
And the respected of persons dwelt therein! 15
Widows hast thou sent away empty;

CHAP. XXII. 4-9.

punishing Job. It cannot be for righteousness. Hence it must be for wickedness.

7. Thus Eliphaz comes at last to his final shot, — the direct charge of wickedness against Job. It is, as we see, merely a conclusion of dialectics, which his doctrine of man's necessary and inevitable corruption bears him out in drawing. Has not the doctrine of total depravity in our own day brought forth just as grave, if not so particular, accusations of sin?

10 sqq. These specific charges are of course wholly theoretic, nor are they inaptly made. They name such things as might be done by a busy rich man like Job, through forgetfulness or indifference, or such things as may have been done in his name by servants. Any of them might take place at the gate of a prince without his knowledge. The expression "man of the strong arm," l. 14, by which Eliphaz characterizes such as Job, shows how he accounts for such sin: the man whose strength and wealth, and whose absorption with his favored friends (l. 15), make him indifferent to needs and distress because removed from them.

And the arms of the fatherless have been broken.
Therefore it is that snares are about thee,
And fear terrifieth thee suddenly.
Or seest thou not the darkness,   20
And the deluge of waters that covereth thee?
Is not God the summit of heaven?
And see the crown of the stars — how high!
And so thou sayest, 'What doth God know?
Can He judge through the thick cloud?   25
Clouds are a covering to Him, and He seeth not;
And He walketh by Himself on the vault of heaven.'

II.

" Wilt thou cherish the way of old,
Wherein trod the men of wickedness?

CHAP. XXII. 9-15.

18, 19. Such is the ground on which Eliphaz interprets Job's dismay and amazement confessed in the previous section (8-11)!

20, 21. As much as to say, Your suffering is a fact, — why do you thus ignore it, and what else can you make of it?

22-27. Another way, this, of accounting for Job's theorized lapse into sin, — he may have supposed that God would not see him, being so far away. To whom so naturally as to Eliphaz would such a reason occur? At the same time it is not improbable that he has in mind Job's complaints of God's remoteness; see sections vi. 20, 21; viii. 99; xii. 12-15.

28 sqq. To Eliphaz Job's candid acknowledgment of

Who were snatched away, and the time was
    not yet; 30
Whose foundation flowed away, a river.
Who said unto God, 'Depart from us;'
And, 'What will the Almighty do unto us?'
And yet — 'He filleth their houses with good,'
    thou sayest;
While also thou sayest, 'The counsel of the
    wicked be far from me!' 35
The righteous see, and are glad;
And the innocent make a by-word of them:
'Verily,' they say, 'our adversaries are cut
    down,
And their remains doth the fire devour.'

Chap. XXII. 16–20.

wicked prosperity seems dangerously near "cherishing" wicked ways.

32, 33. Eliphaz quotes nearly the same questions attributed by Job to the wicked who were prospered (section xiv. 26–28), to characterize the wicked of old who were snatched away. Thus by going back to antiquity he makes his only attempt to disprove Job's appeal to fact.

34. A condensation of what Job has said, section xiv. 14–24.

35. See section xiv. 31.

36–39. Job has viewed the confused order of things with amazement and dismay, nor does he exult over the wicked; and thereby, thinks Eliphaz, he proves himself a sympathizer with evil. A righteous man will curse where God has punished; compare section iii. 49. That is the way to "justify God;" perhaps, also, it is his covert way of defending his treatment of Job.

III.

"Reconcile thyself with Him now, and be at peace;   40
Thereby good shall come unto thee.
Receive now instruction from His mouth,
And lay up His words in thy heart.
If thou wilt return to the Almighty, thou shalt be built up, —
So thou removest iniquity far from thy tents;—
And put thou thy precious ore in the dust,   46
And Ophir in the stones of the brooks;
So shall the Almighty be thy precious ore,
And silver of the mine shalt thou have.

CHAP. XXII. 21–25.

40. *Reconcile thyself.* This word, presupposing guilt and sin on Job's part, is what invalidates the whole force of this beautiful passage, which is the final appeal of the friends to Job. Abstractly there is nothing whatever to be urged against the lines; but in implication, and as here applied, they gather into themselves all the charges that Eliphaz has made.

45. It has been pointed out before (see sections v. 10, note; vii. 27, 28) how in their exhortations the friends put in a sly clause presupposing Job's iniquity.

46. That is, despise earthly riches, renounce the affection for wordly goods which has made thee presumably indifferent to the poor.

47. *Ophir,* — that is, gold of Ophir. The gold was so much spoken of that the country where it was found came to designate it; as we say damask and morocco for products of Damascus and Morocco.

For then shall thy delight be in the Almighty; 50
And thou shalt lift up thy face unto God.
Thou shalt pray to Him, and He will hear thee;
And thy vows shalt thou fully perform.
Thou shalt purpose a thing, and it shall be established to thee;
And upon thy ways shall light shine. 55
Though they lead downward, yet thou sayest, 'Aloft!'
And the lowly of eyes shall He save.
He shall deliver him that is not guiltless;
Who will be delivered through the cleanness of thy hands."

CHAP. XXII. 26–30.

51. Eliphaz has regarded Job as bitter and rebellious against God; see section ix. 22–24. From such hard enmity he promises Job return.

52. Alluding perhaps to Job's complaint, section xii. 12, 13.

55. See section xii. 15.

57. Eliphaz has already asked Job, "Why quiver thine eyes?" (section ix. 23), as if Job were angry and defiant; and this is the contrast that he would inculcate.

58, 59. It is worthy of note that in his closing words Eliphaz prophesies what actually did take place, section xxx.; only the friends were the ones who were "not guiltless," and Job's whole course was on the highest authority justified.

XVI

JOB

AND Job answered, and said:

" Defiant, even to-day, is my complaint,
Though my hand lieth heavy on my groaning.

I.

" Oh that I knew where I might find Him! —
Might come even unto His dwelling-place!   5
I would set in order my cause before Him;
And I would fill my mouth with arguments.
I would know the words He would answer me;
And I would mark what He would say unto
    me.

CHAP. XXIII. 1-5.

LINE 2. *Defiant*, — that is, defying his efforts at repression, and ready to break forth in spite of him.

4 sqq. Job's "complaint" does not begin till l. 14; he delays it long enough to give a brief but fervent response to Eliphaz's exhortation. Eliphaz has bidden him return to God (section xv. 40-44), and given him sweet promises if he will so do; Job takes him at his word, so far forth at least, that he longs supremely after God's presence; though he turns to God not as a sinner, but as a man with a just and righteous cause.

Would He plead against me in the greatness
    of His might? 10
Nay; but surely He would give heed unto me.
There it would be an upright man pleading
    with Him;
And I should be delivered for ever from my
    Judge.

II.

"Behold, I go eastward, but He is not there;
And toward the west, yet I perceive Him
    not; 15
Northward, where He worketh, but I discover
    Him not;
And in the south He hideth Himself, and I
    see Him not.
Yet He knoweth the way that is mine;

CHAP. XXIII. 6–10.

10. This question, with its negative answer, indicates how far Job has advanced in his conviction of God's favor since he conquered his way to the assurance that his Redeemer liveth. He is sure now that if he could find God he would find Him a friend.

12, 13. This utterance of calm confidence is just the opposite of that complaint of Job's earlier days, section vi. 26–29. Something has assuredly wrought to "remove God's hand from upon him" (sections vi. 66; viii. 93); it is that faith which has enabled him to identify God with his Advocate and Redeemer.

18. *Yet*,— literally, *for*. It is an elliptical expression; as if he had said, "Yet I will not despair *for* He knoweth," etc.

He is trying me: I shall come forth as gold.
My foot hath held fast unto His steps; 20
His way have I kept, and turned not aside, —
The precept of His lips, and have not shunned it.
More than aught mine own have I treasured the words of His mouth.
  But He — He abideth the same; who shall turn Him?
Yea, His soul desireth, and He doeth it. 25
For He will accomplish the thing appointed for me,
And like these, many things that are with Him.

CHAP. XXIII. 10–14.

This, too, is a discovery of Job's faith to be carefully noted. It anticipates what Elihu urges afterward, sections xxii. and xxv. Job, on his stoutly maintained ground of integrity, has discovered the solution of his affliction.—*The way that is mine*, literally, *that is with me;* the same particle whose intimacy of relation has been mentioned, section vi. 69, note; my truest, sincerest, most habitual way.

23. *More than aught mine own*, — literally, *more than mine own law* or *behest*. An obscure expression, but seeming to mean, "more than anything to which I give authority or control," that is, whatever is most mine.

24. In the light of Job's new solution note how differently God's dealings look to him. He sees the same changeless, inexorable, inscrutable work that he contemplated in sections vi. 6–27; viii. 27–52; and the sight fills him with trembling awe (compare section xiv. 7–11); but he does not, as then, trace in it God's injustice and persecution; he is content to

Therefore it is that I tremble before Him, —
That I consider, and am afraid of Him;
And it is God that maketh my heart soft; 30
The Almighty it is that confoundeth me.
For I am not dismayed by the face of darkness,
Nor by mine own face, which thick gloom veileth.

III.

"Why are not judgment-times determined by the Almighty?
And they that know Him — why see they not His days? 35

CHAP. XXIII. 15 — XXIV. 1.

let it be so, though wondering at its darkness. This is his only remaining problem, and it is to this that the LORD addresses His words from the whirlwind, sections xxvi. and xxviii.

32. Job has long ago taken leave of personal fear (see sections vi. 40; viii. 77-80); he has approached death with calm readiness (see section x. 71 sqq. note); and now he has got beyond the dismay due to disease and blasted hope (contrast sections vi. 32-35; 54; 105-107; x. 14-34; xii. 16-19). Surely a great advance; he has almost reached his goal.

34, 35. Here Job propounds his one remaining problem. It is the problem that dismayed him in the previous section (xiv. 10-13), and that is "defiant" in this (ll. 2, 3), namely, why God does not, in His dealings with men, so determine the bounds of right and wrong, that those who know Him can trace the principles of His working. Why are things so

> There are who remove landmarks;
> Who seize upon flocks and pasture them;
> The ass of the fatherless they drive away;
> They take for pledge the ox of the widow.
> They thrust the needy out of the way; 40
> The poor of the land must hide themselves together.
> Behold these then! wild asses in the desert;

CHAP. XXIV. 2-5.

turned around — the righteous afflicted, the wicked secure in impunity? The former of these he has just answered *for himself* (ll. 18, 19); now he addresses himself to the latter.

36 sqq. The ensuing lines portray forms of wickedness that were doubtless most prevalent at the time when the Book of Job was written. They seem to indicate a time when classes were sharply distinguished; the rich becoming richer and more heartless, the poor thrust into a more grinding and hopeless poverty. Such times consist best with long settled national prosperity, free from political and social upheavals, such as we can most reasonably associate with the later years of the Jewish monarchy.

36. *There are who remove landmarks.* It is noteworthy that in the first appendix to the original Solomonic Proverbs, made near the time when the Book of Job was supposably written, the injunction is twice given "not to remove the ancient landmark" (Prov. xxii. 28; xxiii. 10); and that in Deuteronomy, whose composition (or at least publication) dates from a time not long after, the same injunction is both given as a commandment (Deut. xix. 14) and sanctioned by a curse (Deut. xxvii. 17). This would seem to indicate that the removal of landmarks, that is, wicked and unscrupulous enlargement of property-holdings, was one of the crying evils of this time. See Introductory Study, pp. 104, 108 sq.

42. Namely, the poor of the land, who are forced to be-

They go forth in their work, seeking eagerly
    for prey;
The waste must be to them bread for their
    children.
In the field they reap, each one, his fodder; 45
And they glean the vineyard of the wicked.
Naked all night they lie, from lack of clothing;
And they have no covering in the cold.
They are wet with the storm of the mountain;
And for lack of shelter they cling to the rock.
  There are who tear away the fatherless from
    the breast, 51
And take what the poor have on for pledge.
So these go about naked for lack of clothing,
And hungry they carry the sheaf;
Between their walls these press out the oil; 55
They tread the wine-vats and suffer thirst.
Groans arise from the city of the dying,
And the soul of the wounded crieth out;
And God regardeth not the enormity.
  There are of them that rebel against light, 60

CHAP. XXIV. 5-13.

come wanderers and outlaws, gathering a precarious subsistence from land that is not theirs.

  55. *Between their walls*, — namely, the walls of the rich wicked, by whom they are so ground down with labor and enslaved, that they have to go hungry in the midst of abundance

  59. *Enormity*, — in choosing this word I follow the translation of Dr. Tayler Lewis. The original is the same word translated "aught unbeseeming," in section i. 88, where see

XVI.   JOB   263

That regard not the ways thereof.
Nor abide in its trodden paths.
With the light riseth up the murderer;
He slayeth the poor and the needy;
And in the night he is as a thief.   65
The eye of the adulterer, too, watcheth for the
    gloom,
Saying, No eye shall spy me out!
And he putteth a covering upon his face.
Men dig through houses in the darkness;
In the daytime they shut themselves up;   70
They know not the light.
For morning to them is just like midnight;
Yea, they know well the terrors of the mid-
    night!

IV.

"'Fleeting he is,' ye say, 'on the face of the
    waters;

CHAP. XXIV. 13-18.

note. The same root occurs in its literal meaning, section iv. 11, where it is translated "tasteless." From "tastelessness" the word may get the meaning *absurdity, anomaly*, or, to use an analogous derivation, *enormity* (*e-norma*), something monstrous, outside of orderly law and custom.

61. The *ways* and *trodden paths* of light are simply the customs of right living, to which murder and adultery and robbery are opposed.

73. *Midnight*, which may contain terrors for others, is just the working-time and congenial season of these; compare John iii. 20, 21.

74-84. In these lines Job draws, I think, on the body of

Cursed the portion of such in the land ; 75
He turneth not the way of the vineyards.
Drought and heat bear away the snow-water, —
The grave also them that have sinned.
There the womb will forget him,
While the worm batteneth upon him. 80
No more will he be remembered ;
And like the tree iniquity shall be broken, —
Even he who devoureth the barren that beareth not,
And doeth no kindness to the widow.'

   Nay ; but He continueth the mighty by His power ; 85
They rise up when they believed not that they would live.
He giveth them to be secure, and they are at rest ;
And His eyes are on their ways.

CHAP. XXIV. 18-23.

Wisdom utterances from which the friends have freely quoted (see sections v. 21–38 ; ix. 38–71), and which we may presume to have been equally familiar to him (compare sections viii. 6 ; 53–56 ; x. 2). From the same body of Wisdom he may have drawn, section viii. 27–52 ; and section xviii. 8–25 reads like a passage from the same collection of truth. The present passage, while it does not quote words that the friends have actually used, maintains the same general tenor of thought, and might well be put alongside of the words of Bildad, section v., or Eliphaz, section ix. It is as if Job had said, I call in question the whole Wisdom teaching on this point.

   85-91. Having made his quotation, Job shows how one-

They rise to eminence; — a little while, and
   they are not!
They are brought low; like all others they are
   gathered in,   90
And are cut off, like the heads of corn.

v.

"If it be not so, who then will prove me false,
And make my words come to nought?"

CHAP. XXIV. 24, 25.

sided it is by stating the actual fact. This passage is virtually a repetition of what he has said, section xiv.

92. Job's conclusive and triumphant victory over his friends is indicated by the challenge with which he here seals his words. No one takes it up; for though Bildad yet speaks, his words are so aside from the issue as to be a virtual confession of defeat.

XVII

BILDAD

And Bildad the Shuhite answered, and said:

" Dominion and dread are with Him;
Who maketh peace in His high places.
Is there any number to His armies?
And on whom riseth not His light? 5
How then shall mortal man be just with God?
And how shall the woman-born be clean?

Chap. xxv. 1–4.

Bildad responds wholly without the rancor and bitterness that have characterized the friends' answers hitherto, and with general considerations quite apart from the question at issue. Perhaps it is Job's persistent affirmation of his integrity, section xvi. 20–23, that immediately calls them forth; but Bildad no longer makes it a personal matter, and seems to repeat his lesson almost mechanically, the chapter from his well-conned Wisdom which is least to be called in question.

Line 3. An allusion, apparently, to some traditional conflict in heaven wherein God was victor; compare section vi. 25, and note.

6. The same doctrine that Eliphaz has twice propounded, once as the oracle of a vision (section iii. 33–43), and again as the sacred word which it were impiety to deny (section ix. 26–31). All have taken it for granted, as the most indubitable

Behold, even the moon — it shineth not;
And the stars are not pure in His eyes;
How much less mortal man — a worm! 10
And the son of man — a caterpillar!"

CHAP. XXV. 5, 6.

conclusion of orthodoxy; besides, it is the doctrine that the Wise Men can least afford to relinquish, being their convenient solvent of the world's mysteries of evil and retribution. And it is this doctrine that Job's bold self-defense most radically traverses. Not that Job really denies it; see, on the contrary, Job's words in section viii. 116, 117; but his point (see section vi. 33, note), that the proportion between man's doings and God's dealings with him is too obviously uurelated to be made a criterion of justice, is lost on them.

XVIII

JOB

And Job answered, and said:

" How hast thou given help to the powerless!
How succored the nerveless arm!
How hast thou counseled the unwise,
And made known truth in abundance!
To whom directest thou words?
And whose breath goeth forth from thee?

I.

" The giant shades tremble
Beneath the waters and their inhabitants.

CHAP. XXVI. 1-5.

Job begins his answer by ridiculing Bildad's speech, intimating ironically that there is no savor, no depth or life, to his words.

LINE 6. Job's way of intimating that Bildad's words do not fit the case; they have no direction.

7. *Whose breath,* — that is, as inspiration. Evidently not the breath of Him whose words reach their aim, and impart knowledge and guidance.

8. *The giant shades,* — the word translated *shades* (*rephaim*) is from a root meaning *weak, powerless.* But the same word is used to designate a race of giants, Genesis xiv. 5; xv. 20;

Naked lieth Sheol before Him, 10
And there is no covering to Abaddon.
He stretcheth out the North over the void;
He hangeth the earth upon nothing.
He bindeth the waters in His thick clouds,

CHAP. XXVI. 6-8.

Isaiah xvii. 5. "Here, in fact," says Dr. Tayler Lewis, "the true force of the passage is best given by combining the two ideas: the once mighty men of old now feeble wailing ghosts."

8 sqq. In the rest of the section Job takes up a strain similar to Bildad's, perhaps indeed a continuation of the same well-known chapter of Wisdom, which, beginning with the description of the heavens above, may have gone on to portray God's control over the regions beneath. Both discourses have the same mythological cast, quite different from the rest of the book; both are parts of the same general theme. Job carries on Bildad's unfinished thought, as if he had said: O yes; I know the old story; do not stop there, go on to the end, it is just as applicable.

10, 11. Beneath the sea somewhere, according to the old mythology, lay the world of the shades: Sheol, the general place of departed spirits; Abaddon, the place where destruction is decreed. It is like the Greek conception of Hades and Tartarus:—

> "Down to rayless Tartarus,
> Deep, deep, in the great Gulf below the earth,—
> As far beneath the Shades as earth from heaven."

But how definite and localized these conceptions of the shades and their dwelling-place had become at the time when the Book of Job was written, it is impossible to say.

12. *The North*,—that is, probably the northern heavens. The void seems to be the great empty space between the earth and the stars.

14. The phenomenon of clouds, wherein vast bodies of

And the cloud is not rent under them. 15
He closeth fast the face of His throne,
Spreading out His cloud over it.
He hath circled a bound on the face of the
    waters,
Unto the margin of light with darkness.
The pillars of heaven rock, 20
And are aghast at His rebuke.
By His power He quelleth the sea;
And by His skill He smiteth through Rahab.
By His breath the heavens become serene;
His hand pierceth the flying serpent. 25

II.

"Behold, these are the outskirts of His ways;

CHAP. XXVI. 8–14.

water hung suspended over the earth, seems to have been an object of great wonder and interest to the Hebrews; compare sections xxv. 55–64; xxvi. 54–59.

18. This seems to be a poetic description of the horizon, especially as observed at sea.

23. *Rahab,* — literally, *the proud one,* has already been mentioned by Job, section vi. 25. Some tradition, well known to Job's hearers, but lost to us, is referred to.

24. To the Hebrews the wind was God's breath.

25. *The flying serpent,* — "according to the ancient mythology, it is the Dragon, or Serpent, which eclipses the sun by winding itself round it, and seeking to devour it." — *Cox.* In Isaiah li. 9, the dragon and Rahab are associated, very much as they are here; see Cheyne's notes on Isaiah xxvii. 1 and li. 9.

And what whisper of a word have we heard of Him!
But the thunder of His power, who can understand?"

CHAP. XXVI. 14.

28. What Job has described, drawing on the mythological ideas of the time, seems occult, but is in reality very easy compared with the great things that so perplex him.

XIX

JOB

AND Job took up his discourse further, and said :

I.

"As God liveth, who hath taken away my right,
And the Almighty, who hath embittered my soul, —
For yet whole is my breath within me,

CHAP. XXVII. 1–3.

LINE 1. *His discourse,* — the Hebrew word *mashal* means discourse in sententious or gnomic style, as represented in proverbs and maxims. This was the style adopted as the vehicle of the Hebrew Wisdom (see Introductory Study, p. 97), a style well adapted, with its condensed parallelisms, to the utterance of weighty and memorable truths.

2. To what Job has yet to say, which may be regarded as a summary of his views and life, he prefixes the most solemn form of the Hebrew oath, "As God liveth." So sure is he of the integrity that the friends have so attacked, and of his true interpretation of God's workings.

4, 5. This asseveration he makes, moreover, in full assurance of his spiritual soundness and sanity. Of this he has been certain all along (see sections iv. 59-61 ; viii. 23-26) ; and

And the spirit of God in my nostril, —
So surely my lips speak not perverseness,
Nor doth my tongue murmur deceit.
Far be it from me that I should justify you;
Till my breath is gone will I not let depart
    mine integrity from me.
My righteousness I hold fast, and will not let
    it go;   10
My heart shall not reproach one of my days.

II.

" Be mine enemy as the wicked man,
And he that riseth against me as the unright-
    eous.

CHAP. XXVII. 3–7.

by reason of it he could detect and rebuke their blindness (see sections x. 56, 57 ; 69, 70; xii. 57–61) ; but they, on their part, have regarded his vision as perverted (see sections iii. 44, and note; ix. 14–19; xv. 20, 21). A diseased body he may have, but it is no diseased utterance that he is to make.

8. *Justify you,* — that is, in their identification of him with the wicked, and by consequence, in the general view of God's world, which this fundamental error of theirs darkens and perverts.

12. So far from being a wicked man, he holds, as do they, the wicked in abhorrence. This he has already said (section xiv. 31) ; but they could not understand how he could attribute such prosperity to the wicked and yet not be in sympathy with them (section xv. 28–35). The mention of the wicked here gives occasion to introduce the subject again, and to settle it according to the insight of truth. Against their intemperate and one-sided portrayals he has already

For what is the hope of the godless, when He cutteth off, —
When God draweth forth his soul? 15
Will God hear his cry,
When distress cometh upon him?
Doth he delight himself in the Almighty?
Doth he call upon God at every time?
I will teach you of the hand of God; 20
What is with the Almighty will I not conceal.
Behold, ye, all ye, have seen it; —
Wherefore then this vanity, that ye vapor forth?

CHAP. XXVII. 8-12.

answered negatively, what the fate of the wicked is *not;* now, free from the heat of controversy, he will give his view of what their fate *is.*

14. *What is the hope?* — This is the keynote of Job's portrayal of the wicked: they have no hope, no abiding future; the permanency of things is not theirs. Job can see this clearly now, having conquered his way by faith to a hope beyond this life.

18. These words furnish an expressive indication of the pure standard of Job's righteousness: it is not merely service for reward, but delight in God, unselfish devotion to God for His own sake. The friends' conception has been distinctly lower than this; and it is this that Job has maintained against Satan's sneer of the beginning. And now Job's conception of wickedness is just its opposite. To him nothing can be more deplorable than not to delight in God.

20-23. Job gives now his view of the real facts of life, a view which also they have pursued blindly; but with their view has been mingled much "vanity;" they have not seen the case in its real ground and perspective. How could

> This is the portion of a wicked man with God,
> And the heritage of the violent, which they shall receive from the Almighty. 25
> If his children increase, it is for the sword;
> And his offspring shall not be satisfied with bread.
> The remnants of his house shall be buried in pestilence,
> And his widows shall not make mourning.
> Though he heap up silver as the dust, 30
> And prepare raiment as the clay, —
>
> CHAP. XXVII. 13-16.

they, when they even viewed Job as wicked, and when they were entangled in the erroneous law of Wisdom, about prosperity and calamity?

24 sqq. Job's portrayal, here beginning, is an exposition in poetic language of what we call the logic of events. It is the truth that only righteousness is well-built and permanent; the logic of wickedness is decay and destruction. Violence begets and succumbs to violence; being itself a tearing-down, it has no future to count upon. To this idea is naturally reducible all that Job here says, and all that is true in what the friends have said, sections v., ix., xi., and xiii.

25. In considering these lines, bear in mind that the special aspect of wickedness that Job contemplates is violence, oppression, the aspect that was probably most prevalent in Job's time, and that was most directly opposed to his ideal of life.

26. Of those who take the sword, the sword, sooner or later, is the doom.

29. Violence and tyranny is a disintegrator even of natural affection.

He will prepare, and the righteous shall wear it;
And the silver shall the innocent divide.
He buildeth his house as doth the moth,
And like a booth that a watchman maketh. 35
He lieth down rich — and never again!
He openeth his eyes — and he is not!
Terrors overtake him as the waters;
By night a tempest stealeth him away;
An east wind lifteth him up, and he vanisheth. 40
It stormeth him forth from his place;
It hurleth against him, and spareth not;
Hither and thither he fleeth from its hand.
Men clap their hands at him,
And hiss at him from his desolated place. 45

III.

"There is indeed a vein for the silver,
And a place for the gold that they refine.

CHAP. XXVII. 17 — XXVIII. 1.

32, 33. "But the meek shall inherit the earth."

35. *A booth*, — such as were built for temporary shelter in vineyards and gardens; compare Isaiah i. 8.

37-45. The rest of the passage is an amplification, Oriental, but with this large interpretation not overwrought, of the same general idea of the instability and transitoriness of whatever is built on evil.

46. *Indeed*, — literally, "*for* there is." The *for* I am inclined to view as equivalent to our idiom of a concessive

Iron is taken out of the soil,
And molten stone becometh copper.
Man setteth an end to darkness, 50
And to the utmost limit he searcheth out
The stone of darkness and of the shadow of death.
He breaketh the ravine remote from the settler;
And there, forgotten of the passer's foot,

CHAP. XXVIII. 2-4.

(indeed) preparing for a coming adversative (but) : "There is *indeed* a vein for the silver, . . . *but* wisdom, where shall it be found?"

The connection of this 28th chapter with the rest of the book has been a puzzle to some. But does it not follow naturally? Having portrayed the extreme of unwisdom (with which in the old philosophy wickedness was identified), the life that has not the future nor is built therefor, it is natural that Job should next speak of its contrast, the true wisdom and foresight whereby to build human life and character. There are many marvelous things that man may know or search out; but many also are unsearchable. He cannot see as God sees, perhaps cannot reach absolute truth. But there is a wisdom *for him*, which points to the absolute good as the needle points to the pole.

The description of mining operations, ll. 46-69, is given with the vividness and accuracy of an eye-witness, and indicates that the writer was familiar with the mines of Egypt and the Sinai peninsula.

50. *An end to darkness,* — that is, by illuminating it and discovering its secrets.

52. *Of the shadow of death,* — this phrase indicates the uncanniness that the Hebrew associated with darkness.

They hang and swing, far off from mortal
    man.
The earth — out of it cometh bread, 56
And underneath it is upturned as it were by
    fire.
Its stones are the place of the sapphire,
And clods of gold are there ; —
A path that no eagle hath known, 60
Nor hath the vulture's eye looked upon it.
The proud beast of prey hath not explored
    it,
Nor hath passed over it the roaring lion.
He putteth forth his hand to the flinty rock ;
He overturneth mountains from their root ; 65
He cutteth channels in the rocks ;
And every precious thing his eye seeth.
He bindeth up the streams from weeping ;
And the hidden thing he bringeth forth to
    light.
    But WISDOM — where shall *it* be found ? 70

CHAP. XXVIII. 4-12.

  55. A vivid picture of miners hanging suspended from the precipice and working so far below as to be unseen.

  60. Man does indeed do wonders in exploring secret things, but there is a mystery far beyond him, — the mystery of wisdom.

  68. *From weeping*, — that is, dripping. A miner's metaphor, referring to the dripping of water into mines ; but well worth translating literally for its beauty.

  70. Though Job has freely criticised the conclusions of the

And where is the place of understanding?
Mortal man knoweth not the price of it;
Nor is it found in the land of the living.
The deep saith, It is not in me;
The sea saith likewise, Not with me. 75
Fine gold shall not be given for it,
Nor shall silver be weighed as the exchange
 thereof;
It cannot be bought with the stamped gold of
 Ophir,
With the precious onyx and the sapphire;
Gold and glass cannot be prized with it, 80
Nor is its exchange vases of fine gold.
Corals and crystal are not to be named with
 it;
And the possession of wisdom is above pearls.
The topaz of Ethiopia cannot be bartered for
 it;

CHAP. XXVIII. 12-19.

Hebrew Wisdom, as brought forth by the friends, and perhaps even as quoted by himself (see section xvi. 74 sqq. note), yet of the true Wisdom he is still the loyal devotee. And as the Book of Job is the ripest product of the Hebrew Wisdom, so it is fitting that this chapter, its culmination and crown, should be devoted to the definition and praise of Wisdom.

78. The several Hebrew words for gold can be at best but awkwardly reproduced in English; but some attempt at discrimination can be made, as here, by a recourse to the root-meanings. The "stamped gold" may refer to the peculiar mark put upon the gold of Ophir.

It cannot be put in the balance with gold of
    purest stamp.   85
  But Wisdom — whence then cometh it?
And where is the place of understanding? —
Since it is hid from the eyes of all living,
And kept secret from the bird of the heaven?
Abaddon and Death say,   90
'We have heard but a rumor of it with our
    ears.'
God understandeth the way thereto,
And He knoweth its place.
For He looketh to the ends of the earth;
Under the whole heaven He seeth.   95
When He gave the wind its weight,
And meted out the waters in a measure, —
When He gave a law to the rain,
And a way to the flash of the thunder, —
Then did He see, and declare it;   100
He established it, yea, He searched it out.
  And unto man He said,

CHAP. XXVIII. 19-28.

  90. *Abaddon*, — or destruction. See section xviii. 10, 11, and note.

  96-99. Just as everything in nature is precisely determined, just as the rain has its law and the lightning its appointed direction (compare section xxv. 65, 66), so man has a law which is his wisdom, a way of life in which alone he finds his goal.

  102. *Unto man*, — whatever is the law of other creatures and forces, here is what alone concerns man.

' Behold, the fear of the Lord, that is Wisdom,
And to shun evil is understanding.' "

CHAP. XXVIII. 20-28.

103. *The Lord*, — the original word is not the name Jehovah, but a word meaning more specifically Lord or Master, and perhaps especially appropriate here where as Creator He is viewed in relation to His great works.

103, 104. These are just what Job started with, section i. 2, 3; but they have reached a significance far beyond what they had then. He has tested and maintained them through the fiercest fires of struggle and affliction; and not only has he proved them true, but he has defined as never before *what it involves* to fear God and shun evil, — even all that Satan doubted of him. Further, that very integrity has been to Job for insight into the deeps of things; the faith that was born of his loyalty to what was holy and loving has indeed proved itself " understanding." This, then, is the highest expression of Job's vindication.

XX

JOB

AND Job took up his discourse yet further, and said:

I.

"Oh that I were as in months of old,
As in the days when God watched over me;
When His lamp shone over my head,
When by His light I walked through darkness; 5
As I was in mine autumn days,
When the friendship of God was over my tent;
While yet the Almighty was with me,
And round about me were my children;
When my steps were washed with cream, 10

CHAP. XXIX. 1–6.

Having thus reached the culmination of his argument, Job here, in a retrospect, gathers up the threads of his past life and his present affliction, to present them as his vindication before God.

LINE 4. Compare section xi. 11, 12, and note.

6. *Mine autumn days,* — days of ripeness and fruitfulness.

7. *The friendship of God,* — literally, "the *secret* of God." Compare section xii 38, and note.

And the rock poured forth beside me streams of oil;
When I went forth to the gate by the city;
When I fixed my seat in the open place.
Young men saw me, and withdrew themselves,
And old men arose and stood up; 15
Princes checked their words,
And laid their hand upon their mouth;
The voice of nobles was hushed,
And their tongue cleaved to their palate.

For the ear that heard blessed me; 20
And the eye that saw bare witness for me;
Because I had delivered the poor when he cried,
The fatherless also, and him that had no helper.
The blessing of the perishing came upon me,
And I made the widow's heart sing for joy. 25

CHAP. XXIX. 6-13.

12. The city gate was the place where counsel was held and judgment pronounced. Job was eminent among the judges and wise men.

13. *The open place*, near the gate, was more specifically the place of judgment and assembly.

14-19. Marks of respect from various ages and ranks, indicating that Job had been recognized as "the greatest of all the sons of the East" (section i. 10).

22-33. One of the most beautiful ancient portrayals of virtue, founded on a Christian ideal of love and mercy, rather than on the ideal of mere justice and law-keeping, such as afterward obtained among the Scribes and Pharisees.

I clothed myself in justice, and it clothed itself
    with me ;
As a mantle and as a turban was my judg-
    ment.
I was eyes to the blind,
And feet to the lame was I ;
A father was I to the needy, 30
And I searched out the cause of him that I
    knew not.
And I brake the fangs of the wicked,
And from his teeth I snatched the prey.
    And I said, 'I shall expire in my nest,
And like the phœnix I shall multiply days. 35
My root shall be spread out to the waters,
And the dew shall lie all night on my branch.
My glory shall be fresh within me,
And my bow shall be renewed in my hand.'
    Unto me they gave ear, and waited ; 40
And they were silent, listening for my counsel.

CHAP. XXIX. 14–21.

26. "Job clothed himself with righteousness, so that as a man he was lost in the justice that clothed him ; and justice clothed itself in him, — he on the other hand was justice become a person." — *Davidson.*

31. Job's helpful spirit was not dependent on the attraction of relatives and personal friends: he that was a stranger and had no natural claims fared just as well.

35. *The phœnix,* — the original word is not certainly known, but seems to refer to that fabulous bird which is said to renew its youth and attain a great age.

After my words they spake not again;
For upon them my speech descended gently,
And they waited for me as for the rain,
And opened their mouths wide as for the latter rain. 45
I laughed upon them when they were doubtful,
And the light of my countenance they cast not down.
I chose their way, and sat as their head;
And I dwelt as a king in the multitude, —
As one that comforteth mourners. 50

II.

"And now they mock at me, — men younger in days than I,
Whose fathers I disdained to set with the dogs of my flock.
Nay, the strength of their hands — what is that to me?
Men to whom the vigor of age is lost;
Gaunt they are with want and hunger; 55

CHAP. XXIX. 22 — XXX. 3.

42. *They spake not again,* — because the best and conclusive word had been spoken, and needed no supplement.

45. Like young birds opening their mouths for food.

51. The second division of Job's retrospect, here beginning, draws the sad contrast between that past and the joyless present.

54-60. Job describes the outlaws and vagabonds of a pastoral country, whose refuge is the desert; the same class, per-

Who gnaw the dry ground in the gloom of
    wild and wilderness;
Who pluck up the purslain by the sprouts,
And the root of the broom is their bread.
They are driven forth from society;
Men cry after them as after a thief.   60
In the horror of the ravines must they dwell;
In holes of the earth, and among the crags.
They bray among the thickets;
Under the nettles they herd together.
Children of folly, yea, children of nameless
    men, —   65
They are scourged out of the land.
    And now their song of derision am I be-
    come;

CHAP. XXX. 3-9.

haps, which he has represented, section xvi. 41-50, as added to by the tyranny of the unscrupulous wicked around him.

56. *Wild and wilderness,* — in this translation an attempt is made to reproduce something of the meaning and word-play effect of the original.

67. Even such men, the very dregs of humanity, despise him because he is smitten of God. Even they, though under the ban of men, are ready to curse where God has set His mark of displeasure. Edmund Burke, speaking of the Catholic disabilities of his time, thus describes the disposition of men to persecute: "This desire of having some one below them descends to those who are the very lowest of all; and a Protestant cobbler, debased by his poverty, but exalted by his share of the ruling Church, feels a pride in knowing it is by his generosity alone that the peer whose footman's instep he measures is able to keep his chaplain from a jail."

And I am to them for a byword.
They abhor me, they stand afar off from me;
And from my face they withhold not their spittle. 70
Because He hath loosed my cord and bowed me down,
They also have cast off the bridle before me.
On my right hand they rise — a rabble;
They thrust my feet aside;
They cast up against me their destructive ways. 75
They break up my path;
They help forward my hurt;
They — who themselves have no helper.
As through a wide breach they come in;
Under the crash they roll themselves along; —
All overturned upon me — terrors — 81
They chase away mine honor like the wind;
And like a cloud my prosperity passeth.

And now my soul within me is poured out;
Days of affliction take fast hold upon me. 85

CHAP. XXX. 9-16.

71, 72. This it is that has caused Job's sensitive and loving heart the most poignant pain, — because men's treatment of him does not proceed from genuine heart-feeling, but from a conventional idea of what God's disposition is. Compare section iv. 43, note.

75-80. The old figure of a host against him and a siege, only now associated with men rather than with God's unseen agencies.

Night pierceth out my bones away from me;
And my gnawing pains lie not down to rest.
It is by great exertion that my garment is changed;
Like the collar of my tunic it clingeth about me.
He hath cast me into the mire;   90
And I have taken the semblance of dust and ashes.
I cry unto Thee, and Thou answerest me not;
I stand before Thee, and Thou beholdest me;
Yet Thou art become cruel unto me;
By the might of Thy hand Thou fetterest me. 95
Thou liftest me up on the wind, where Thou makest me ride;
And Thou dissolvest me in the crash of the storm.
For I know that Thou turnest me back to death,

CHAP. XXX. 17-23.

86. A vivid description of his fearful emaciation.

96, 97. The momentum of Job's vivid thought bears him onward into very bold imagery; descriptive probably of the whirling, bewildering, perilous seeming spiritual experience that he is compelled to undergo.

98. We will bear in mind that Job's greater calmness and hopefulness of late have not been due to release from death or suffering; he still accepts the prospect of death, and draws near to it with the assured hope of one who knows that his Redeemer liveth.

To the house of assembly for all living.
  Surely, will not a man in ruins·stretch out his hand? 100
Or in his calamity will he not cry out therefore?
Have not *I* wept for him whose day was hard?
Hath not *my* soul grieved for the needy?
Yet I looked for good, and there came evil;
I waited for light, and there came darkness. 105
  My bowels boil, and are not still;
Days of anguish overtake me.
I go about darkened, but not with the sun's glow;
When I stand in the assembly I must cry out for pain.
Brother am I to the jackals, 110
And companion to the daughters of the ostrich.
My blackened skin falleth from me,
And my bones burn up with heat.

CHAP. XXX. 23-30.

102-105. An appeal to the compassion that should exist above, corresponding to the like emotions of men. Such anthropopathism is the only basis on which man can philosophize; and the fact that Job can find in the darkness no counterpart to his highest self is the deepest cause of his perplexity.

106 sqq. All this paragraph contains observed symptoms and characteristics of elephantiasis.

110. He is cast out of society, and so compelled to be like the beasts and birds of the desert.

So is my harp turned to mourning,
And my pipe to the voice of them that weep. 115

III.

" I made a covenant for mine eyes;
How then should I look upon a maid?
For what is the allotment of God from above,
And the heritage of the Almighty from on high?
Is it not destruction to the wicked, 120
And disaster to the workers of iniquity?
Is He not seeing my way,
And numbering all my steps?
If I have walked with vanity,
And my foot hath made haste to deceit, — 125

CHAP. XXX. 31 — XXXI. 5.

116. This third division of the section, here beginning, contains Job's last and strongest asseverations of righteousness, a kind of solemn testimony which is to be lifted up before God (ll. 187-192,) to be seen and judged.

118-121. Job alludes to Zophar's description of the doom of the wicked (see section xiii. 59, 60), the strongest that has yet been given, as defining, whether exaggeratedly or not, the stern warning by which he has kept himself from evil.

122. Thus he contradicts Eliphaz's accusation, section xv. 22-27; nay, it has been one element of his complaint that God has watched him, all too closely (sections iv. 100-104; viii. 106-109), and his longing to be laid away in the grave has been sharpened by the thought that the watching and numbering of steps would cease (section viii. 145-148). Yet such consciousness has determined his whole life.

124, 125. The Hebrew manner of designating falseness of life and word; compare Psalm xxiv. 4.

Let Him weigh me in scales of righteousness,
And let God know mine integrity! —
If my step hath turned from the way,
And after mine eyes hath walked my heart,
And a stain hath cleaved to my hands, —   130
Let me sow, and another eat,
And my sprouted grain — let it be rooted out.

If my heart have been befooled by a woman,
And I have lain in wait at my neighbor's door,
Let my wife grind for another,   135
And let others crouch over her;
For that were an infamous thing, —
Yea, a crime that, for them that pass judgment.
For it is a fire; unto Abaddon it devoureth;
And all mine increase it would root out.   140
If I have spurned the right of my servant and my handmaid,
When they have had controversy with me,
What then shall I do when God ariseth?
And when He visiteth, what shall I answer Him?

CHAP. XXXI. 6-14.

126, 127. This parenthesis invites the strictest standard of judgment, as it accepts the severest penalty.

135. Grinding was the representative occupation of the female slave, hence chosen as the mark that his wife is domiciled and degraded in another house.

139. *Unto Abaddon*, — see section xviii. 10, 11, note.

Did not He that made me in the womb make him? 145
And did not one Being fashion us in the belly?
    If I have kept back the poor from their desire,
And caused the widow's eyes to fail,
And have eaten my morsel alone,
And the fatherless hath not eaten thereof, — 150
Nay, from my youth he grew up to me as to a father,
And from my mother's womb I protected her; —
If I have seen one perishing for lack of clothing,
And the poor without covering, —
Nay, rather his loins blessed me, 155
And from the fleece of my lambs he warmed himself; —

CHAP. XXXI. 15–20.

145. Job retains the pure ideal of the oneness of all the race, — an ideal which, it would seem, was fading in the general tendency of the time to separate classes; compare section xvi. 36 sqq. note.

151. The fact of Job's compassion and benevolence is so evident that he cannot finish bringing up the contemplation of its opposite even as a supposition; so again below, ll. 155, 175. He doubtless has in mind Eliphaz's vague accusations, section xv. 10–17, which as he passes them in review are so palpably false that he thus breaks them off.

If I have lifted up my hand against the fatherless,
When I saw mine ally in the gate,
Let my shoulder fall from the shoulder-blade,
And let mine arm be broken from its bone. 160
For fear was upon me of calamity from God;
And because of His majesty I could not.
If I have made gold my trust,
And to the coined gold said, 'My confidence thou;' 164
If I have rejoiced because my wealth was great,
And because my hand had gotten much; —
If when I saw the sunlight as it shone,
And the moon walking in splendor,
My heart was enticed in secret,
And my hand kissed my mouth, 170

CHAP. XXXI. 21–27.

158. *Mine ally*,— another reminiscence of Eliphaz's accusation, section xv. 15, who represented that Job had neglected the needy because others, "the respected of person," were his closer favorites.

161, 162. This same fear was mentioned as the constant attendant of his life, section ii. 51–54, where see note; and God's "majesty" has kept him from falseness and impelled him to rebuke his friends for time-serving, section viii. 73.

163. Eliphaz's exhortation to Job, section xv. 46–48, has seemed to imply that Job was too fond of money; perhaps this is introduced in allusion and answer to that.

167–170. A reference to the worship of the heavenly bodies, which before the Babylonian exile, as Jeremiah xliv. 17 sqq. indicates, was prevalent in Palestine.

This too were a crime for the judges,
For so I had been false to God on high.
  If I have rejoiced at the calamity of him that hated me,
And have exulted because evil befell him, —
Nay, but I gave not my mouth to sin,   175
By invoking a curse on his life;
In sooth, the men of my tent say,
'Who will show us one not filled with his flesh?'
The stranger lodged never without;
I opened my doors to the wayfarer.   180
  If like Adam I have covered my transgressions,
To hide mine iniquity in my bosom,
Because I feared the great multitude,
And the contempt of clans terrified me,
So that I was silent, went not out of the gate, —   185
. . . Oh that I had one to hear me! —

CHAP. XXXI. 28-35.

173-176. Here Job avows a higher ideal than Eliphaz has inculcated, for Eliphaz makes it a test of righteousness to rejoice at the calamity of the wicked; see section xv. 36-39; also section iii. 49. Job is too merciful to rejoice at calamity.

175. See note on l. 151 above.

181. *Like Adam*, — see Genesis iii. 8-11.

186. At this point in his retrospect Job comes suddenly to realize that in no reasonable point has he failed. The sum of his life, so far as he can compute it, has come out right;

Behold my sign! let the Almighty answer me! —
And the charge that mine Adversary hath written!
Surely, I will lift it upon my shoulder;
I will bind it unto me like a crown; 190
I will declare unto Him the number of my steps;
I will draw near unto Him like a prince.
    If against me my land crieth out,
And its furrows weep together; —
If I have eaten its strength without silver, 195
And caused its tenant to pant out his life; —

CHAP. XXXI. 36–39.

and he is ready to present the account to God for judgment and award.

    187 sq. *My sign . . . and the charge,* — this record of an upright life, Job means. It is this record which constitutes his only offense; and as it has been visited by punishment, it may be ironically named a "charge," an accusation, that in all things he has been "a man perfect and upright, one that feareth God and shunneth evil."

    189 sq. Of such a charge he has no fear. He is proud to come before God as a prince, on equal terms, as one who has a just cause and is sure of vindication. This, all told off, is the "number of his steps" which God has noted so narrowly (see l. 123), the "bitter things" which God has written against him (see section viii. 103), no longer some unknown and fearful sin, but a life of honor and integrity.

    193–198. It seems probable that this last paragraph is displaced, as the previous passage forms the fitting and triumphant close to Job's words.

Instead of wheat let briars come up,
And cockle instead of barley."

THE WORDS OF JOB ARE ENDED.

CHAP. XXXI. 40.

198. *Cockle,* — from the derivation of the word the more accurate translation would be *stinkweed*, which, however, it was not thought best to adopt in the text.

XXI

TRANSITION

AND these three men ceased to answer Job, because he was righteous in his own eyes.

Then was kindled the wrath of Elihu, son of Barachel the Buzite, of the family of Ram. 5

CHAP. XXXII. 1, 2.

So far as the friends are concerned, Job has proved himself invincible: his righteousness, as he by the loftiest standards defines righteousness, they cannot successfully impugn. The fact that he has silenced them, however, is not in itself conclusive. There still remains the question how the two parties stand in the absolute light; and we have yet to learn the result alike of Job's impassioned appeals for judgment, and of the friends' confident assurance that they represent the mind of God. To bring in the friends' cause anew, and in its best and strongest statement, a fourth speaker, hitherto unmentioned, is here introduced.

LINE 4. Elihu's family and descent are given with much particularity, as if he were a veritable historical personage; which of course we can neither affirm nor deny. Buz, who is mentioned as his ancestor, was a son of Nahor (Genesis xxii. 21), and the Buzites are evidently regarded by Jeremiah (xxv. 23), along with Tema, as an Arab tribe.

5. *The family of Ram.* In 2 Chronicles xxii. 5, the Syrians, whose ordinary designation is Aramites, are called Ram-

Against Job was his wrath kindled, because he justified himself rather than God; and against his three friends was his wrath kindled, because they found no answer wherewith to condemn Job. Now Elihu had waited for Job with his words, because they were older than he; and when Elihu saw that there was no answer in the mouth of the three men, his wrath was kindled.

CHAP. XXXII. 2-5.

ites: this fact, together with the fact that the dialectic peculiarities of Elihu's speech are supposably Aramæan, would make it most probable that Elihu was an Aramæan; yet the Buzite descent, mentioned in the foregoing note, is not clearly in favor of this.

6. From Elihu's and the friends' point of view Job's justification of himself would be of necessity condemnation of God; though Job has merely maintained his ways (compare section viii. 81-84) regardless of logical consequences, and with increasing trust in God's goodness and love.

9. It is not because the friends are wrong that Elihu is angry with them, but because their argument is not strong enough. His whole attitude is essentially one with theirs; he merely enters the lists as a better representative of their cause.

12-14. Elihu has the fire and impatience of youth; he is irritated because their words, moving cautiously in the lines of the ancient Wisdom, and keeping within the bounds of tradition, are not like a direct "answer" fitted to the present case. Speaking broadly, we may say, Elihu may be regarded as furnishing the test whether the Wisdom philosophy will have resources enough, in the hands of a new interpreter, to meet the strain which Job's case and his valiant self-defense impose upon it.

XXII

ELIHU

AND Elihu, son of Barachel the Buzite, answered and said:

I.

"Young am I in days, and ye are hoary;
Wherefore I shrank and was afraid
To utter unto you what I know.
I said, Days should speak,
And multitude of years should make known wisdom.
But truly, a spirit there is in mortal man,
And a breath of the Almighty, that giveth understanding.

CHAP. XXXII. 6–8.

LINE 2. Elihu's youth, while it explains his delay and diffidence, also determines the character of his thought, which is self-confident, constructive, unconventional, less bound by tradition and precedent than that of the friends.

7, 8. Through this reflection he leaps from excessive hesitation, which after all has a kind of egotism about it, to excessive boldness, even wordiness. He says so much about his modesty that we begin to distrust it, — a clever bit of characterization on the part of the author.

Not the great alone are wise,
Nor is it the aged that understand judgment. 10
Therefore I say, Listen unto me;
I will utter knowledge, even I.
 Behold, I waited for your words;
I gave ear unto your reasonings,
Until ye should search out what to say. 15
Yea, unto you I gave attention,
And behold — none that convinced Job,
None of you that answered his words.
Lest ye should say, We have found wisdom,
God will vanquish him, not man; 20
For not against me hath he directed words,
Nor will I answer him with your arguments.
They are dismayed, they do not answer more;
Words have fled away from them.
And I waited — for they did not speak, — 25

Chap. xxxii. 9-16.

9, 10. This reflection that age is not necessarily a requisite to wisdom is no more than Job has already made; see section viii. 25, 26.

13 sqq. The present paragraph is made intentionally verbose, in order to set forth the character of the man. Consider how little is really said, and how many repetitions there are.

20, 21. Elihu is so "stung by the splendor of a sudden thought" that his self-confidence overleaps itself; he identifies his thoughts with God's thoughts, and regards himself as the mouthpiece of a divine communication.

25-29. The idea of being the vehicle of absolute truth raises his conceit, and the pronoun *I* begins to play an important part.

For they stood still, and did not answer more.
I will answer, yea I, for my part;
I will utter knowledge, even I.
For I am full of words;
The spirit in my breast constraineth me; 30
Behold, my heart is as wine that hath no vent,
As new bottles that are ready to burst.
I will speak, and it will be a relief to me;
I will open my lips and answer.
Let me not now accept the person of men, 35
Nor let me use flattery unto human kind;
For I know not how to flatter, —
Else would my Maker soon take me away.

II.

"Yet hear now, O Job, my speech,
And unto all my words give ear. 40

CHAP. XXXII. 16 — XXXIII. 1.

32. Alas! he mistakes tumidity for inspiration; let not this fact, however, blind us to the real worth of his words. The reader does not need to be reminded here that Elihu has in mind the skin-bottles of the East.

35. Elihu prides himself on his impartiality and his original views. Job accused the friends of special pleading for God (see section viii. 65-68), and perhaps Elihu alludes to that; but he turns it around. He will not accept either Job's person or the person of the friends. Eliphaz's wisdom, Bildad's learning, Zophar's eloquence, are nothing except as they embody reason and truth.

38. *My Maker*, — this designation of God is peculiar to Elihu; see sections xxiv. 18; xxv. 5.

Behold now, I have opened my mouth;
My tongue hath spoken in my palate.
The uprightness of my heart are these words
 of mine,
And my lips shall speak their knowledge sin-
 cerely.
The spirit of God hath made me; 45
And the breath of the Almighty giveth me life.
If thou art able, answer me;
Set words in array before me, take thy stand.
Behold, I, according to thy word, stand for
 God;
Out of clay am I moulded, also I; 50
Behold *my* terror shall not unman thee,
Nor will my burden upon thee be heavy.

CHAP. XXXIII. 2-7.

45, 46. By these same characteristics he has identified him-self, ll. 7, 8, with mankind; here he simply reminds Job that it is as a man that he represents the mind of God. This he says in preparation for the assumption that he is about to make.

49. A reference to Job's wish for a Daysman, section vi. 62-69. Elihu is so sure of knowing God's mind that he assumes to fulfill Job's wish; as a man he will stand between Job and God, and mitigate the divine terrors. This of course puts the whole idea of a Daysman on a lower plane, and entirely ignores the conquering faith by which Job found what he sought. Job is beyond the need of what Elihu can offer; while Elihu is blind to the higher reaches of the Messianic idea with which Job has been comforted.

III.

"Verily, thou hast said in mine ears,
And I have heard the voice of thy words:
'Pure am I, without transgression; 55
Clean am I, and there is no iniquity in me.
Behold, He findeth occasions against me;
He counteth me for His enemy;
He putteth my feet in the stocks;
He marketh all my paths.' 60
  Behold, in this, I answer thee, thou art not just;
For greater is God than mortal man.
Why makest thou complaint against Him,
That He answereth thee by no word of His?

CHAP. XXXIII. 8–13.

55, 56. Compare Job's words, sections vi. 40, 84; viii. 81, 82; x. 39, 40; xii. 59 (see note). The assertions of innocence that Job has made in reference to his excess of punishment Elihu takes as having been made in the absolute sense.

57. Not an exact quotation, but reproducing the sense of such passages as section vi. 96–107.

58. Compare section xii. 21.

59, 60. Compare section viii. 105, 106.

62. That is, enough greater to have a transcendent standard of judgment which man cannot discover. We have no business, therefore, to say either what is human righteousness or what is divine punishment.

64. This has been a very poignant element of Job's bewilderment; in fact, he has condensed his whole longing into a desire for an answer. Elihu refers more immediately, per-

For God speaketh — once,   65
Yea, twice, while man regardeth it not:
In dream, in vision of the night,
When falleth deep sleep upon men,
In slumberings upon the bed,
Then uncovereth He the ear of men,   70
And setteth a seal upon the warning,
To make man put away his evil deed,
And to hide pride from the strong man;
To keep back his soul from the pit,
And his life from passing by the dart.   75
He is chastened also with anguish upon his
    bed,

CHAP. XXXIII. 14-19.

haps, to Job's words, section xx. 92; compare also section xii. 12, 13.

67. The first way in which God answers. Elihu means dreams in general, with perhaps a reference to Eliphaz's vision, section iii. 22-32, which was well utilized for instruction, and to Job's terrifying visions, section iv. 90, 91, in which Job has found no meaning.

71. *Setteth a seal*, — that is, gives it some mark or sign whereby it can be interpreted as from God.

74. *The pit*, — a favorite expression of Elihu's, occurring no fewer than five times in the present section. By it he seems to mean, not necessarily death, but that extreme depth of trial and affliction which would issue in death were it not for deliverance.

75. The dart is the dart of Death, as the instrument of retribution.

76. The second means whereby God speaks, — affliction. This is a direct reference to Job's suffering, which Elihu in-

And the strife of his bones is unceasing;
And his life abhorreth bread,
And his soul dainty meat;
His flesh consumeth away, out of sight, 80
And laid bare are his bones, that before were
    not seen;
And his soul draweth near to the pit,
And his life to the Destroying Ones.

IV.

" If then there be with him a messenger,
An interpreter, one of a thousand, 85
To show unto man what is right for him, —

terprets, not as punishment, but as a vehicle of instruction and warning. Some of the main features of Job's disease are specified in Elihu's description, so that the reference may be made plain.

83. *The Destroying Ones,* — angels or agencies of fate; perhaps the mysterious " they " to which Job has several times referred.

84. Here is introduced Elihu's theory of the way in which these messages of God are to be made intelligible. Some messenger is needed to trace God's mind and will through the dream and the affliction. The word translated literally *messenger* is the same word used to designate *angel;* but in the present case Elihu, who carefully ignores the supernatural, seems to mean himself, as a representative of God. This is quite in accordance with his assumption of the Daysman's office, ll. 49-52, and with his general exalted opinion of himself. He has arrived just in time to set things right.

85. *One of a thousand,* — that is, one exceptionally quali-

So doth He show grace, and say,
'Deliver him from going down to the pit;
I have found a ransom.'
Fresher than a child's then cometh his flesh;
He returneth to the days of his young vigor.
He prayeth unto God, who accepteth him,
And maketh him see His face with joy,
And giveth back to the mortal his righteousness.
Then he singeth before men, and saith:
'I sinned, and perverted the right,
Yet retribution came not upon me.
He hath delivered my soul from going to the pit,
And my life shall behold the light.'

Chap. xxxiii. 24-28.

fied, by gifts and by the divine authorization that lies in his endowments.

90-94. A prophecy of what actually took place, but not by Elihu's intercession nor recognizing his principles.

96 sqq. Elihu has here a full-fledged theory of atonement, — a theory which, like his Messiah-theory, is thoroughly rationalistic. There is no supernatural element in it, except what inheres in his theory of the Daysman. Observe also its crudeness: it contemplates merely release from the punishment of sin, and its highest ideal is restoration to the welfare of this life. In this respect it moves on a much lower plane than does Job, with his confidence in a Redeemer and his hopeful readiness to meet death; while it is also thoroughly identical with the other friends' idea of blessing.

Lo, all these things worketh God, 100
Twice, three times, with man ;
To bring back his soul from the pit,
To enlighten him with the light of life.

v.

" Attend then, O Job, give ear unto me ;
Keep thou silence, and I will speak. 105
If there are words to be said, answer me ;
Speak, for I desire to justify thee.
If not, listen unto me thou ;
Be silent, and I will teach thee wisdom."

CHAP. XXXIII. 29–33.

101. *Twice, three times,*—a climax on ll. 65, 66, with perhaps an allusion to Elihu's intercession as messenger and interpreter, as the third way of God's working with man.

XXIII

ELIHU

And Elihu answered further, and said:

"Hear, O wise men, my words,
And men of knowledge, give ear unto me.
For the ear testeth words,
As the palate tasteth what is eaten.   5
Let us choose to ourselves judgment;
Let us know between us what is good.

1.

" For Job saith, 'I am righteous,
And God hath taken away my right.

Chap. XXXIV. 1-5.

Line 2. This section is addressed to the friends, with the exception of a short diversion, ll. 31-34, in which Job is brought into the audience with them.

4, 5. This is evidently a well-known Wisdom maxim; Job has already quoted it, section viii. 23, 24, as containing a self-evident truth.

6, 7. Elihu's object in addressing the friends is to find common ground with them, on which he can admonish Job. He evidently regards himself as the champion of the friends' cause.

8-11. These words, though (with the exception of l. 9, see

Against my right I am made to lie; 10
Incurable is my wound, yet without crime of
    mine.'
Who is a mighty man like Job? —
Who drinketh in scorning like water,
Who consorteth with workers of iniquity,
And walketh with men of wickedness. 15
For he hath said it availeth not a man,
That he should delight himself with God.

    Therefore, men of understanding, hear me:
Far be it — far be God from wickedness,
And the Almighty from iniquity. 20
For the work of man will He requite unto him,
And make every man find according to his way.
Yea, verily, God will not do wickedly,

CHAP. XXXIV. 6-12.

section xix. 2) not literally quoted, are a not unfair representation of the general tenor of Job's complaint.

13-17. This passage gives Elihu's idea of the logical outcome of Job's position. As Eliphaz has already complained (see section ix. 6, 7), it seems to break down the barriers between devoutness and scorn, and thus to make Job a companion of wicked men. Job has indeed disclaimed sympathy with wickedness (section xiv. 30, 31), and this same sneer, "What availeth?" he has attributed to them (section xiv. 26-29); but Elihu ignores this fact, because the whole logic of Job's complaint seems to him to belie it.

18 sqq. In this paragraph Elihu occupies the friends' ground of indiscriminate justification of God; and for this he urges only the reason of God's power, as if might made right This of course is just the idea that Job has contested.

Nor will the Almighty pervert judgment.
Who laid upon Him the charge of the earth, 25
And who disposed the whole world?
If He should set His heart upon Himself,
And gather unto Himself His spirit and His
    breath, —
All flesh would gasp out its life together,
And man would return to dust. 30

II.

"Oh, if thou wilt understand then, hear this;
Give ear to the voice of my words.
Shall even a hater of right have dominion?
And wilt thou condemn the Just, the Mighty? —
Who saith to a king, Thou worthless! 35
To nobles, Thou wicked one!
Who regardeth not the face of princes,
Nor heedeth the rich before the poor;
For the work of His hands they are, all of
    them.

CHAP. XXXIV. 12-19.

33, 34. *A hater of right,* — so Job appears to Elihu. Job has condemned wrong wherever he saw it, even in God; but when it came to judging God, Elihu, who blindly identified His justice and His might, regards Job's words as condemning the right itself.

35 sqq. This paragraph merely amplifies the argument outlined in ll. 25-30. The statements are true enough; but they ascribe to God nothing higher than arbitrary power.

In a moment they die; and at midnight, ⁴⁰
The people rise in tumult, and rush to and fro;
And the mighty is removed — yet not with
    hands.
For His eyes are on the ways of each man,
And all his goings doth He see.
There is no darkness, and there is no shadow
    of death, ⁴⁵
Where workers of iniquity may hide them-
    selves.
For He needeth not to set thought on a man
    the second time,
That he should come to God in judgment.
He breaketh in pieces mighty men, inscruta-
    bly,
And setteth up others in their stead. ⁵⁰
Therefore He taketh note of their works,
And He overturneth in the night, and they
    are crushed.
He beateth them as He beateth the wicked,
In the place where all may see;
Because they have turned back from Him, ⁵⁵

CHAP. XXXIV. 20-27.

40-42. Description of the national disturbance occasioned by the death of a prince.

46. Because the first stroke does the work thoroughly; compare Milton, Lycidas, ll. 130, 131: —

> " But that two-handed engine at the door
> Stands ready to smite once and smite no more."

And all His ways they have heeded not;
That they may bring before Him the cry of
    the poor;
And the cry of the afflicted He will hear.
  When He giveth quietness, who shall disturb?
When He hideth His face, who shall spy Him
    out?   60
Be it with nation, or with man, He dealeth
    alike;
That the godless man may not bear rule,
Nor they that ensnare the people.

III.

" For oh, had he but said unto God,
'I bear it — I will not offend —   65
Beyond what I see, teach me Thou, —
If I have wrought iniquity, I will no more!' ...

CHAP. XXXIV. 27-32.

57. The end of God's way, after all, is righteousness and mercy; herein the parties are not in dispute, though Job does not work out the problem so clearly, nor does he pass so lightly as do the friends over such disturbing elements as are suggested in ll. 62, 63.

64. Addressed to the friends again.

65 sqq. What Elihu deprecates here is Job's hardness of tone and lack of humility in asserting his right. He ought to have been more ready to confess ignorance and take the attitude of a sinner.

Shall He requite on thine own terms, and say,
'Whether thou spurnest, whether thou choosest,
Be it thou, and not I,   70
'And, what thou knowest, speak'?
    Men of understanding will say to me,
And the strong wise man, hearkening to me;
'It is not in wisdom that Job hath spoken,
Nor have his words been in insight.   75
Would that Job might be tried to the utmost,
Because of his answers after the manner of
       wicked men;
For he addeth outrage to his sin;
He clappeth his hands among us,
And multiplieth words against God.'"   80

CHAP. XXXIV. 33-37.

68–71. This passage is one of the most obscure in the poem; the above seems to me its most probable meaning. I take it as Elihu's way of turning back upon himself Job's general arrogance toward God, which is to the friends the most offensive feature of Job's behavior.

73. *The wise man,* — it is in the interests of wisdom and in the dialect of the "wise men" that Elihu is speaking.

76 sqq. Although Elihu is ordinarily very courteous in addressing Job, yet here he brings forth the harshest seeming judgment that has been pronounced. We will remember, however, that he regards Job's affliction merely as a trial wherein the latter is to be brought to hear and accept an interpreter, through whom he is to be restored (section xxii. 84–89). What he wishes here, therefore, is that Job's arrogance, desperate as it is, may have a desperate enough remedy to cure it. It is not Job's death that he is wishing; it is the heroic treatment which will effectually humble him.

XXIV

ELIHU

AGAIN Elihu answered, and said:

I.

" Countest thou this for judgment,
When thou sayest, ' My justice is more than
    God's ' ? —
For thou sayest, What advantage hast thou ? —
' What am I profited more than by my sin ? ' 5
I will answer thee words,
And thy companions with thee.
  Look unto the heavens, and see,
And survey the skies — high above thee they
    are, —

CHAP. XXXV. 1–5.

LINE 2. *For judgment*, — that is, for a true discrimination of things, a right estimate of where justice lies between him and God.

3. *Thou sayest*, — that is, virtually. From the friends' point of view Job's complaint has involved such assertion.

7. Elihu's answer in this section is directed both to Job and the friends. It deals more with general truths, which it is of interest for all to know, than with Job's particular case.

8-15. To Elihu and the friends the heavens are the symbol

XXIV.   *ELIHU*   315

If thou sinnest, what workest thou against
    Him? ₁₀
And if thy transgressions be multiplied, what
    doest thou to Him?
If thou art righteous, what givest thou Him?
Or what receiveth He from thy hand?
It is to man such as thou that thy wickedness
    cometh,
And to the son of man thy righteousness. ₁₅

II.

" From the multitude of the oppressed men cry
    out ;
They groan because of the arm of the mighty.
Yet no one saith, ' Where is God my Maker,
Who giveth songs in the night ; —

CHAP. XXXV. 6-10.

of God's inaccessible distance. Eliphaz, in section xv. 22-27, has used this same feeling of God's remoteness to account for Job's imputed sin; and indeed he has brought forth in outline, and without application, this argument of Elihu's, section xv. 2-5. Elihu seems to adduce it here in order to rebuke Job for trying to judge God on human standards of justice and make Him like man. God is not one to be benefited or defrauded by man's little doings; hence Job's whole implied demand of reciprocal relations between God and man is a presumption.

16, 17. These two lines bring up, in very brief form, Job's complaint of the oppression of the poor by the wicked, which Elihu answers in his own way.

18-25. Elihu's explanation of this problem is similar to his

Who teacheth us more than the beasts of the
    earth, 20
And more than the fowls of heaven maketh us
    wise?'
Therefore it is He heareth not,
When they cry because of the pride of the
    wicked.
For surely, vanity will not God hear,
Nor will the Almighty regard it. 25
Yet no less when thou sayest thou discernest
    Him not,
The cause is before Him: wait thou for Him.
  And now, because He visiteth not in His
    anger,
And doth not strictly regard transgression, —
Job openeth his mouth in vanity, 30
And multiplieth words without knowledge."

Chap. XXXV. 11–16.

explanation of Job's affliction. When the poor are oppressed, it is their discipline, to draw them to God; if they fail to learn the lesson, their cry for help is vain.

20 sq. This question on the part of the poor implies doubt of any Power to give them more than a brutish life, and is an excuse for cherishing a lower existence than they are made for.

28–31. The upshot of Elihu's criticism in this section seems to be that Job is wrong in bringing God to the bar of justice and right, because it leaves God's failure to punish the wicked unexplained. Elihu is trying to justify God in all His ways, and to make His dark dealings clear too; and because Job honestly calls them insoluble, Job's words are vanity.

XXV

ELIHU

And Elihu continued, and said:

" Wait for me a little, and I will show thee;
For there are yet words for God.
I will fetch my knowledge from afar,
And to my Maker will I ascribe justice;
For of a surety my words are no lie; —
It is the Perfect in knowledge that is with thee.

I.

" Behold, God is mighty, yet despiseth not, —
Is mighty in strength of understanding.

CHAP. XXXVI. 1-5.

In the present section Elihu elaborates into a general doctrine that idea of submission which he has inculcated upon Job.

LINE 5. Elihu is much concerned to "justify the ways of God to man;" this in special reference to Job, whose affirmations of innocence it was, with the sequent implication of God's injustice to him, that kindled his wrath; section xxi.

7. *The Perfect in Knowledge*, — by this term Elihu identifies his thoughts with the mind of God; he is as confident of his doctrine as if it were a veritable oracle. A delicate touch of the author, — to make Elihu's conceit prepare his humiliation.

He will not let the wicked live; 10
And justice will He give to the afflicted.
He withdraweth not His eyes from the righteous;
But with kings upon the throne
He maketh them sit for ever, and they are exalted.
And if, bound in fetters, 15
They be taken in toils of affliction,
And He showeth them their deed,
And their transgressions, that they have been overweening,
And openeth their ear to discipline,
And speaketh, that they turn back from iniquity, — 20

CHAP. XXXVI. 6–10.

10, 11. These two lines comprise Elihu's doctrine, which is the general Wisdom doctrine, of God's final purpose. As it contemplates no adjustment of things beyond this life, it is merely the doctrine that Job has called in doubt, nor does it make any advance on what the friends have maintained.

15. But here begins Elihu's own resolution of the doctrine. The statement of the problem he draws from Job's case, which embodies the difficulty in point. Affliction, he says, is intended by God to produce confession of sin and a docile, obedient spirit, responsive to discipline. This too is quite consistent with the friends' system; for, as in their view man is of necessity corrupt, he can never fail to have sins to confess. And in general it contains a noble and helpful truth. But it falls short of the case of Job, who by the hypothesis is pure and upright, and who finds, both in his affliction and in the world, evils out of all proportion to any reasonable purpose

If then they hearken, and be obedient,
They shall fill out their days in good,
And their years in pleasantness.
And if they hearken not, they shall perish by the dart,
And they shall expire without knowledge. 25
Also the godless of heart, that cherish wrath,
That cry not out when He bindeth them, —
Their soul dieth in youth,
And their life is with the obscene.

He delivereth the afflicted by his affliction, 30
And openeth, by suffering, their ear;
And thee also He lureth from the jaws of distress,
Unto a broad place, where there is no straitness;
And the furnishing of thy table shall be full of fatness.

Chap. XXXVI. 11–16.

of justice or discipline. It still fails to answer the question, What of the man who, perfect in integrity and honest with himself, will not confess to a sin that he does not feel?

21–25. The end that Elihu contemplates is either restoration or utter ruin in death; his thoughts are bounded by this life, and leave no room for a solution beyond.

24. *The dart*, — Elihu's chosen symbol of God's vengeance and retribution; see section xxii. 75.

26–29. The same doctrine applied to the afflicted wicked; a repetition, essentially, of what Elihu has propounded, section xxiv. 16–25.

32. *And thee also,* — the thought gracefully turned from the

But hast thou filled the judgment of the wicked, 35
Judgment and justice shall lay hold of thee.
For beware lest anger stir thee up against the stroke,
And abundance of ransom shall not deliver thee.
Shall then thy cry set thee forth out of distress,
And all the resources of wealth? 40
  Sigh not thou for the night,
When the nations go up from their place.
Keep thyself, lest thou turn unto iniquity;
For thereto thou inclinest more than to affliction.

II.

"Behold, God worketh loftily in His power; 45

CHAP XXXVI. 17–22.

general to Job, by an idiom similar to section viii. 115, where see note.

  37. It is Job's "anger" (so they interpret his clear-eyed indignation) which is the greatest difficulty both to Elihu and to the friends; compare section iii. 46.

  41. This seems to refer to Job's wish for death, with its rest and its dark oblivion.

  44. Elihu strikes Job's balance as toward iniquity. He does not accuse him directly of sin, as do the friends; but in thus judging Job's inclination of spirit he is at one with them: he is as blind as they are to the real determination toward God which underlies all Job's earnest remonstrances and all his achievements of faith.

  45. At this point, it seems most reasonable to conclude,

Who is a teacher like unto Him?
Who hath laid upon Him His way?
And who saith, Thou hast done iniquity?
Take heed that thou magnify His work,
Which men celebrate in song. 50
All mankind gaze wonderingly thereon;
Mortal man beholdeth it from afar.
  Behold, God is exalted, and we know Him
      not;
The number of His years is unsearchable.
For He draweth up the water-drops, 55

CHAP. XXXVI. 22-27.

Elihu's attention is turned to the glory of God, perhaps by the impressiveness of a distant storm, which he employs as furnishing material for a didactic discourse.

47-50. The same view of God that Elihu has taken before; see section xxiii. 25 sq. A true enough view in itself; but it betrays, whether intentionally or not, the radical discordance between the friends and Job. The truth of God's resistless power over the world Job himself, far from disputing, affirms with all emphasis, as a point whereon he accepts their doctrine; see section viii. 15-56. But that, because God is mighty, all His dealings, whatever their mysterious inconsistency, must be called justice, — this, Job is too honest to avow, and the disposition to avow it blindly and indiscriminately, as Elihu is now doing, Job has censured in the friends, as the disposition to be special pleaders for God; see section viii. 63-76. So this didactic discourse of Elihu's, true and eloquent though it is, really opens the whole issue between the friends and Job, and prepares the two parties to appear before the God of the whirlwind in their contrasted spiritual attitudes.

55. With this line Elihu begins to recognize the storm as

And they distil rain in place of the mist;
Which then the skies pour down,
And drop upon men abundantly.
Yea, is there that understandeth the spreadings of the cloud,
The crashings of His pavilion? 60
Behold, He spreadeth thereon His light,
And the roots of the sea He covereth up;
For by them He judgeth the nations;
He giveth food in abundance.
Over both hands He wrappeth lightning, 65
And giveth it command where to strike.
His thunder-cry maketh report thereof,
The herd also, of the flame that ascendeth.
Yea, at this my heart trembleth,
And shuddereth from its place. 70
Hear ye, oh, hear the roar of His voice,
And the rumbling that goeth forth from His mouth.

CHAP. XXXVI. 27 — XXXVII. 2.

the occasion of his discourse; and while the storm is yet distant he can, in a leisurely manner, draw other objects into his disquisition, such as the sea, l. 62, snow and ice, ll. 80, 88.

63. God judges the nations, Elihu says, by clouds and rain, which indicate His will by giving or withholding their supply.

68. This seems to refer to the perturbation of beasts in a thunder-storm, or at the approach of a hurricane.

69-72. These lines seem to indicate definitely the approach of the storm, at which he is disturbed, but not yet enough to intermit his discourse.

Under all the heavens He sendeth it forth,
And His lightning to the edges of the earth.
After it resoundeth a voice, — 75
He thundereth with the voice of His majesty,
Nor doth He stay them when His voice is heard.
God thundereth with His voice marvelously,
Doing great things, and we comprehend Him not.
For to the snow He saith, Be thou upon the earth, 80
And the rain-flood, yea, the flood of His mighty rains.
On the hand of every man He setteth a seal,
That all mortals whom He hath made may know.
And the beast goeth into his covert,
And in his lair abideth. 85
Out of His chamber cometh the hurricane,

CHAP. XXXVII. 3–9.

77. *Nor doth He stay them*, — the reference of *them* is obscure; perhaps it means the lightnings.

80 sqq. In this paragraph the signs of the coming whirlwind, or hurricane, become more definite; which, so long as he can look upon them calmly, Elihu associates didactically with snow and ice.

82. God *setteth a seal* on men's hands; that is, in the winter and in the rainy season causes them to suspend work and activity, going into their houses as the beasts go into their coverts.

And cold from the cloud-dispersers.
From the breath of God ice is given;
And the broadness of the waters is straitened.
Also He loadeth the cloud with moisture; 90
He spreadeth the lightning-cloud abroad;
And at His guidance it turneth itself about,
To do all that He commandeth it,
On the face of the terrestrial world;
Whether for a scourge, or for the land, — 95
If for mercy He causeth it to come.

III.

"Give ear unto this, O Job;
Stand, and ponder the marvelous things of God.
Knowest thou how God layeth command upon them,
And maketh shine forth the light of His cloud? 100
Knowest thou the poisings of the thick cloud,
The wonders of the Perfect in knowledge? —

CHAP. XXXVII. 9-16.

87. *The cloud-dispersers,* — the clear cold winds that drive away the clouds and leave the heavens serene.

97 sqq. Elihu's didactic spirit rises with the oncoming of the storm, until it reaches its highest pitch of patronizing wisdom, even to the extent of naming again (l. 102) the Perfect in knowledge, with whom, as he has previously identified his thought (l. 7), he now identifies the portents and marvels of the storm.

Thou whose garments are hot,
Because from the south the earth lieth sultry
    still, —
Canst thou spread out with Him the skies,   105
Firm, as a molten mirror?
. . . Oh teach us what we may say to Him!
We cannot order it — it groweth so dark . . .
Hath one told Him that I am speaking? . . .
Or hath a man said . . . for he shall be
    swallowed up!   110

.   "   .   .   .   .

And now they no longer see the light, —
That splendor in the skies,
For a wind hath passed, and scattered them.
. . . From the north a golden glory cometh! . . .

CHAP. XXXVII. 17–22.

    103, 104. One sign of the whirlwind, which is preceded by sultry heat and stillness.

    106. Another sign, — the peculiar metallic appearance of the sky.

    107. At this point, as it would seem, the storm bursts upon them, and with such exceptional features that Elihu must regard it as betokening the immediate presence of Jehovah. For this he is not prepared, nor has any of his discourse manifested either desire for or conception of such a thing. His succeeding words, accordingly, are confused and incoherent, indicating a vague terror of impending destruction.

    111. With the passing of the mysterious light which accompanied the storm, Elihu's spirit rebounds, and in comparative calm he is resuming his disquisition.

    114. *From the north*, — a new quarter of the heavens (compare l. 104), and with manifestations wholly portentous. —

Oh, with God is terrible majesty! 115
The Almighty — we have not found Him out;
Vast in power, and in judgment,
And in abundance of righteousness; —
He will not afflict;
Therefore do men fear Him; 120
He regardeth not any wise in their own con-
    ceit."

Chap. XXXVII. 22-24.

A golden glory, — literally, *gold;* but in this connection it can hardly refer to anything but the exceptionally splendid light.

116. At which Elihu begins to retract his pretensions, and in a kind of wheedling terror to bring God's mercies to mind, as if in a confused attempt thereby to turn away the wrath that seems so imminent. Quite in contrast to the self-respecting boldness of Job when he took his life in his hand (section viii. 80), in order to speak out to God's face what was in him.

121. *Wise in their own conceit*, — literally, *wise of heart*. Thus he characterizes himself, making thereby abject confession of the futile pretensions of his wisdom.

This is the last of Elihu. He is self-judged. Though he has said many noble things, and represented the highest and the truest that the friends could bring forth from the treasures of their Wisdom, yet, because of its unspiritual and essentially selfish basis in their character, it does not enable them to stand before the searching light of God's immediate presence. A God who is undesired is unbearable; it is only aspiring love and purity of heart that can endure His face.

XXVI

THE LORD

AND the LORD answered Job out of the whirlwind, and said:

"Who is this, darkening counsel
With words, — but without knowledge?
Gird up thy loins now, like a strong man,
And I will ask thee; and inform Me thou.   5

CHAP. XXXVIII. 1-3.

The first words from the whirlwind dismiss Elihu abruptly with a judgment just adapted to his pretensions. Full of words he confessedly has been (section xxii. 29); but to set up as the mouthpiece of the Perfect in knowledge (section xxv. 7) is a presumption too great to pass unrebuked. "Without knowledge," — thus on Elihu the Divine verdict is passed.

Not so with Job. He is left rather to judge himself. From his impregnable citadel of integrity he has looked into the world of God's mysterious dealings, and while blinking none of its difficulties his faith has imaged a God who is his Friend and the Friend of righteousness. One difficulty remained, however, which caused him dismay (section xvi. 24-33): the sight of God's changeless, inexorable, inscrutable work in the world, where wicked and righteous live together in the same apparently undiscriminating government. To this problem we may regard the LORD's discourse as addressed; not by

I.

"Where wast thou, when I laid the founda-
    tions of the earth?
Declare, if by knowledge thou understandest:
Who set its measurements, so thou knowest;
Or who stretched the line over it?
On what were its piers deep-laid,   10
Or who placed its corner-stone, —
When the morning-stars sang together,
And all the sons of God shouted for joy?
    Who shut up the sea with doors,
When it brake forth — issued from the
    womb, —   15
When I made cloud its garment,

CHAP. XXXVIII. 4-9.

way of a narrow answer why, but rather, by passing in review before Job the greatness and variety of created things, it raises him to a point where he has a broader horizon, and can better judge of his position in the sum of things. His vision is right (compare section xxx. 6), therefore he shall have more to see; "to him that hath shall be given."

LINES 6 sqq. This first part of the address deals with the transcendent things: earth and sea, light and darkness, — things too great and too ancient to reveal their origin to man. The earth is represented under the figure of a vast building.

13. The sons of God are mentioned in the Prologue (ll. 22, 89) as God's ministering spirits, reporting on themselves and the creation.

14 sqq. The sea, under the figure of a vast Being, born of Chaos, full of proud ambition, but submissively in the power of God.

And thick gloom its swaddling-band, —
When I established over it my decree,
And set bars and doors,
And said, 'Thus far shalt thou come, and no farther, 20
And here the pride of thy waves shall cease'?
  Hast thou, since thy days began, commanded the morning,
And taught the day-spring his place,
That he should lay hold of the skirts of the earth,
And the wicked be shaken out of it? 25
That it should be changed as clay under the seal,
And all things stand forth as in festal attire?
That their light should be withholden from the wicked,
And the uplifted arm be broken?
  Hast thou made thy way to the sources of the sea, 30
And walked in the recesses of the deep?

CHAP. XXXVIII. 9-16.

23. The Day-spring, or Dawn, personified as one who "seizes the coverlet under which the earth has slept at its four ends and shakes the evil-doers out of it like flies; upon which form and color return to the earth, as clay (a Babylonian image) receives a definite form from the seal, and as the sad-colored night-wrapper is exchanged for the bright, embroidered holiday-robe." — *Cheyne.*

28. *Their light,* — which is darkness, their deeds being evil.

Have the gates of death been revealed to thee?
And the gates of the shadow of death — hast
    thou seen them?
Hast thou comprehended the breadths of the
    earth?.
Tell, if thou knowest it all, —   35
Where is the way to where light dwelleth,
And darkness, where is its place, —
That thou shouldst trace it to its boundary,
And shouldst be acquainted with the paths to
    its house.
Thou know! — then thou wast already born, 40
And the number of thy days must be great!

II.

"Hast thou visited the treasuries of the snow?
And the treasuries of the hail, hast thou seen
    them, —
Which I have reserved for the time of distress,
For the day of onset and war?   45
  Where is the way to where the light is dis-
    persed,
When the East spreadeth abroad. over the
    earth?

Chap. xxxviii. 17-24.

45. Compare Joshua x. 11. The hail is represented as stored up in treasuries for direct use in human affairs.

47. Compare Tennyson: —

"The wither'd moon
Smote by the fresh beam of the springing east."

Who hath riven a channel for the rain-flood,
And a way for the lightning of the thunder?
To bring rain on a land where no man is, 50
On the desert, where no son of Adam dwelleth;
To satisfy waste and wilderness,
And to cause the springing grass to grow?
  Is there indeed a father to the rain?
Or who hath begotten the drops of dew? 55
Out of whose womb came the ice,
And the hoar-frost of heaven, who brought it forth?
As in stone the waters hide themselves,
And the face of the deep congealeth.
  Canst thou bind the fetters of the Pleiades, 60
Or loose the cords of Orion?
Canst thou bring forth the Signs in their season,
And canst thou guide the Bear with her sons?
Knowest thou the laws of the heavens,

CHAP. XXXVIII. 25-33.

50, 51. Yet quite apart from human requirements, too, God's natural powers are working in silence, doing just as great and beneficent things where there is no eye to see.

60–63. In these lines there may be allusions to mythological ideas now unknown; nor is the meaning of all the names certain. The name of Orion, the "fool-hardy" giant, seems to have come from some such myth. *The Signs* (*Mazzaroth*) are supposably the signs of the Zodiac.

Or wilt thou dispose their empire over the
    earth?
Wilt thou raise thy voice unto the cloud,
That a flood of waters may cover thee?
Wilt thou send forth lightnings, that they may
    go,
And may say unto thee, Here we are?
Who hath put wisdom into their reins?
Or who hath given understanding to the me-
    teor?
Who numbereth the clouds in wisdom?
And the bottles of heaven, who poureth them
    out, —
When dust is molten into a mass,
And clods cleave fast together?

III.

"Wilt thou hunt prey for the lioness,
And still the craving of the young lions, —

CHAP. XXXVIII. 33-39.

65. The always prevalent idea taken for granted, that the heavens have influence on the seasons and affairs of earth.

70, 71. This passage, which is very obscure in the original, is here given in what from derivation and context seems the most probable meaning.

76 sqq. The succeeding examples illustrate the variety of the providential care and wisdom manifest in the animal creation, and by contrast man's utter lack of wisdom either to control or to interpret. The lions and ravens are fed, yet by means wholly inscrutable to man.

When they lie crouching in their lairs,
When they lurk in the covert for ambush?
   Who provideth his prey for the raven,   80
When his young cry out unto God,
And wander here and there, without meat?
   Knowest thou the bearing-time of the wild goats of the rock?
Wilt thou direct the travail of the hinds?
Is it thou who numberest the months they fulfill,   85
And hast thou known the time for them to calve?
They bow themselves, let their young cleave the womb,
And thus they cast away their labor-pangs.
Their young ones fatten, grow up in the field,
Go forth, and return not again.   90
   Who hath sent forth the wild-ass free,
And the bands of the fleet one who hath loosed?
Whose house I have made the wilderness,
And the salt-waste his lodging-place.

CHAP. XXXVIII. 40 — XXXIX. 6.

83 sqq. The wild goats live a complete life, from birth to death, in a Care just adapted to them, yet far apart from the knowledge of man.

91 sqq. In the wild-ass is a freedom that scorns all control; yet there is some mysterious Wisdom that has "sent him forth free."

He laugheth at the tumult of the city, 95
And the clamors of the driver will he not hear.
The choice spots of the mountain are his pasture;
And after every green thing he searcheth.
　Will the wild-ox be content to serve thee,
Or will he pass the night at thy crib? 100
Wilt thou bind the wild-ox with his cord in the furrow,
Or will he harrow the valleys after thee?
Wilt thou trust him because his strength is great,
And wilt thou commit unto him thy toil?
Wilt thou rely on him to bring home thy seed,
And to gather thy threshing-floor? 106
　The wing of the ostrich beateth joyously,
But is it a kindly pinion and plume?
For she leaveth her eggs to the earth,
And warmeth them upon the dust, 110
And forgetteth that a foot may crush them,

CHAP. XXXIX. 7-15.

99 sqq. In the wild-ox, likewise, we see provided in nature a strength whose purpose no domestication can utilize or human insight comprehend.

107 sqq. In the ostrich is seen a variety of contradictory traits, which no man is wise enough to reconcile and explain. How interpret the Wisdom that would see fit to create a bird at once wonderfully endowed with swiftness, to escape her enemies, yet so foolish as to leave her young at the mercy of every hostile foot?

And that the wild beast of the field may trample them.
She dealeth hardly with her young, as though they were not hers.
In vain her labor, being without fear;
For God hath denied her wisdom, 115
Nor hath she portion in understanding.
Yet what time she lasheth her pinions on high,
She scorneth the horse and his rider.
  Givest thou might unto the horse,
Or clothest thou his neck with the quivering mane? 120
Dost thou make him spring as a locust?
The glory of his snorting is terrible.
He paweth in the valley, and rejoiceth in strength;
He goeth to meet the weapons of war.
He mocketh at fear, and is not dismayed; 125
And he turneth not back for the sword.
Upon him rattleth the quiver, —
Flaming of spear and javelin.
With rage and fury he devoureth the earth,

CHAP. XXXIX. 15-24.

119 sqq. The war-horse, which seems to be created for battle, and to delight in the turmoil from which most animals would flee, was an object of peculiar wonder to the Hebrew mind, perhaps on account of the scarcity of horses in Palestine. There is no other description of animals in this section in which the imaginative spirit expresses itself in such bold and lofty terms.

And he standeth not still, — for it is the voice
 of the trumpet.   130
At every trumpet-blast he saith, Aha!
And from afar he scenteth battle,
Thunder of captains, and shouting.
 Is it by thy wisdom that the hawk soareth
  aloft,
And spreadeth her wings toward the south? 135
Or is it at thy word that the eagle mounteth
 upward,
And that he buildeth his nest on high?
He dwelleth on the rock, and maketh his home
 there,
On the tooth of the rock, and the strong hold.
From thence he spyeth out his prey;   140
His eyes discern it from afar.
And his young ones suck up blood;
And where the slain are, there is he."

CHAP. XXXIX. 24-30.

 134 sqq. From one source of wisdom, which cannot be man's, the hawk receives the instinct that directs her southward, and the eagle is guided to his rocky home, whence he can spy out prey.

 139. *The tooth of the rock,* — the Hebrew metaphor for the sharp-pointed rocky summit.

IV.

So the LORD answered Job, and said:

"Will the reprover contend with the Almighty? 145
He that censureth God, let him answer it."

CHAP. XL. 1, 2.

144. This should not be printed as the beginning of a new discourse, as is generally done; it simply summarizes and applies the foregoing section.

145. Job has desired to "bring his cause" before God (see section xvi. 4-13); this indeed has been his most constant longing, and for this we left him all ready, when he ceased speaking (section xx. 186-192). Has he still the same desire, after all this view of the various Wisdom inlaid in nature? Will he still "contend" (the legal term, see section vi. 4, note) as a reprover and critic, after he has seen so much that is beyond and above him? The following words of Robert Buchanan interpret well the significance of the LORD's question here, as related to the review of creation that has just been given: "Because there is sin and misery in the world, because hearts ache and bodies die, shall we turn upon this sublimely exhaustless Being, and demand explanation? Is it not something to know how He delights in making, in endless creating, and that One who thus delights cannot be cruel? The explanation will come."

146. He that is great enough to "censure," to pass judgment on God, is great enough to answer his own questions; if to him God's way is not self-justifying, no answer from outside himself would justify it.

XXVII

JOB

AND Job answered the LORD, and said:

"Behold, I am too small: what shall I answer
    Thee?
I lay my hand upon my mouth.
Once have I spoken, and I will not answer;
And twice, but I will not add thereto."

CHAP. XL. 3-5.

LINE 2. The speech from the whirlwind has wrought its purpose thus far: it has made Job see God's world in something of its true perspective, and that he is not the centre of the system, but only a very small unit in the infinite sum of things. He does not presume to present his cause; how could he, so small, give it its true relation to the vast universe of God's working?

4. It is to be observed, however, that Job does not retract what he has said; he simply ventures, with humility and awe, to let it remain before God just as it has been spoken.

XXVIII

THE LORD

AND the LORD answered Job out of the whirlwind, and said:

" Gird up thy loins now, like a strong man;
I will ask thee; and inform Me thou.

I.

" Wilt thou even disannul my right?
Wilt thou condemn me, that thou mayest be justified? 5

CHAP. XL. 6-8.

LINES 4, 5. Job has come to see that he has no wisdom wherewith to enter the lists against the infinite Wisdom of the world, and pass judgment on what is so complex. The LORD now takes him one step further back, and asks him why he should separate God's cause from his own, as if they must be antagonists. Is there not room, in such a universe, for both God's right and Job's? Nay, and such belligerent assertion of a mortal's "rights,"—which assertion we will remember Job has not yet withdrawn,—is *that* the attitude for utter weakness to assume before infinite Power? Questioning like this, and from such a source, fulfills Elihu's wish (section xxiii. 76) as no words of the friends could do; it

Doth an arm like God's belong to thee?
And wilt thou thunder with a voice like His?
Put on now thy grandeur and majesty,
And array thyself with splendor and glory;
Pour forth the overflowings of thy wrath,   10
And behold all that is lofty, — and abase it;
Behold all that is lofty, — bring it low,
And tread down the wicked where they stand.
Hide them in the dust together;
Bind up their faces in the hidden place;   15
And then will I with praise confess to thee
That thine own right hand can save thee.

II.

" Behold now Behemoth, which I made along with thee:

CHAP. XL. 9-15.

"tries Job to the utmost," revealing and refining the real gold of his character; compare section xvi. 19. This is doubtless its purpose, rather than to prove Job in the wrong.

6. The previous discourse of the LORD'S has treated of the various aspects of Divine wisdom; this has to do more with portrayals of God's power. With the power of God, as with the wisdom, Job must measure himself.

17. As Job's assumed wisdom ought to be sufficient to resolve its own problems (section xxvi. 146), so Job's assumed power, implied in this attitude of condemning God for the sake of his own rights, ought to be sufficient to save him. Why should he be selfish any farther than he is really sufficient to himself?

18. " The word *behemoth* may be a Heb. *plur.* of intensity, signifying *the beast* or *ox, par excellence;* but probably it is an

Grass, like the ox, doth he eat.
Behold now his strength in his loins,   20
And his power in the muscles of his belly.
He moveth his tail like a cedar;
The sinews of his thigh are knit together;
His bones are tubes of brass;
His ribs like a bar of iron.   25
He — chief of the ways of God; —
Only He that made him can make His sword
    approach him.
Yet the mountains furnish him food;
And all the beasts of the field may sport there.
Under the lotus-trees he lieth,   30
In the covert of reed and fen.
The lotus-trees weave him a shadow;
And the willows of the brook encompass him.
Behold, the river rageth, and he trembleth not;
He is steadfast though a Jordan rush against
    his mouth.   35

CHAP. XL. 15–23.

Egyptian name Hebraized. It has been supposed to be the Egyptian *p-ehe-mout*, i. e., 'the *water* or *river ox*. At all events the animal referred to appears to be the hippopotamus, or river-horse, of the Greeks." — *Davidson*.

   26–29. A beast of immense power, yet inoffensive; unsubduable by any but God, yet living in harmony with other beasts.

   34–37. Nor is he lacking in courage: he resists fearlessly the raging of the river; yet he lets himself be captured and subdued by man. Such is one manifestation of God's power in nature.

Yet before his very eyes men capture him,
And pierce through his nose with snares.

III.

" Wilt thou draw out Leviathan with a hook?
Or with a cord wilt thou press down his tongue?
Wilt thou put a rope into his nose,   40
Or with a spike bore through his jaw?
Will he multiply supplications unto thee,
Or will he speak unto thee soft things?
Will he make a covenant with thee,
That thou mayest take him as a servant for ever?   45
Wilt thou sport with him as with a sparrow,
And bind him for thy maidens?
Will the fisher-bands traffic over him,
And retail him among the Canaanites?
Wilt thou fill his skin with barbed irons,   50
And with fish-spears his head?
Lay but thine hand upon him, —
And of battle think thereafter no more!

CHAP. XL. 24 — XLI. 8.

38. *Leviathan*, — probably the crocodile, the animal that answers most nearly to the present description, though some of the details are idealized.

49. The Canaanites, or Phœnicians, were the typical merchants of antiquity; so that the words Canaanite and merchant became almost synonymous; see Zechariah xiv. 21; Proverbs xxxi. 24.

53. That is, one who attempts to vanquish him once will never live to join battle with him again.

Behold, one's hope is belied;
Nay, at very sight of him one is cast down; 55
None so desperate as to stir him up, —
And who is he then that will take his stand before ME?
Who hath first put Me in his debt, that I should requite?
Nay, under all the heaven — whosoever he is, he is mine.
I will not pass over in silence his limbs, 60
Nor the fame of his strength, nor the beauty of his build.
Who will uncover the front of his array?

CHAP. XLI. 9–13.

54. That is, one's hope to capture or subdue him.

56. Here, then, is a beast no greater in power, perhaps, than behemoth, yet wholly contrasted in traits, being utterly unsubduable; this beast also, as well as behemoth, being the handiwork of God, made along with man.

57–59. The lesson of these portrayals drawn. Both beasts are vastly more powerful than man, the one mild, the other fierce, yet both owing all they are to God. Shall man alone, who belongs to God in the same sum of things, bring to his Maker an unpaid demand? In all these things, has God left man's life unprovided for? We are reminded of the lesson drawn in Isaiah xl. 26–28.

60 sqq. To me there is no other passage in the Book of Job so doubtful as is the remainder of this section. All the rest of the book has the unity of tissue belonging to one literary idea; and at this point the argument naturally culminates. Not that ll. 60–105 are discordant with the previous; they simply seem like a later addition put on to satisfy some

Into that twofold bridle who will enter?
The gates of his face who shall open?
The circuits of his teeth are terror. 65
A pride are the rows of his shields,
A seal each one, shut close and bound.
One cometh so near to the other
That no air can come between them;
Each to his fellow, they are close joined; 70
They cleave so together that they cannot be sundered.
His neesings flash forth light,
And his eyes are like the eyelids of the morning.
From his mouth go forth burning torches,—
Sparks of fire issue forth. 75
Out of his nostrils goeth smoke,
Like a pot kindled, and like a rush-fire.
His breath setteth coals aflame,

CHAP. XLI. 13-21.

writer's love of description, but not adding to the argument either in idea or in emotional effect.

63. His rows of teeth, "the term 'bridle' referring particularly perhaps to the corners of his jaws."

66. The rows of his shields are the crocodile's armor of scales.

72. *His neesings*,—the breath from his nostrils, which in the sun is said to flash light.

73. "In the Egyptian hieroglyphs the eyes of the crocodile are a symbol of the dawn." — *Davidson*. This same expression, "eyelids of the morning," is used in section ii. 20, to signify the dawn.

And a tongue of flame issueth from his mouth.
On his neck lodgeth Might, 80
And before him Horror leapeth.
The flanks of his flesh cleave together,
Molten upon him, immovable.
His heart is molten firm, like a stone; —
Yea, molten firm, like a nether millstone. 85
When he riseth up, mighty ones are afraid;
They lose their senses for terror.
Though one reach him with the sword, it holdeth not;
Nor the spear, nor the dart, nor the coat of mail.
He accounteth iron as straw, 90
And brass as rotten wood.
The son of the bow cannot make him flee;
To chaff are sling-stones turned before him;
As chaff too he regardeth a club,
And he laugheth at the shaking of a spear. 95
His under parts are sharpened shards;

CHAP. XLI. 21-30.

82. "The parts beneath his neck and belly, which in most animals are soft and pendulous; in him they are firm and hard." — *Davidson.*

92. *The son of the bow,* — the Hebrew metaphor for *arrow.*

96, 97. "The scales of his belly, though smoother than those on the back, still are sharp, particularly those under the tail, and leave an impression on the mire where he has lain as if a sharp threshing-sledge with teeth had stood on it or gone over it (Isaiah xli. 15)." — *Ib.*

He spreadeth out a threshing-wain over the mire.
He maketh the deep to boil like a cauldron;
The sea he maketh like a pot of ointment.
After him shineth a pathway; 100
One would think the deep turned to hoary hair.
There is none on earth his master, —
He — created without fear.
On all that is high he looketh, —
He — king over all the sons of pride." 105

CHAP. XLI. 30-34.

105. In section xix. 62, the "proud beast of prey" is literally "the sons of pride;" and here doubtless the expression refers to the proud beasts.

XXIX

JOB

AND Job answered the LORD, and said :

"I know that Thou canst do everything ;
Nor is withholden from Thee any design.
'Who is this that hideth counsel without knowledge ?' —
Therefore have I uttered, and understood not, 5
Things too wonderful for me, and I knew not.
'Hear now,' Thou sayest, 'and I will speak ;
I will ask thee ; and inform Me thou ;' —

CHAP. XLII. 1-4.

LINES 2, 3. Job's eyes are open at last to perceive the universality both of God's power and wisdom; an all-pervading Care in which he is content to take his place, hushing all complaints and trusting where he cannot see. This is the grand outcome of Job's experience; an outcome not merely in a completed argument, but in a chastened, obedient, enlightened character.

4. Quotation of the question regarding Elihu, section xxvi. 2, 3; which Job humbly takes up and applies to himself, thus virtually assuming the burden not only of what he has rashly uttered, but of the short-sighted speculations of his friends also.

7, 8. The LORD's words to Job; sections xxvi. 5; xxviii. 3.

I had heard of Thee by hearing of the ear,
But now mine eye seeth Thee;   10
Wherefore I loathe me, and repent,
In dust and ashes."

Chap. xlii. 5, 6.

9-12. The past hard experience has brought Job immeasurably nearer to God. Between this and his former spiritual state there is all the difference between sight and hearsay. God is no more a conventional God, the God of a philosophy, but the real and actual Presence after which Job has longed; and the attitude that befits such communion is not the self-complacent attitude of one who has triumphed, but the lowly self-abasement of repentant, trustful love.

Job's repentance is not to be referred to some definite error or event in which he has been proved wrong; it is due to that feeling of earthly impurity which cannot but rise when the heart is laid bare before infinite Holiness, — like the feeling which prompted the poet's prayer at the end of his work: —

> "Forgive what seem'd my sin in me;
> What seem'd my worth since I began."

XXX

EPILOGUE

I.

AND so it was, after the LORD had spoken these words to Job, that the LORD said to Eliphaz the Temanite, " My wrath is kindled against thee, and against thy two friends; for ye have not spoken concerning Me that   5

CHAP. XLII. 7.

The Epilogue, to which many have objected, is not without its justification in logical necessity. It does not indeed portray Job's real reward, which was inward and spiritual; but it does reveal to his unspiritual friends the one vindication which they have shown themselves able to appreciate, — the vindication of prosperity in this life. If they could so confidently promise restoration as the reward of his coming to God by their prescribed way of repentance and confession of sin, surely no smaller or less palpable blessing should follow his brave maintenance of his righteous ways until God Himself pronounces his course right.

LINE 5. *That which is right*, — the whole trend of their words toward God (for it is literally, " Ye have not spoken *to* Me ") has been wrong; for it has had its spring in a selfish desire to secure God's favor by indiscriminate praise (see section viii. 63–76), and that selfish desire has led them to deny Job's evident integrity, to manufacture for him a sin of which he was not guilty, and to deny the obvious prosperity of the which is right, as hath my servant Job. And now take unto you seven bullocks and seven rams, and go to my servant Job, and offer a burnt-offering for yourselves, and my servant Job will pray for you; for his face will I accept, — lest I deal with you after your folly. For ye have not spoken concerning me that which is right, as my servant Job hath."

And Eliphaz the Temanite, and Bildad the Shuhite, and Zophar the Naamathite went and did as the LORD spake unto them; and the LORD accepted the face of Job.

And the LORD turned the captivity of Job when he prayed for his friends. And the LORD added to all that had been Job's twofold.

CHAP. XLII. 7-10.

wicked in the world. On the other hand, Job's words, bold and outspoken though they were, have been honest, speaking the truth as he saw truth, and charged through and through with loyalty to what is just and loving and Godlike.

10. Job's intercession for the friends is a remarkable fulfillment of what they promised him he might do if he would " reconcile himself " with God; see section xv. 52, 58, 59.

15, 16. The *three* friends are mentioned; why not Elihu also, who championed their cause? Because he has already judged himself. There would be the same propriety in making him appear again that there would be in making a character in a drama who has just died reappear and receive the plaudits of the audience.

19. This is merely the fulfillment of the friends' numerous

XXX. *EPILOGUE* 351

II.

And there came to him all his brethren, and all his sisters, and all who had known him before; and they ate bread with him in his house, and mourned with him, and comforted him for all the evil that the Lord had brought upon him. And they gave him, each man a kesita, and each man a ring of gold.

And the Lord blessed the latter end of Job more than his beginning; for he had fourteen thousand sheep, and six thousand camels, and a thousand yoke of oxen, and a thousand she-asses. And he had seven sons and three daughters. And he called the name of the first daughter Jemima, and the name of the second Kezia, and the name of the third Keren-happuch; and in all the land there were not found women so fair as the daughters of Job; and their father gave them inheritance among their brethren.

Chap. XLII. 11-15.

promises; see sections iii. 78-97; v. 8-14; vii. 25-38; xv. 40-59; xxii. 90-94.

29. *A kesita,*— an uncoined piece of money, which was reckoned by weight; Genesis xxxiii. 19; Joshua xxiv. 32. The mention of the *kesita*, which evidently belonged to patriarchal times, is perhaps one mark of the author's imitation of patriarchal customs.

III.

And Job lived after this a hundred and forty years; and he saw his sons and his sons' sons, four generations. And Job died, 45 old and full of days.

CHAP. XLII. 16, 17.

43. Job's long life, conformed to the generous patriarchal standard, is one of the illustrations of that slight framework of legend on which our author presumably built; a framework that it would be a task both baffling and thankless to reconstruct, because the whole soul of the poem is preëminently an outgrowth of the Wisdom thinking. Its interest for us lies in its invention rather than in its legendary basis.

45. Compare Eliphaz's promise, section iii. 96, 97.

Volumes of Criticism on Life.

Fannie Nichols Benjamin.
The Sunny Side of Shadow. Reveries of a Convalescent. 18mo, $1.00.

Dangerous Tendencies
in American Life, and Other Papers. 16mo, gilt top, $1.25.

Thomas Davidson.
Prolegomena to In Memoriam. With an Index to the Poem. Crown 8vo, gilt top, $1.25.

Ralph Waldo Emerson.
Conduct of Life. 12mo, gilt top, $1.50.

Charles Carroll Everett.
Poetry, Comedy, and Duty. Crown 8vo, gilt top, $1.50.

CONTENTS: I. Poetry; The Imagination; The Philosophy of Poetry; The Poetic Aspect of Nature; The Tragic Forces in Life and Literature. II. Comedy; The Philosophy of the Comic. III. The Ultimate Facts of Ethics; The New Ethics. IV. Conclusion: Poetry, Comedy, and Duty, considered in their Relation to One Another.

John Fiske.
The Destiny of Man. 16mo, gilt top, $1.00.

The Idea of God, as affected by Modern Knowledge. With Notes, etc. 16mo, gilt top, $1.00.

John F. Genung.
Tennyson's In Memoriam. Its Purpose and its Structure. A Study. Crown 8vo, gilt top, $1.25.

The Epic of the Inner Life. Being the Book of Job, translated anew. With Introductory Study, Notes, etc. Crown 8vo, gilt top.

Applied Christianity. Moral Aspects of Social Questions. 16mo, gilt top, $1.25.

CONTENTS: Christianity and Wealth; Is Labor a Commodity? The Strength and Weakness of Socialism; Is it Peace or War? The Wage-Workers and the Churches; Three Dangers; Christianity and Social Science; Christianity and Popular Amusements; Christianity and Popular Education.

William Elliot Griffis, D. D.
The Lily among Thorns. A Study of the Song of Solomon. 16mo, $1.25; in white cloth, gilt top, $1.50.

Oliver Wendell Holmes.
Pages from an Old Volume of Life. A Collection of Essays. 1857-1881. Including Soundings from the Atlantic, and Mechanism in Thought and Morals, etc. Crown 8vo, gilt top, $2.00.

Rossiter Johnson (editor).
Life. Vol. 4 of Little Classics. New Edition, bound in new and artistic style. 18mo, $1.00.

Thomas Starr King.
Substance and Show, and other Lectures. Edited, with Introduction, by E. P. Whipple. New Edition. 12mo, gilt top, $1.50.

George Henry Lewes.
Problems of Life and Mind. 5 vols. 8vo. Vols. 1, 2, and 3, each $3.00; Vol. 4, $2.00; Vol. 5, $3.00. The set, $14.00.
Vols. 1 and 2. First Series. The Foundation of a Creed.

CONTENTS: Vol. 1. Part I. The Method of Science and its Application to Metaphysics. Part II. The Rules of Philosophizing. Problem I. The Limitations of Knowledge.

Vol. 2. Problem II. The Principles of Certitude. Problem III. From the Known to the Unknown; Problem IV. Matter and Force; Problem V. Force and Cause; Problem VI. The Absolute in the Correlations of Feeling and Motion.

Vol. 3. Second Series. The Physical Basis of Mind.
Vols. 4 and 5. Third Series.

CONTENTS: Vol. 4. The Study of Psychology.
Vol. 5. Mind as a Function of the Organism; The Sphere of

Sense and Logic of Feeling; The Sphere of Intellect and Logic of Signs.

Elisha Mulford.
The Republic of God: An Institute of Theology. 8vo, $2.00.

> We do not remember that this country has lately produced a speculative work of more originality and force. . . . The book is a noble one — broad-minded, deep, breathing forth an ever-present consciousness of things unseen. — *The Critic* (New York).

William Mountford.
Euthanasy; or, Happy Talks towards the End of Life. New Edition. Crown 8vo, gilt top, $2.00.

Rev. Theodore T. Munger.
On the Threshold. Familiar Lectures to Young People. 16mo, gilt top, $1.00.

> A book of thoroughly sensible, judicious, sympathetic, helpful talks to young People on Purpose, Friends and Companions, Manners, Thrift, Self-Reliance and Courage, Health, Reading and Intellectual Life, Amusements, and Faith.

Elizabeth Stuart Phelps.
The Struggle for Immortality. 16mo, $1.25.

> CONTENTS: What is a Fact? Is God good? What does Revelation reveal? The Struggle for Immortality; The Christianity of Christ; Psychical Opportunity; The Psychical Wave.

Agnes Repplier.
Books and Men. 16mo, gilt top, $1.25.

> CONTENTS: Children, Past and Present; On the Benefits of Superstition; What Children Read; The Decay of Sentiment; Curiosities of Criticism; Some Aspects of Pessimism; The Cavalier.

Horace E. Scudder.
Men and Letters. Essays in Characterization and Criticism. 12mo, gilt top, $1.25.

> CONTENTS: Elisha Mulford; Longfellow and his Art; A Modern Prophet; Landor as a Classic; Dr. Muhlenberg; American History on the Stage; The Shaping of Excelsior; Emerson's Self; Aspects of Historical Work; Anne Gilchrist; The Future of Shakespeare.

Newman Smyth.
Social Problems. Three Sermons for Workingmen. 8vo, paper covers, 20 cents.

Henry D. Thoreau.

Walden: or, Life in the Woods. 12mo, gilt top, $1.50. In Riverside Aldine Series, 2 vols. 16mo, $2.00.

CONTENTS: Economy; Where I Lived and What I Lived for; Reading; Sounds; Solitude; Visitors; The Bean-Field; The Village; The Ponds; Baker Farm; Higher Laws; Brute Neighbors; House-Warming; Former Inhabitants and Winter Visitors; The Pond in Winter; Spring; Conclusion.

Kate Gannett Wells.

About People. 18mo, $1.25.

CONTENTS: Average People; Individuality; Striving; Loyalty and Liberality; Transitional Woman; Personal Influence; Who's Who; Caste in American Society.

Edwin P. Whipple.

Literature and Life. 12mo, gilt top, $1.50.

CONTENTS: Authors in their Relations to Life; Novels and Novelists; Charles Dickens; Wit and Humor; The Ludicrous Side of Life; Genius; Intellectual Health and Disease; Use and Misuse of Words; Wordsworth; Bryant; Stupid Conservatism and Malignant Reform.

Character and Characteristic Men. 12mo, gilt top, $1.50.

CONTENTS: Character; Eccentric Character; Intellectual Character; Heroic Character; The American Mind; The English Mind; Thackeray; Nathaniel Hawthorne; Edward Everett; Thomas Starr King; Agassiz; Washington and the Principles of the American Revolution.

Success and its Conditions. 12mo, gilt top, $1.50.

CONTENTS: Young Men in History; Ethics of Popularity; Grit; The Vital and the Mechanical; The Economy of Invective; The Sale of Souls; The Tricks of Imagination; Cheerfulness; Mental and Moral Pauperism; The Genius of Dickens; Shoddy; John A. Andrew.

Outlooks on Society, Literature, and Politics. Crown 8vo, gilt top, $1.50; half calf, $3.00.

George E. Woodberry.

Studies in Letters and Life. 16mo, $1.25.

⁎ *For sale by all Booksellers. Sent, post-paid, on receipt of price by the Publishers,*

Houghton, Mifflin & Company,

ND - #0022 - 100625 - C0 - 229/152/20 - PB - 9781331024958 - Gloss Lamination